Rearview Mirror

Alana Stewart

Rearview Mirror

A Memoir

Vanguard Press
A Member of the Perseus Books Group

Published by Vanguard Press
A Member of the Perseus Books Group

Designed by Trish Wilkinson
Set in 12 point Adobe Garamond Pro

Cataloging-in-Publication data for this book is available from the Library of Congress.
ISBN 978-1-59315-707-4 (hardcover)
ISBN 978-1-59315-723-4 (e-book)

Vanguard Press books are available at special discounts for bulk purchases in the U.S. by corporations, institutions, and other organizations. For more information, please contact the Special Markets Department at the Perseus Books Group, 2300 Chestnut Street, Suite 200, Philadelphia, PA 19103, or call (800) 810-4145, ext. 5000, or e-mail special.markets @perseusbooks.com.

10 9 8 7 6 5 4 3 2 1

To Delilah—the light of my life

Contents

Acknowledgments, ix

Prologue: A Rude Awakening, xi

PART I

Mama's Girl, 1

PART II

The Glamorous Life, 29

PART III

Rock 'n' Roll Royalty, 103

PART IV

The Unraveling, 161

PART V

Starting to Heal, 199

PART VI

Finding Peace, 265

Acknowledgments

When I look back on my life, I truly see that there are many people who factor into the decisions I've made and the path I've taken, and who are really threads in the fabric of who I am. And when you create a book, there are many people that lend a hand in taking it from an idea you had to tell your story to actually making the book (or e-book) you're holding now. It is to both these groups of people that I am so thankful, namely:

Roger Cooper, my publisher, whom I affectionately call "Papa Bear." I knew from the minute we met and started to talk about the possibility of this book that we were on the same page (pardon the pun) and we shared the same vision of what it should be. I've so appreciated your guiding hand during this process, Roger.

Melanie Mitzman and the team at Perseus Books—my deepest gratitude for your dedication, commitment, and creative input.

My friend and literary agent, Joel Gotler, who gave me great advice and support and who connected me to Papa Bear.

Francine LaSala, my brilliant and patient editor who helped keep me sane and who encouraged me through what I thought was an impossible deadline. And, most of all, for giving me confidence in my writing.

Christine Romeo—my associate and friend. You made it possible for me to get through this process. I couldn't have done it without you.

Liam Collopy of Levine Communications—for all your support, loyalty, and dedication.

Eileen Ford—thank you for being my mentor and my friend and for believing in me.

My children—Ashley, Kimberly, and Sean. I can't imagine my life without you. Because of you I have learned the meaning of unconditional love.

Mama, I'm eternally grateful to you for taking me in and instilling in me your values, your strength, your courage, and your faith. I don't think I would have made it through life without your influence. I wish more than anything my children could have known you.

Mother, I hope that you are soaring with the angels, free of your earthly burdens. I love you.

All of my friends—I've learned through the course of my life the importance of friendship. I've been so blessed to have so much loving support in my life and I cherish each and every one of you.

Lesley, thank you for your friendship and unfailing support through some very difficult times.

Jacquie Eastlund—in loving memory. You always told me I would write one day.

Marianne Williamson, I can never thank you enough for the contribution you've made to my spiritual growth. I would not be the woman I am today without your friendship and support.

Deepak Chopra, who started me on the road to healing and spiritual enlightenment all those many years ago.

Dr. Mark Vierra, thank you for your continuing spiritual support and for always being there for me.

Lameice Harding, my wonderful friend and teacher. Thank you for your assistance on my road to healing and for giving me a deeper understanding of God.

And finally, to all of the therapists who helped me see more clearly along the way.

Prologue
A Rude Awakening

I felt the cold, steel blade of a knife pressed against my throat. In the blackness of the night I could barely make out a shadowy figure leaning over me. I jumped up and opened my mouth to scream, but it was like one of those nightmares in which you try to scream but nothing comes out.

The intruder hit me so hard with his fist that I flew backward across the room, slamming the back of my head onto the chest of drawers as I fell to the floor. He pounced on me, holding me down, the knife tight against my throat.

"Don't make another move or I'll kill you," he threatened.

He mounted me and forced himself inside me. "Please, God," I prayed to myself, "Don't let him kill me." I kept praying silently, over and over, trying to astral-project myself away from what was happening to my body. When he was done, he held the knife against my throat again.

"Don't move." He ripped the sheet off the bed and tore it into pieces. He blindfolded me, put a gag in my mouth, and tied my hands and feet together. I could feel him standing over me in the dark. Then he did a strange thing—he turned on the light.

"Oh my God," I heard him gasp, and he quickly turned it off again. Then there was only silence.

I lay there, afraid to move, afraid he might still be in my small apartment and make good on his threat. I waited another minute or two, maybe more, as I listened for any sign of his presence. It was dead quiet. I managed to turn myself over and inch my way toward the bathroom. I struggled to free my hands and pulled myself up on the sink, my feet still bound by the torn sheet.

As I removed my blindfold and gag, I too gasped at what I saw in the mirror. My face was swollen and bloody; my hair was caked with blood. I untied my feet and shakily walked back to the bedroom. A three-foot radius of the carpet was soaked with blood. I reached for the back of my head and felt the sticky, gaping gash that was still bleeding profusely.

I called a friend of mine who lived in the next apartment building. "We have to call the police," he told me.

"No, please!" I protested. I felt horrified and disgusted that I'd been raped. It was such a stigma in those days in Texas. He insisted, however, and two policemen arrived within half an hour.

"Did you know the man? Did you let him in?" the first officer asked.

"I don't think it was anyone I know," I said, "but I can't be completely sure. It was so dark . . . "

I told them I had chain-locked the door when my date had left earlier, and I showed them the open window over the sink where the screen had been pulled off and was still lying outside on the ground. It didn't take Sherlock Holmes to figure out where the guy had broken in. They continued to question me, but there was a suspicious, almost accusatory element to their questioning. I started to feel like I was the one who had committed the crime.

Finally, they took me to the emergency room. The doctor examined my head and said I needed a number of stitches. He did a vaginal examination and took a specimen of the semen. That disgusted me more than anything, to think I had this creepy rapist's sperm inside me—what if I got pregnant?

When the doctor left the examining room, the two policemen returned to grill me.

"What did you do tonight?" one of the officers asked, a suspicious tone still in his voice.

I told them I had been on a date with a pilot from Trans Texas Airlines, for whom I was working as a stewardess. I told them it had been our first date and I didn't really know him that well. I guessed he was probably about thirty, which to me, eighteen at the time, was an "older man."

Over dinner we had shared one of those giant Scorpions in a bowl with two straws, and I was pretty smashed by the time we got back to my apartment. We were kissing passionately on my sofa when his hands started wandering down my body. Drunk or not, I knew I wasn't about to go any further.

"I think maybe you should go now," I told him. He argued with me, but I was insistent. He left in a huff, slamming the door behind him. After that, I chain-locked the door and went to bed. I fell into a deep sleep, and the next thing I knew I felt the knife at my throat.

The police asked if I'd take a lie detector test. Thinking back, I'm not even sure why it would have mattered if I'd let him in, which I didn't. He still beat me up, raped me, and left me tied up and gagged, lying in a pool of blood.

"Yes, of course!" I tried to act confident, but I was so nervous I was shaking badly.

Afterward, the policemen smugly informed me that the test showed I had lied about letting him in. I felt like I was being gaslighted. I clearly remember chain-locking the door after my date and I knew without a doubt that I hadn't let anyone in. I didn't hear from the police again, and my rapist was never caught.

I felt terrible shame about being raped and I never told a soul. I knew I needed to get as far away from Texas as possible—away from the unhappy memories of my childhood, my drug-addicted mother, and this humiliating experience. What I didn't know is that you can't run forever . . .

This is not a story of rape, of surviving and coping with rape. I chose to open my memoir with this because in many ways it marked a beginning for me. Because of it, I made the decision to leave Texas and start over again in New York, and that's when my life changed.

For me, leaving home not only meant creating distance between myself and this event but also creating distance between myself and a painful childhood—a young girl struggling with abandonment, neglect, and parental alcoholism and addiction, a girl who grew into a young woman poised to become a model, actress, and wife and mother.

They say into every life a little rain must fall. Some of us get a trickle, others a deluge. In the end it's the shelter we build within that keeps us safe and dry. It's the way we put together what we've experienced and learned from our experiences that decides if we weather the storm or crumble into rubble.

I spent roughly the first forty years of my life hiding the pain, pretending it didn't exist, running as far away from it as I could get. After my second marriage failed, I fell to pieces. It was only after I discovered how to rebuild myself, my soul, through a deep sense of spirituality that I have been able to stand strong. I owe the peace I have in my life to the structure I have built within.

I resisted writing a book for a long time because I didn't want to invade anyone else's privacy or hurt anyone or anger anyone. I never wanted to write a "Hollywood tell-all," and I've tried to avoid doing that here. I only wanted to tell the truth.

One of the commitments I made to myself when I decided to write a book was to be brutally honest, particularly about myself. Writing about a lot of what happened in my life and in my children's lives has been hard for me because I don't want to hurt anyone by bringing up the past, but if I'm going to tell the truth, I really feel I have to be completely open and honest.

Everything I've written here has been taken directly from the diaries that I have been keeping since I was nine years old, not from selective or vague memories. I'm not proud of a lot of the things I did or didn't do before I worked on myself, but I am proud of my transformation from a young woman who may have looked like she had it all but was desperately trying to find some kind of magic "glue" to hold her life together to the woman I am today. Through a long and painful process I've learned that happiness is an inside job—not based on anything or anyone in the outer material world. I've become a different and better person—not perfect, but still a work in progress.

On the surface my life seems as if out of a storybook. A Texas girl who grew up in terrible poverty, I ended up leading a pretty glamorous life. I have rubbed elbows with luminaries. I was married to two very famous men. But I have also endured plenty of heartache under that sheen of glamour people generally see when they look at me—darkness, fear, and deep, horrible pain.

Just because you "live a fairytale" doesn't mean "happily ever after" is a given; "happy" is something you have to make.

Which leads me to the most important reason I'm writing this book. As I explained earlier, I used to deal with pain by running away, ignoring it, or burying it deep within. Those tendencies of mine nearly caused me to self-destruct. It was only when I was actually able to stand and face the pain, to really deal with my demons, that I was able to find peace.

Finding peace and a sense of well-being from the strength that comes from within is my hope for anyone who reads this book.

PART I

Mama's Girl

Chapter 1

My very first memory was one of fear. I was only fourteen months old, but I remember it vividly. My mother and I were on a train traveling from California back to her home in Nacogdoches, Texas. She had just left my father, and they would never speak again nor would I ever see him. My mother held me up to the window so I could look out. We were crossing a trestle over a river far below, and to me it seemed as if we were suspended in air. I felt like I couldn't breathe and that I would fall into the vast open space and never stop falling. It's a feeling of fear and panic that has been a familiar thread throughout my life—a feeling of having no foundation beneath me.

I began to scream and cry hysterically. My mother couldn't figure out what was the matter and became frustrated and impatient with me. She was barely twenty years old with an infant daughter, no husband, no source of income, and an uncertain future; she was probably as scared as I was.

My mother, Lela Kathryn Gossage, had grown up in Huntsville, Texas, the middle child between brothers—the serious one, Eugene (Gene), and the fun-loving one, Radford, whom I called Uncle Duck. Their father, James Thomas Gossage, was my grandmother's second husband. Her first husband had died in World War I, just one week before the war ended.

James Gossage had been married twice before and already had four children. He was a farmer. When he died suddenly from a heart attack at age fifty-two, Mother was only seven years old. My grandmother was left destitute, and people tried to convince her to give her three children away because she wouldn't be able to support them. But she wouldn't hear of it. She took a loan from her sister's husband

and moved to Nacogdoches, where she rented a tiny, ramshackle house on the outskirts of town. She got a job in a garment factory and worked long, hard hours, then came home and cooked, cleaned, washed, and ironed at night.

My mother never felt my grandmother loved her or gave her the kind of attention she gave the two boys. She felt she was particularly tough on her, and my grandmother always told me how difficult and rebellious my mother was. I'm sure the truth was a little bit of both. I think my mother was strong willed and hot tempered, but she was also sensitive and desperately craved love. Even later in life, my mother always went home to my grandmother in times of distress, always seeking that affection my grandmother seemed never able to give.

My grandmother, who I called Mama, was part Cherokee. Her mother, my great-grandmother, actually grew up on a Cherokee reservation. She wore two long braids and would come stay with us sometimes and tell me stories about growing up on the reservation. I was always fascinated by her stories and begged her to tell them to me over and over again.

Mama was also a very religious woman, quiet and strict, and after coming home from a grueling day's work, and not affectionate by nature, it's doubtful she had much energy left over to support her children emotionally.

After five years of overwhelmingly hard work, my grandmother became ill and was told she couldn't go back to work. So my Uncle Gene, who was seventeen at the time, dropped out of high school and went to work for the Texas Power and Light Company. When World War II broke out, Gene joined the army and was sent out to Los Angeles before beginning active duty in Okinawa. Uncle Duck ran away and joined the navy at age fifteen, nearly breaking my grandmother's heart. He'd return from time to time for holidays and other occasions, and it was always much more fun when he was there, but mostly it was my Uncle Gene who was around when I was growing up.

When Mother graduated from high school, she got a job as a waitress in a small local café. Restless, she went to Los Angeles to visit my uncle and ended up getting a job as a cocktail waitress. It was there that she met my father, a handsome, charming ladies' man who was a sergeant in the army. She fell madly in love with him and soon found out she was pregnant with me. They married and Mother went to live with his parents, Hestro and Gladys Collins, in Santa Ana while my father was stationed at an Army base in Washington State.

I never got the full story of what happened between my parents from my mother, but my grandmother later told me there had been a bitter breakup. Mother had told me often that it was plain to see he didn't care about me, as he'd never sent me so much as a Christmas or birthday card. I often wondered why, but I never asked questions.

When I was two and in town with Mama, she said I ran into the street and threw my arms around the legs of the sheriff, who was directing traffic. Plaintively I asked him, "Are you my Daddy?" I suppose that was the beginning of my lifelong search for that magical "daddy," for a Prince Charming who would make me feel safe and loved.

When I was six, I sent my father my school picture. On the back I wrote, "Daddy, I just wanted you to see what I look like." He never responded. I guess after that I just accepted that I didn't have a father like other kids.

I have learned now, through reading and years of therapy, that for a woman, never knowing her father is more difficult than losing him through death because women who never know their fathers tend to look for that fantasy figure their whole lives. Consequently, they desperately seek men who they think will fill that void in their lives, yet rarely are these men able to do that because they're generally workaholics, alcoholics, philanderers, or unavailable in some way. This has certainly been my pattern for most of my life—looking for that "powerful daddy" who would love me and make me feel safe, yet choosing men who couldn't possibly fill those shoes.

My uncle and grandmother lived in a tiny, wooden shack. There were only two rooms: a bedroom and a kitchen with a wood-burning stove. There was no running water and no indoor plumbing, which meant we had to use an outhouse. The house was located miles away from town on a red-dirt country road surrounded by piney woods. I remember being fascinated by the color of the earth, and I loved to play in it. When I'd come back in the house, my white dress and underwear would be covered with the red mud, and I'd get a good scolding.

Mother left me with my grandmother, who took care of me while my mom left for Houston to work as a cocktail waitress. When I was almost three, Mother remarried and brought me to Houston to live with her and her new husband, a butcher, in a one-room garage apartment. He drank a lot, had a terrible temper, and didn't care for me.

One night he came home drunk and went into a rage because I had left my doll carriage on the steps.

"That kid and her crap are always in the way! I swear to God, I'm going to throw this down the stairs and her after it!"

"If you lay one hand on her, I'll kill you!" she screamed back at him.

Mother then took me out into the night to walk for what seemed like hours, my small hand clutching onto hers. When she felt it was safe to return, we quietly snuck into the kitchen and she made me some white rice with milk, sugar, and cinnamon in it. It was my favorite thing to eat—poor man's rice pudding. I remember lots of nights like that—walking in the dark with Mother holding my hand as we waited for him to calm down or pass out. I couldn't understand what I did wrong, why he didn't like me. I desperately wanted him to love me and be my daddy.

When I was four, my mother divorced the butcher and I was sent back to live with Mama. (I have to mention here that my mother was married a total of four times: To my father, to the butcher, and, during this short period of time that I was sent back to live with

Mama, briefly to another man—so briefly in fact, that I never met him. She soon married my stepfather, but I'll talk about that later.)

Uncle Gene built a larger (and I use the term "larger" loosely) house for us down the road. It had a small living room, two tiny bedrooms, and a small kitchen. There was still no running water or indoor toilet, though. Mama would give me a bath at night in an aluminum washtub filled with water from the well that she heated on the stove.

We had no telephone and no television, just a large brown radio with an outside antenna, which brought us one station. We often listened to revival meetings, Amos and Andy, or Hank Williams music. Other nights we would sit outside on the front steps and listen to the crickets and the whip-poor-wills and the sounds of the night. A game of Dominoes with my grandmother was a big exciting evening for me.

But of this time I think I remember the loneliness most of all; there were no children my age to play with. I used to take my doll and have tea parties and long conversations with the neighbor's cows at the top of the hill, until my grandmother heard a rabid fox had been spotted in the woods so I was no longer allowed to play there.

I also amused myself by playing in the chicken coop. My best friends were two big black hens, which I named Lulu and Tulu. I loved those hens with all my heart, and they would come running to see me every morning when I went out to the chicken yard (or, more likely, to get the chicken feed I was bringing to them). One day, they disappeared and I was heartbroken. My grandmother told me that the fox had gotten them. I was devastated when I was older and learned she had made chicken and dumplings out of them.

My grandmother was a strict, no-nonsense, devout Southern Baptist woman. She had a gigantic bible and she would read to me from it often. My grandmother didn't talk a lot, but when she read all those bible stories to me, I felt like we communicated and connected. (I actually still have that bible; my uncle gave it to me when she died years later.)

When we could get a ride, my grandmother liked to take me to church. It was far too long to walk, and it wasn't often that she could take me, but it was always special for both of us when we could go.

That early religious grounding actually gave me many of the tools I would need later, making me better able to tap into the spirituality that helped me refocus my life.

But there were also drawbacks to such a strict religious upbringing, especially when it came to sexuality. When I was about six, a boy in my class drew a crude cartoon of a naked man and woman pressed up against each other.

"This is what your parents did to have you," he told me. The picture troubled and confused me, and I brought it home to show Mama.

She was absolutely aghast. "Don't you ever let anyone give you a filthy picture like this again!" she said. "It's sinful!" I could see she was upset. She looked me square in the eyes and pointed her finger at me. "Lana Kaye, I am telling you this now. You should not even so much as kiss a boy unless you are engaged! Otherwise it's a sin and you won't go to Heaven!" Her strict ideas about sexuality stayed with me for years, and pretty much affected any relationship I had until later in my life, when I was finally able to break free of my inhibitions.

Mama kept a .38 pistol in her dresser drawer. (I still sleep with a similar .38 in my night table.) If ever we heard any noises outside at night, she never hesitated to pull it right out and march into the darkness to investigate.

Although she seemed to be pretty fearless herself, Mama instilled a hell of a lot of fear in me. There were so many things to be frightened of: falling into the well, rabid foxes or dogs with foam coming from their mouths, snakes, strangers, getting hit by a car, the Russians invading us, and, most of all, catching polio. Every time I'd get one of those growing-pain cramps in my leg I was sure I'd be spending the rest of my life in an iron lung.

The other fear she instilled in me was poverty. I remember once, after she had, yet again, made her dire prediction that "We were going to end up in the poorhouse," looking around and thinking, "Aren't we already there?"

Most of the time my grandmother and I lived alone, but when my uncles were around, they'd take us into town on Saturday night and buy me a strawberry ice cream cone at the local café. At Christmastime they'd drive us up to North Street, where all the big houses were brightly decorated with colorful lights. It was my favorite thing to do. I imagined how thrilling it must be to be "rich" and live in one of those fabulous "mansions."

Every time I go back to Nacogdoches to visit my Uncle Gene, who at the time of this writing is ninety-one, I drive down North Street and marvel at these small, wooden Victorian houses that seemed so impressive back then.

Those memories instilled something else in me: a love for Christmastime. To this day it is the most important time of year for me, and I take great pains to make it special. It's one of the most memorable things I take away from my childhood, and it is something I have instilled in my kids as well.

When we needed groceries, Mama and I would walk three miles to the country store along the red dirt road in the blazing Texas sun. Sometimes we lived on potato soup for a week or more when my grandmother's social security check hadn't come in, because she was too proud to ask the store for credit. In the summer we always had fresh vegetables from the garden, and Mama would spend hours canning them in mason jars so we'd have something for the winter months. When we ran out, it was back to potato soup.

Every Sunday we had chicken. I'd watch as Mama wrung the poor chicken by the neck until the head literally came off in her hand. Blood would gush out while the body would continue to jump and writhe around on the ground for what seemed like forever. It was a gruesome sight. Sometimes she'd put the chicken down on a log and chop its neck off with a hatchet. Needless to say, my grandmother was not a squeamish woman. I was just glad we didn't have pigs to slaughter like the neighbors down the road.

Just before I started school, a black and white cat started coming around our house, and it was soon clear he was looking to join our family. Mama, who was not particularly fond of animals, let me keep him, and I called him "Puddy Tat," after Sylvester the cat in cartoons. I just loved him and he loved me. Aside from the cows and the chickens, he really was my first friend. To show how much he loved us back, one day Puddy Tat caught a five-foot snake and presented it to us as a "gift." He was a big highlight in my life.

However, an even bigger highlight was Mother's occasional visits. Every Friday night I'd sneak out of my bed and wait hopefully by the window for the sound of a car approaching down the lonely dirt road. When she did come, it was always late at night. She'd take the bus from Houston, and a taxi would bring her out to our house. When that taxi pulled into our driveway, it was the happiest moment of my life. I'd fly out the door into her arms.

Life was fun and exciting when Mother was around. She always seemed so full of life, and I thought she was the most exciting, glamorous woman in the world. She was movie-star beautiful, with long, auburn hair, large green eyes, and a beauty mark above her lips. She always wore high-heeled ankle-strap shoes and dresses with shoulder pads and nipped-in waists. Mother said people told her all the time that she looked like Hedy Lamarr or Gene Tierney.

My grandmother had made most of my dresses from flour sacks. In those days, flour came in large printed cotton sacks, and poor people would make clothes out of them when the flour was finished. But just before I began first grade, Mother took me shopping and bought me several pretty, although inexpensive, dresses and a warm coat for the winter. I felt like a little princess in my beautiful new dresses, and I particularly loved them because my mother had bought them for me.

I became friends with another little girl, Rose, who lived about a mile down the road from me. Sometimes her family would pick me up on Sunday mornings and take me to church with them. They belonged to a Pentecostal Church, and the women weren't allowed to wear makeup or cut their hair. I also went to church occasionally with Mama's sister, Daisy, and her husband, Frank, who were also Pentecostals. Sometimes people would get so overcome with the Holy Spirit during the service that they would start waving their arms and speaking "in tongues." I'd sit back and watch in wide-eyed astonishment as the "holy rollers" writhed all over the floor of the church. It was kind of scary to a six-year-old and maybe also a little confusing, but it was entertaining all the same—and it sure beat staying at home doing nothing.

When I got home from church, Mama would have Sunday dinner ready: fried chicken or chicken and dumplings, potato salad, turnip greens, black-eyed peas, and cornbread. And because it was Sunday, she'd make lemon or coconut meringue pie or, sometimes, my very favorite, banana pudding.

When I was a kid, I loved to eat. Maybe it was because there wasn't very much else to do. Mama and Uncle Gene used to laugh at the breakfasts I'd eat: a big bowl of oatmeal, two fried eggs, bacon, and toast. And I just kept growing taller and skinnier. Mama's sister Maude always said that I surely had a tapeworm, because I ate more than most grown-ups and never gained a pound.

I loved school. I couldn't wait to get on the bus every morning, even though it was still dark when it came. The bus took an hour and a half to wind its way along the country roads from my house to the school.

The following year, my second-grade teacher, Mrs. Dover, was impressed by my advanced reading and ability to learn so quickly.

"I honestly think she should skip the next grade," she told my grandmother. "She's ready for fourth grade."

My grandmother, who didn't usually show very much emotion, was proud. I was the only student who would be skipping a grade, and I was really excited that my teacher thought so well of me.

But just before the next school year began, my mother decided she was going to bring me to Houston to live with her.

"How could you do this?" Mama asked. She was really hurt and angry that Mother was taking me away. "I've raised that little girl from a baby. She's like my own child . . ."

My mother let my grandmother know in no uncertain terms that she was the mother, and if she wanted me to live with her, that was her right.

"Is this what you want?" Mama asked me.

I felt torn because of my loyalty and love for my Mama, but I wanted to be with Mother more than anything in the world. "Yes, Mama," I said, and that was the end of living with Mama. At least for now.

It's interesting and, in hindsight, also painfully ironic that I had spent so much time longing for Mother, and now, it seemed, my dream was coming true—I was going to be with Mother always. Unfortunately, things were not going to be as I wanted them to be, and as my life went on, this longing for something unavailable would ultimately become a familiar and self-destructive pattern.

Chapter 2

It was the middle of the summer when Mama packed up my few belongings as well as my precious Puddy Tat and took me to Houston.

Mother lived in a small dingy apartment over the television repair shop where she worked. It was like living in luxury for me—it even had an actual bathroom, with a tub and running water. But the most exciting thing was that we had a tiny black-and-white television. I'd never seen television before, and I couldn't wait for four o'clock to roll around, when Superman came on.

Sadly though, within a few days Puddy Tat ran away and I never saw him again. I was heartbroken, but at least I had my mother now. Being with her was wonderful.

In the fall I started school, and Mother walked me in the morning. It was all new, strange, and kind of intimidating. The classes were much larger, and I didn't get the kind of doting attention I'd gotten in Nacogdoches.

Shortly after, Mother introduced me to a new man she was dating, Al Ahrens. This Al was very nice and seemed to like me. I really liked him too, though I didn't get that much time to get to know him before he and Mother married. I was excited. At last I had a "Daddy" and now we'd be a real family.

Mother, Al, and I moved into an apartment in Bellaire, Texas, a small middle-class neighborhood, where I had my very own bedroom for the first time in my life. I was just turning nine and finishing the third grade. After school, I'd walk over to the bar where Mother was now working with my new daddy, and I'd have a barbecue pork sandwich and listen to the jukebox. My mother was crazy about this new singer named Elvis Presley, and she'd play "Hound Dog" or "That's All Right, Mama" and dance with me on the wooden floor. I'd stay there until almost dark. Then she'd walk me home and cook dinner while I played or did my homework.

When summer came, I played all day with kids who lived nearby until my mother came home to cook dinner. On Saturdays, sometimes as a special treat, my parents would take me to the drugstore for a banana split or a chocolate malted.

Occasionally on a Saturday we'd go to the San Jacinto River, where we'd sit for hours in a rickety wooden motor boat and fish. If we were lucky, we'd go home with a small catch of bass, which my stepfather would cook for dinner. Or we'd go crabbing in nearby Kemah. When we got home, my parents would cook the crabs we caught in a huge boiling pot of water.

After living in Bellaire almost a year, we moved into a house on a quiet street named Golfcrest in a lower-middle-class section of Southeast Houston. That meant starting another new school, but I liked it a lot and made friends right away. My parents bought me a bicycle, and I rode to school every day. I could even come home for lunch most days. Mother would have a big bowl of hot soup or a bologna or Vienna sausage sandwich waiting for me.

My stepfather bought a bar in a run-down section of town near the docks, and he worked there every night until late. We didn't have a lot of money, but to me, we were living a pretty great life. He drove a used Pontiac and bought my mother a used blue '51 Ford.

They even got me a dog that was the love of my young life. Her name was Dixie, and she was part Chow and part Chesapeake Bay retriever. She got pregnant by some stray dog down the street and gave birth to eight puppies in the shed under the carport. I watched in fascination with my parents as each wet, squirming baby was born.

As the puppies grew, and housing them in the tiny toolshed became impossible, my stepfather made a decision that devastated me. He took them all in a box and drowned them. I followed him almost all the way to the creek.

"Daddy! Stop! Please stop!" I cried as I chased him. "Please don't kill my puppies!"

As much as I cried, as much as I begged, I couldn't stop him. He just ignored me except to wave me aside. I ran crying hysterically back to the house. I couldn't believe anyone could do such a thing.

I was heartbroken that my stepfather could be so cruel about the puppies, but it wasn't that he was a bad man. It was just the way things went in those days, especially in the country. People just didn't hold animals in the high regard they do today. Al had his problems, but he was always very good to my mother and me. Even after he and my mother split up and he remarried, he was still a part of my life.

Around the time I turned ten, things started to change in our house. Mother started getting sick a lot, usually with some kind of virus, and she began going to a doctor who had an office in the back of a pharmacy near our house. He would give her various prescriptions, and she spent more and more time in bed and less time with my stepdad and me. She and Al started to argue frequently. Al started drinking more and, on occasion, would come home drunk at late hours.

One night I was sleeping soundly when I was awakened by the sound of a loud explosion. I jumped out of bed and ran, my heart pounding out of my chest, into the kitchen.

"Let go of that! Dammit!" I heard my stepfather shout. I saw him trying to wrestle a shotgun away from my mother, who had tried to fire it at him. He had grabbed it, and the shot had gone into the kitchen floor, blasting a huge hole in the linoleum.

I began crying hysterically. Finally, they stopped arguing.

"Go back to bed, Alana," my mother said. Trembling, I crept into my bed and lay there for what seemed like hours, my heart still pounding, tears running down my face. I wished she would come in and comfort me, but she never did. I just lay alone there in the dark, terrified and confused.

Another night, I was awakened again by loud arguing in the kitchen. This time my mother had attacked my stepfather with a large butcher knife. But again, he was able to get it away from her. Once she hit him over the head with an iron skillet, breaking the handle off the skillet and leaving him with a huge lump on his head.

My stepdad was not a violent man and never struck her back. He only tried to defend himself by disarming her of whatever weapon she was attempting to use. I don't know if she truly intended to hurt him or kill him or only to threaten him. All I know is that her prescription drug use got continually worse, his drinking escalated, and they blamed each other for their problems.

"I know you're having an affair! With that whore at the bar. I know you are!" she'd shout at him.

"Those pills are making you nuts!" he'd shout back.

Mother's behavior began getting stranger. The drugs made her suspicious and paranoid, and she spent most of the time in her room sleeping. When she came out, she would more often than not stumble and slur her words.

One night, she grabbed me by the arm and told me to be very quiet as she pulled me in the dark over to the window. "He's having me watched," she whispered, slurring. "I just saw someone light up a cigarette out there in the trees. You see?"

I didn't see anything. There was nothing there. But it scared me, and I didn't understand what was going on or why someone would be outside spying on my mother. I went to bed, my heart beating furiously, dreading the fight that would surely ensue when my stepfather came home.

Mother and I moved back to Mama's little house in Nacogdoches, but within a few months my mother and stepfather made up and we went back to the house on Golfcrest. I had high hopes that we would be a happy family again, and for a very brief while we were. Then the old patterns started repeating. When the arguing and fighting got too bad, Mother would occasionally take me and check into some shabby motel somewhere, spending her days in the dark room, huddled under the covers. I would go to a nearby café to get food for us. Then, my stepfather would come and get us and we'd go home again and, for a short time, things would look up.

By the time the latter part of the sixth grade rolled around, Mother packed our bags, my dog Dixie, and me into the old blue Ford and back we went to Mama's house. Mother seemed to get somewhat better out in the country, and as soon as she regrouped, she'd head back to Houston and my stepfather. Things were still pretty tenuous between them, I suppose, so I was left behind to finish out sixth grade in Nacogdoches.

I was lonely out in the country. I came home on the school bus, did my homework, had a simple dinner, which often consisted of a fried potato and sausage sandwich, and went to bed.

Mama didn't allow Dixie in the house. Instead, she built a pen for her out in the garden, where Dixie barked and howled a lot, in protest at being banished so far away from me.

"Dixie belongs inside with me!" I pleaded. "She's my friend!"

"She belongs in the yard. She's a *dog*," she said firmly. When Mama put her foot down, that was that.

I could see now why she and Mother had not gotten along. I never doubted for a moment that my grandmother loved and adored me, and to this day I believe it was through her that I gained the strength, feistiness, faith, and values that have gotten me through some very difficult periods of my life. But sometimes, especially as I got older, communicating with her got harder and harder. She was so set in her ways that it was hard to make her come around and see the world from another angle.

After the summer, Mother and Daddy came to get me to move back to Houston with them. Hard times had forced them to give up the Golfcrest house that I'd loved, and they were now renting a one-bedroom garage apartment in a run-down neighborhood near the bar my stepfather owned. I slept on a pullout bed in the living room, but I was so happy to be back with them again that it didn't matter.

Just as I was turning thirteen, my parents bought a house a block away from the old house on Golfcrest. It was a white wooden house with a front and backyard, two bedrooms, one bathroom, a small living room, and large den in the back.

I was ecstatic. We had a real home now, and things seemed to be going well between my parents. Mother wasn't sick as much, and although she still spent a lot of time in her room, we'd sometimes go fishing and crabbing or out to a drive-in movie.

I made friends right away and enrolled in Hartman Junior High, where some of my friends from grade school were now going. I wasn't one of the "in crowd," however. There was a small group of pretty popular girls who made good grades, wore pretty dresses, were elected cheerleaders, and whose parents were well-off and lived in Glenbrook Valley, a ritzy section of Southeast Houston not far from the school. I longed to be one of them. They had slumber parties and all the cute boys at school wanted to hang out with them. I was tall, skinny, and flat-chested; the boys clearly weren't paying any attention to me. I desperately wanted to be short and cute and have boobs.

Within a year things took a bad turn. Mother was always sick and was being given many different prescriptions. She'd hide them from my stepfather, who would get furious whenever he'd find them. Again, his drinking escalated. Mother would sometimes take off and go to Mama's for a visit, and I'd be sent to stay over with a neighbor because my stepfather was at the bar very late.

On one of those mornings I could hear Al's alarm clock going off as I walked past our house to school. I wondered why he didn't wake up and turn it off. That afternoon, the people I was staying with greeted me with worried faces. "Your stepfather's been in a very bad automobile accident and he's in the hospital," they told me. "Your mother's on her way."

When Mother found out that the woman who worked in the bar with him had also been in the car, she was furious. When Al came home from the hospital, the atmosphere around the house was tense, to say the least. Before he was even fully recuperated, he started drinking again. Soon, he was carrying a pint of Old Crow in his hip pocket and drinking all day until he passed out. He'd sleep in the late afternoon until it was time to go to work. Mother's pill-taking escalated again, to the point at which she seldom came out of her room, and when she did, she was unstable and slurred her words. My stepfather slept in the den.

My room was right next to Mother's, and sometimes, when Al came home, I'd hear her door open and I'd hold my breath, fearing what would happen next.

She would always start in on him and he would try to get her to leave him alone. Sometimes she'd go back to her room, momentarily, and I'd pray she'd just let it go and go to sleep. But no such luck. She was like a dog with a bone, determined to keep going at him until, eventually, a fight ensued.

Al had gotten rid of the gun, but there was always something she could attack him with. She was too drugged to do much damage, but it was always terrifying to me to hear them yelling and scuffling in the other room.

Sometimes she'd come stumbling into my room. "Are you hearing this?" she'd ask. "Do you see what that bastard just did to me?"

Usually, it was merely where he'd grabbed her wrist in order to stop her from hitting him with whatever object was handy. As I said before, he wasn't a violent man, and he disliked confrontation. He only wanted to finish his bottle of whiskey and pass out.

Chapter 3

By the time I started my sophomore year at Austin High School, things had become unbearable at home, but I found ways to escape. When I was fifteen, I got my beginner's driving license and started driving the beat-up old blue Ford to school. I should have had an adult driving with me, but my parents were so out of it that they didn't pay much attention to what I was doing. I was the only sophomore who had a car, and even though it was a junker, it gave me a certain status. Luckily, the cops never stopped me.

By now I was pretty but I hadn't even realized it. Boys had never paid attention to me before, but that year I was named "Most Beautiful Sophomore." I also became popular and finally joined the "cool" group.

When my mother wasn't staying with Mama, she was usually locked in her room with her pills. So I did all the grocery shopping, the cooking, and most of the housework, including the washing and ironing, which I had been doing since I was thirteen. Mother also spent a fair amount of time in the hospital. On several occasions I'd come into Mother's room after school and find her limp and lifeless. Hysterical, I'd track down my stepfather, and he'd call for an ambulance. I guess they would pump her stomach and keep her for a few days, sometimes as long as a week or more.

When Mother came home, she'd be clean of all drugs, my stepfather would try to curtail his drinking, and I would make myself hopeful that we were going to be happy again. But it never lasted long. The "other shoe" would always drop, and soon it would be back to business as usual—drinking and taking pills and fighting.

Throughout my life, no matter how well things seem to have been going, I've always had this deep fear that it wouldn't last, that the "other shoe" would soon drop. Interestingly enough, that always seemed to be the case. Perhaps it's true that we get what we expect.

I've read that children who grow up in homes where there is alcoholism, drug use, and/or violence often develop post-traumatic stress disorder, much like vets coming home from a war. I can certainly relate to that. Often my home felt like a war zone, and even during times of truce I could never rest easy and let down my guard because I was so afraid that at any moment there could be another explosion.

I escaped into school and being with my friends. My teachers always considered me a little "wild" because I didn't have much supervision at home. Skipping class from time to time and forging notes from my mother probably didn't endear me to them, but I was fortunate that I was smart and could keep up.

The dress code at my school was very strict. I couldn't wear a dress above the knees and my shoulders couldn't show. My shoulders! I, of course, constantly tested the limits and would wear a dress with bare arms and, invariably, get sent to Mrs. LeGros, the ancient dean, who had bright dyed red hair and never smiled—not at me, anyway.

"Alana Collins, you'll never amount to anything more than a carhop!" she once told me.

I made up my mind, then and there, that I would show her! I wasn't sure how that was going to happen, as I couldn't see any way out of my circumstances, but still, I had big dreams.

Sometimes my girlfriends and I would drive into River Oaks, the wealthy section of Houston, where the houses were grand and beautiful and set far back from the street behind large, forbidding gates and surrounded by beautiful manicured lawns and colorful flower beds. I was sure the people who lived in these lovely homes in River Oaks had magical, happy lives, wore fabulous clothes, and drove shiny new cars. I loved to park in front of my favorite, an impressive gray stone house that looked like a castle out of a fairy tale, and I'd dream that one day I would live in a house like that. Little did I know then that someday I would—and more than one.

My biggest escape from reality, though, was to have crushes on boys, and the more unavailable, the better. The pattern of striving for "unavailable" men, mainly emotionally unavailable men, would repeat often in my life. I would learn later it had to do with the feelings of abandonment from my early childhood; at this point in my life, though, I probably made myself think I just liked a challenge.

No matter how many boys I had crushes on or dated, though, I never "went all the way." This had a lot to do with my religious upbringing. My grandmother's reaction to that boy's silly cartoon had stuck with me all these years. And I lost a few potential boyfriends because of it.

One thing I had wanted desperately was to be a cheerleader during my senior year, and by the end of my junior year, when elections were held, there was little doubt with the kids at school that I'd be elected. The only glitch was that the faculty had to pass me.

I had spent hours practicing my routine and speech, and I felt fairly confident about it, although I was still pretty nervous. When it was my turn, I ran from the back of the gymnasium to the appointed spot in front of the bleachers. The faculty all seemed to be looking at me disapprovingly, and in that moment, I knew they weren't going to pass me no matter what.

I barely remember getting through my cheer. It felt like my arms and legs were filled with lead. I somehow got through my speech, although I felt like my words were barely audible. My heart was pounding out of my chest, and I wanted to get away as fast as I could.

When I learned I didn't make it, I was crushed, but I kept the disappointment and pain locked up inside me. I didn't go to school the next day, or the following day. The weekend came, and some of my friends came by to see if I was okay. When I saw their car pull up, I immediately went outside so as not to risk them coming in and possibly seeing Mother stumble around the house. I talked to them a few minutes, but not about the cheerleading audition, and certainly not about Mother. I was too deeply ashamed of both.

This experience of not making cheerleader was a defining moment in my life, and the panic I had felt in front of those teachers stayed with me. Years later, on auditions, I'd get that same cold, clammy, frozen feeling of being judged. If I'd been able to open up about the cheerleading experience at the time it happened, if I'd had the support of a functioning mother who could reassure me, would my stage fright have been less severe? In those days, people didn't talk about those kinds of things. If anyone in my family—my mother or stepfather, my grandmother or uncle—had ever talked about their feelings, would I have not developed such a toxic tendency to always stuff my feelings down in me? I wonder.

Summer finally came, and with it, another devastating event. My stepfather and mother split up. He was broke and couldn't afford to keep the house, so they decided that he would move my mother and me to Nacogdoches and rent us a small house there. I couldn't believe this was happening. I had to leave my home, my school, and my friends and finish my senior year at a new school in another town.

If any good could come from this, I had hoped perhaps Mother would be better here. But her pattern didn't change. She closed herself off in the bedroom and continued taking the pills that kept her asleep most of the time.

When my stepfather visited, I was so miserable. "Daddy, please, please let me come back to Houston," I begged him. Not only was Mother not improving; there was nothing for me to connect to here, no place for me to escape. On top of that, now that my grandmother was living close to us, she could see what my mother was up to, and she strongly disapproved. As I explained, Mama was virtuous and religious and didn't believe in alcohol or drug use. As much as my mother craved her own mother's attention, she was not getting the attention she needed from Mama. So back to Houston we went.

Mother and I moved into a small, one-bedroom apartment in a shabby complex on Golfcrest, across the street from the house we had once lived in. I slept on the sofa in the tiny living room; Mother stayed in the small bedroom with the curtains drawn shut and seldom came out. When she did, she was completely loaded on the numerous pills she kept by her bedside.

We had very little money, and I desperately wanted to have nice clothes like the other girls, so I started shoplifting. Just after school started, a girlfriend and I went on a "shopping spree" in downtown Houston. We were just leaving the large department store when a woman walked up to us, flashed a badge, and said, "You girls will need to come with me." The store detectives took us into a back room, where they took photographs of us and our fingerprints. We were shocked and humiliated and ashamed. My girlfriend wasn't allowed to talk to me anymore, and to make matters worse, word leaked out at school and everyone knew.

The only bright spot in my life was that football season had started, and Bill, a popular football player I had a crush on, asked me to several of his football games. After one of them, we had parked on a dark road and were doing some pretty heavy necking in the front seat of his pick-up truck. When he tried to go a little further than kissing, I stopped him.

"I can't do this," I told him.

"Come on, you know you want to," he whispered.

The truth was that I didn't really want to. For one, there was Mama's influence. But I also firmly believed "nice" girls didn't let boys go too far and that if they did, the boy would never respect them again.

He drove me home in stony silence and didn't call me again after that. Soon after I heard he was going out with a girl who hadn't turned him down. It seemed like my life couldn't get much unhappier.

Before the end of my senior year, things started to look up again. I became the editor of the school newspaper and reunited with my friends. The shoplifting scandal was behind me, and I was selected

"Most Beautiful Senior." On graduation day, however, I was the only one who had no family present to see me receive my diploma.

My friends were all going away to college, but because I couldn't afford to go, I got a job as a receptionist at Home Savings and Loan Company in downtown Houston. My mother was in really bad shape now, taking more pills than ever, and had started hallucinating. One day I found her huddled in a corner of her bedroom in her dirty nightgown, eyes feral, a butcher knife clutched in her hand. "Come any closer and I'll kill you," she slurred.

I didn't know what to do. I had never seen her this crazy before. I decided to call my stepfather for help, and later that day two men in white uniforms came into the house and forced her into a straitjacket and into the waiting ambulance. She was heavily drugged and barely coherent, but she was struggling against them as they dragged her out. When she saw me, she hissed, "I'm going to kill you for this!"

I didn't cry. I just watched numbly as they took my mother away, screaming and cursing. She was sent to the State Psychiatric Hospital in Austin, Texas, and spent three months there. I went to visit her several times, and it was frightening and excruciatingly painful to see my once-beautiful mother locked away with seriously deranged patients. She kept saying that she shouldn't be there, that she wasn't crazy. In truth, she wasn't.

Many years later a therapist who specialized in drug addiction told me that the doctors never diagnosed her real problem, drug-induced psychosis. What she really needed was a drug rehabilitation program, but the many drug and alcohol treatment centers that we have today didn't exist then. The doctors there treated her with more drugs and even gave her electric shock treatments.

By the time Mother was ready to come home, my stepdad moved us into yet another tiny, one-bedroom apartment. He still cared about my mother, and he loved me and thought of me as his real daughter. He was a good man and didn't abandon us after they broke up, but he had his own problems with alcoholism.

It was a matter of weeks before Mother was back in her dark bedroom. I had hoped and prayed for years that our family situation would change, but it only got worse. I wanted to get away in the worst way.

I found a temporary escape.

My first real boyfriend, Johnny, was a handsome ex-football player who had gone to a neighboring school. We were so crazy about each other; he was my first love, and I thought we would be together forever. I spent all of my free time at his house, and I loved being there. I'd hang around the kitchen with his mom and cook with her. I felt like I was part of a real family at last, and I dreaded going back to that depressing apartment. I hardly ever saw my mother. I'd spend my free time at Johnny's house and stay there until it was time to come home and go to bed.

We always took for granted that we would get married one day, and eventually, we got engaged. I was determined to remain a virgin until we got married, but it was getting more and more difficult. I was just about to turn nineteen when we made love one night on his living room sofa while his parents were out. After all those months of building passion and restraint, it wasn't what I thought it was going to be. It didn't really hurt much, as I'd feared, but it left me feeling empty and guilty. In part, I felt like I had "sinned" because of my grandmother and her beliefs, but beneath that there was more. I wasn't aware of it at the time, but on some level I knew this wasn't going to be the life for me.

Johnny was going to follow in his father's footsteps and become a fireman. We started looking at furniture and even put a blue sofa on layaway. We hadn't picked a date, but we did decide that the wedding would take place the following summer.

Once getting married started to become a reality, I began having terrible migraine headaches and having doubts about my relationship with Johnny. The thought of moving into a small apartment with that blue sofa was starting to make me feel anxious and claustrophobic. I'd sit at work and look out the window, thinking that there must be an exciting world out there that I was missing.

One day while going through the newspaper, I saw a want ad for stewardesses for Trans-Texas Airlines. On a whim I decided to apply, and I was hired immediately. I didn't tell them that I'd never been on an airplane before, though, or that the thought of flying scared me to death. I was actually so terrified of flying in the beginning that the passengers sometimes had to reassure me. On one of my early flights I grabbed a passenger's arm and frantically asked, "What's that noise?"

"Miss," he said, eyeing me suspiciously as he pulled his arm out of my grasp, "It's only the landing gear coming down." Obviously being a flight attendant was not my calling!

Johnny wasn't happy about my new job, but I convinced him it would be fine. Meanwhile, I'd rented an apartment with a girlfriend in a large complex not far from the airport. It was in the back of the building and overlooked a wooded area and a small creek. I was so excited to be out of that horrible apartment with Mother.

I felt myself starting to pull away from Johnny, and the more possessive he became, the more smothered I began to feel. I felt like I had lost a part of myself in the relationship, and I was beginning to resent it.

Soon after I moved into my apartment, Johnny and I had an argument over something trivial—I don't even remember what it was about. All I knew was that I was consciously picking a fight with him, and I was doing it to get out. I took off my engagement ring and threw it at him, telling him I didn't want to get married. I felt a tremendous sense of relief. I felt like a bird being let out of a cage. I never looked back. He tried to reconcile with me, but I refused. Life was waiting for me out there, and it was time I moved on.

Of course, this sense of "moving on" after breaking up with Johnny was only the tip of the iceberg. I was finally away from Mother. I had an exciting new job. My future was open and filled with possibilities—as I was to learn, both good and bad . . .

After I was raped, I never went through a period of falling apart. I simply shut the experience down, buried it deep within. It would take years of therapy for me to stop doing that, to actually stop running and trying to escape. To face my demons head on, to acknowledge my pain and allow myself to feel it, and to finally start to heal. But for now, I was still running.

I considered my options.

At this point in time Jean Shrimpton, the English model, was on the cover of every fashion magazine, and I dreamed one day that could be me. I always thought about moving away, but now I started seriously thinking about going to New York to become a model. I just didn't have a clue how to begin.

In my life, things have had a tendency to fall into place when it's time for them to fall into place, and that started happening around this time. I met a man on one of my flights who lived in New York and told me to call him if I ever got up there. I knew I could get a free round-trip ticket through Trans-Texas, but I hadn't saved enough money to get by before I found work. Then, a guy rear-ended me on the freeway, and his insurance company paid me five hundred dollars as a settlement. I began making plans.

My friends and family were all concerned about my decision to leave Texas. My mother was so out of it that she had nothing to say, but my grandmother and uncle were not in favor of my decision. They were country folk and didn't trust the city—especially New York City. I wasn't scared, but they were scared for me.

Terrible things could happen to a young girl alone in the city, they argued. What if I couldn't find work? What if I was kidnapped and sold into white slavery? It never occurred to me that I wouldn't start modeling immediately, and as for the dangers that might be lurking there, I put an ice pick in my purse. Luckily, there were no security checks in those days.

At last I was ready. I gave notice to the airlines and set a date to leave for New York to follow my dream.

PART II

The Glamorous Life

Chapter 4

I arrived in New York City in the springtime, though it was cold and raining—not like in Texas. I was nervous and excited, leaving behind me the memory of the rape and my broken engagement.

Most of all, I was finally getting some distance from my untenable family situation. After her latest stay in the mental hospital, my mother returned to Nacogdoches to stay with my grandmother, still seeking the "sweet comfort of home" she was never going to find each and every time she felt lost. I could only hope that somehow she would get better staying with Mama, but a part of me knew Mother would be back to her old ways soon enough.

I got a tiny hotel room for seven dollars a night and walked all around the city, looking in awe at the places I'd only seen in photographs or in the movies—Fifth Avenue, Central Park, the Empire State Building, Times Square, Broadway. I stood on Park Avenue, looking downtown toward the Pan Am Building, and I felt such a sense of freedom, exhilaration, and wonder. I couldn't believe I was actually here!

I called the man I met on the plane. "I made it," I said.

"It's nice to hear from you," he told me. "Do you need a place to stay?"

I wasn't sure if he was coming on to me. I actually got a sense from him that he was gay, but this was New York; I wasn't going to take any stupid chances.

"Actually . . . ," I began, not really knowing what I was going to say.

"Look," he said, "I'm just heading to San Francisco for a month. Leaving tonight. If you need a place to crash until you find something more permanent, you're more than welcome to stay at my place."

"I don't know what to say," I said, and I truly didn't. He gave a friendly laugh. "I have to catch my plane now, but I'll leave the keys with the deli downstairs."

"Thank you so much!" I said. I couldn't believe my good luck.

He gave me the address to a small studio apartment on Madison Avenue in the upper 70s. It was incredible how kind this man was, who didn't even know me. And he never asked for anything in return.

I started looking for a temporary job to support myself until I could get an appointment with the prestigious Ford Modeling Agency. I was nervous about my money running out and extremely cautious about spending much of it. In fact, I bought a book, New York on $5 a Day, and made it my bible. I discovered Lebanese food, Italian meatball sandwiches, and pizza for twenty cents a slice. The most "exotic" food I'd ever eaten in Texas was Tex-Mex, so this was all part of my exciting new adventure.

I'd read about resale shops in this book, and there was actually one nearby. As I was looking through the racks of used clothing, my palms started to itch. I looked down and noticed large red welts beginning to rise on my wrists. Then my face began to itch and my lips started tingling. I found the ladies room, where I looked in the mirror; my face was covered in hives and my lips were huge and swollen. I rushed out of the bathroom, and the owner came over to me to see what was wrong.

"I don't know," I told him. "This has never happened to me before."

He brought me across the street to a pharmacy. The pharmacist took one look at me. "She's got to get to a hospital—now!" he said, and helped the store owner—truly an angel in disguise—rush me into a taxi. The store owner climbed in with me.

"Lenox Hospital, quick!" he barked at the driver. I guess the driver took one look at me and saw the urgency, because he peeled away from the curb and raced to the hospital at top speed.

By now I was gasping for air. The emergency room attendants rushed me onto a stretcher and started pumping adrenaline into me intravenously. The last thing I remember was drifting off to sleep.

When I awakened, the swelling and hives had gone down, and I could finally breathe normally.

"Looks like you went into anaphylactic shock," the doctor explained. "It's very serious. You could have died. Did you eat anything unusual or take any kind of medication today?" he asked.

"I had some cottage cheese and toast for breakfast, that's all," I replied. "I've never been allergic to anything before."

"You know, they use a chemical to treat used clothing before it can be resold. Maybe it was that," he said, and left the room. That was the first time I had had such a reaction, but not the last. Over the years, it's happened to me four other times—twice with antibiotics, twice with fish. I always carry an EpiPen in my purse.

My wonderful "Good Samaritan," the man who owned the clothing store, had waited for me during this whole ordeal. He had a daughter named Laura, whom he wanted me to meet. She was a student at NYU and was looking for a roommate to share her small Greenwich Village apartment. My terrifying near-death experience had a silver lining: I now had a place to live and a really nice roommate.

I found work as a factory model for a clothing manufacturer located on the fourth floor of an old building on Eighteenth Street and Fifth Avenue. My job was to have the sample pieces of clothes fitted on me. It was anything but glamorous, but the people were nice and it paid enough money for me to feel a little more secure in the big city while I pursued my dreams of becoming the next Jean Shrimpton.

The day of my interview with Ford Models, I took the subway uptown then walked over to the brownstone that housed the agency. I walked up to the second floor and nervously entered the reception area. It must have been so obvious that I was a hick from out of town. I was wearing a pink wool dress, tan high heels, and a coat with a little mink collar that I had bought on layaway in Houston. My hair was carefully curled in a flip, held in place by a ton of Aqua Net. I sat nervously clutching my "Most Beautiful Senior" yearbook photo.

The uppity receptionist flipped her hair dismissively at me. "Why don't you wait over there," she told me, pointing to a sofa.

It seemed like I had been waiting an eternity when, suddenly, a woman came out from the back and looked me up and down through glasses perched on her nose. "Why are you keeping this pretty girl waiting?" she asked the receptionist. It was Eileen Ford herself! "Come with me," she said, and I followed her into a small office where an older blonde woman was sitting. She introduced me to Sonny Harnet, who handled all the new models, and left the room.

Sonny looked at my photo.

"Where are you from?" she asked me.

"Nacogdoches, Texas," I said, trying my best to keep smiling through my nervousness.

She looked at me, puzzled. "Naga-what?" she asked.

"Nacogdoches," I said. "Nacog—"

"Texas," she said, and she looked me up and down. "So that's where you learned makeup?" she asked.

"Yes, ma'am," I replied.

"Here's what you need to do," she told me. "You need to head down to Bonwit Teller, to the cosmetics counter, and have the makeup artist there show you how to do makeup."

"Okay . . . ," I said.

Then she took my phone number and sent me on my way. But before I left, she called out to me. "Also, lose five pounds."

I left the office, but I had no idea what had just happened. Did this mean I was now a Ford model? Just like that? Or would I never hear from her again?

As instructed, I went to Bonwit's, where I watched attentively as my makeup was done. When I got home, Sonny called with a list of photographers whom I was to go see, along with their addresses. I learned that these appointments were called "go sees." For a new model starting out, the first prerequisite was to build a portfolio of pictures obtained by "going to see" various photographers, who would then decide if they wanted to photograph you or not.

Like the models sent to them, the photographers were also mostly young and starting out. Unfortunately, most of them weren't very good, and Sonny rejected a great number of the photos they took of me.

My childhood had not exactly equipped me with strong self-esteem, and at the time these photos were being rejected, I didn't consider that it might have been because of the lighting or the inexperience of the photographer; I thought something was wrong with me, that I was ugly, not photogenic. I started to feel like I was under a microscope and that every flaw in my face and body were now magnified. My face was too long, my jaw too prominent, my forehead too high. And I still needed to lose five pounds.

I had never tried to lose weight before. I'd been trying to gain weight all my life! Also, I'd never realized before how food was such a big part of my life, especially when I moved to New York and was so lonely. The main thing I looked forward to was eating, and boy, could I eat. I could put away a whole pizza easily, followed by a pint of ice cream. When I was told I had to take off those pounds, all I could think about was eating. Everywhere I looked there was food.

One night my roommate and her boyfriend offered me a joint, and I was shocked and terrified. No one in Texas, at least that I knew, had ever smoked marijuana. It was something that juvenile delinquents did in movies like *Reefer Madness*, and they were put in jail for it. I thought it was in the same category as heroin.

"Nah, it's really safe," Joey, Laura's boyfriend, told me.

"Seriously," Laura said. "It just makes you feel all giggly and warm and great."

I tentatively took a small puff, fearing what my reaction might be. I guess I was wound pretty tightly, having had to stay in control and keep all my feelings suppressed growing up. I was afraid that any drug might take me out of that controlled persona I worked so hard to maintain. I was scared I might lose my mind, like my mother. And, of course, I hated drugs because of what they had done to her.

But I didn't go insane. I took another puff or two at their urging, and suddenly, I felt relaxed, silly, and giggly. "I'm really hungry," I said, and we all burst out laughing. Then we headed out and consumed endless amounts of pizza and ice cream, and I thoroughly enjoyed it. From then on, I would occasionally indulge whenever they offered it.

Drugs were not going to be a problem for me, but food was definitely becoming a destructive element in my life. The more I tried not to eat, the more obsessed I became about eating. I'd starve myself all day, then I'd eat way too much and feel horribly guilty.

One night, alone in my apartment, I ended up finishing off a pint of ice cream after dinner. I couldn't stop myself. Afterward I felt stuffed and sick, and the ice cream felt like it was almost up to my throat. I leaned over the toilet, sort of belched, and out it all came—the ice cream and the rest of the dinner.

And now I had another problem.

Bulimia wasn't something anyone was really aware of in those days. I'd never heard of it. I just knew I'd found a solution to my overeating and inability to lose weight. I could eat whatever I wanted and get rid of it afterward.

I became a binge-and-purge eater. I could no longer eat two cookies—I had to finish the package, and then I had to get them out of my body so that I didn't gain weight. I began to feel like I couldn't stop. Binging and purging was all I thought about. I always felt horrible afterward, sick and guilty and ashamed of what I was doing, but I couldn't seem to stop, and I certainly couldn't ask anyone else for help or advice.

At this point I began suffering from occasional depressions, especially when nothing seemed to be moving forward in my modeling career. I started to feel strangely disassociated from myself, as if I needed something to hold on to. I needed to feel some sense of a foundation beneath my feet. It was like when I was a baby and felt panicked on the train, that there was nothing that could stop me from falling.

Thinking I could find some sense of security at home, I headed back to Houston for a short trip. My girlfriends were all impressed with my new clothes, my new look, and my glamorous life in New York. They all said they had always known I'd make something of my life, that it had always been clear that I was going to "go places." I didn't tell them that becoming a model wasn't exactly a piece of cake—or about the binging and purging that had become an almost-daily habit in my life.

When I returned to New York, I became even more determined to be a success. That was one thing that saved me and kept me going— my relentless determination to be somebody.

The other was a blind faith that God or someone or something up there was watching over me. Thank God for all those years of going to church and reading the Bible with my grandmother; it gave me something to hold on to.

Chapter 5

As time went on I started to feel more at home in New York, though I still carried my ice pick. One day when I was walking down a very crowded Fifth Avenue, a woman passing by suddenly cried out, "Ouch! I've been stabbed!" As she grabbed her leg, I looked down to see a thin trickle of blood running down her calf, and at the same time I noticed that the tip of my ice pick was sticking right through the side of my canvas modeling bag. I was mortified. I really didn't know what to do, so I just kept walking as fast as I could!

Although I was young and somewhat naive, I had this no-nonsense, feisty, "don't fuck with me" attitude, and that's how I carried myself, especially when it came to men. There were always plenty of men who wanted to go out with young models, but they were mostly "older" men, in their midthirties to midforties. At twenty, I couldn't even imagine being attracted to a man that much older, but if one asked me out to dinner, sometimes I'd go just so I could get a great meal. I'd get taken to fabulous restaurants, like Le Pavillon, La Côte Basque, Lutèce, or Gino's. I'd never been in restaurants like this before, and I ate like a truck driver who hadn't had food in three days. My dates watched in amazement as I devoured everything but the table and washed it all down with a glass of milk.

I typically ended the night with a polite "Thank you for such a lovely evening." Great meal or not, there was no way I was going to do anything I didn't want to do. I couldn't imagine kissing someone good night whom I wasn't attracted to—or even holding their hand for that matter.

Modeling work was not happening very quickly, and I started to lose hope about ever making money as a model. Then a photographer booked me for a five-day job in Acapulco, shooting an eight-page

Eastern Airlines ad campaign for Vogue. I fell in love with Acapulco, a love affair that lasted many years.

That fall, I booked a few more jobs. One was for *Cosmopolitan* with a well-known photographer named Jérôme Ducrot. I was so excited that I could barely contain myself, but I was also nervous. When I arrived on the set, the photographer's assistant showed me where to stand. I was inexperienced, so I didn't really know what to do with my body. I tried striking a couple of poses I'd seen in magazines, but nothing I did pleased him. He made it very obvious that he was not happy. After much whispering on the side, I was told I could get dressed and go. As I was leaving, I saw Lauren Hutton, who was already a very big model, walk in the door. I was crushed and humiliated. I cried all the way home.

When the bookers at Ford sent me over to meet Diana Vreeland at Vogue, my first thought as I walked nervously into her office that October afternoon was that she looked like the Queen of Hearts from *Alice in Wonderland*, and I was feeling more and more like Alice—the small Alice. She barely looked at me over her peanut butter sandwich and then waved me into a dress that was hanging nearby. I thought this was my big break, that I had been booked for a fashion shoot. But I was only there for a run-through so they could select the clothes they wanted to use for the shoot. After she briefly eyeballed me in each outfit, she'd wave me on to the next one. She clearly was much more interested in her sandwich than she was in me.

Just before Christmas I was trying to hail a cab on Fifth Avenue when a taxi pulled up next to me. A distinguished gray-haired gentleman was already sitting in the backseat. "I'm going downtown," he said. "You can share this cab with me if you like." Normally I would not have gotten into a car with a strange man, but it was rush hour and there were no taxis. He didn't seem like a hatchet murderer or a white-slave trader, so I thanked him and hopped in. "Oleg Cassini," he said, holding out his hand.

"Alana," I said. "Alana Collins."

"So nice to meet you, Alana," he said with a warm smile.

On our way downtown, we chatted.

"Where are you from, Alana?" he asked me.

"Nacog . . . Houston," I told him.

"Houston? Really?" he said. "What a coincidence. I'm going to Houston in a few days for my daughter's Coming Out party."

"Really?" I said. "I'm actually heading back there in a couple of days for Christmas."

"Well, in that case, I think you should come to the ball with me."

I was a little surprised. "I'd love to," I said. "But I don't think I have anything to wear to a ball."

"Not to worry," he said. "I'll have a gown sent over for you."

Oleg made good on his promise to have a gown sent, and it was amazing—white and strapless. He picked me up in a limousine, and we went to a fabulous home in River Oaks where his ex-wife, Gene Tierney, the famous movie actress, lived with her new husband. Everyone, including Oleg's daughter, who was only a couple years younger than me, was very nice to me.

Naively, I thought he was just being fatherly, but I don't think Mr. Cassini only had friendship in mind. He told me that he and his brother, Gigi Cassini, had rented a house in Acapulco for the holidays and invited me to come down. I hesitated, but when he told me to please bring a girlfriend and that we would have a room together, I accepted. I was dying to go back to Acapulco.

But first I went to see Mother. After a stay in the state mental institution in Rusk, she had moved into a small, dark apartment in Kilgore, Texas.

On Christmas we drove to Nacogdoches for Christmas dinner with Mama. I was so happy to see her, and she was overjoyed that her "little girl" was home. She cooked her good old Christmas dinner, which I loved—and which I still prepare to this day for my kids: turkey with cornbread stuffing, sweet potatoes, peas, giblet gravy, and coconut meringue pie. I told her about my new career, but mostly she just wanted to know I was safe in New York.

Every time I visited Mama I'd bring her a pretty new dress, and she'd protest that I shouldn't be spending money on her. She never wanted to take anything from anyone, and I always admired that about her.

Mama and I rarely if ever talked about Mother's condition, but I could tell it was wearing on Mama.

"Lana Kaye, I'm sorry. It got so bad, I had no choice. I had to have her committed to Rusk," she said, shaking her head. "I was terrified she might overdose and die."

I felt so bad for my grandmother, having to go through that, watching the men in the white coats take Mother away, remembering how terrible it was when I had to go through it myself. I could tell it was heartbreaking for Mama, but she was stoic, as usual.

When Mother and I got back to Kilgore, she went to bed and stayed there, claiming she was "sick with a virus." It was obvious she was back on the pills. I could hardly wait to get away from there. I felt so helpless and hopeless. I didn't know how to solve it, so my only option seemed to be, as always, just to escape.

At one of the many parties my girlfriend and I attended in Acapulco, I met a Mexican playboy and actor named Hugo Stiglitz. He was half-Austrian with blond hair and blue eyes, and I thought he was just gorgeous. But while we were dancing, flashbulbs suddenly started popping, the crowd parted, and into the party walked George Hamilton with Lynda Bird Johnson, Merle Oberon, and her husband, Bruno Paglia, and John Wayne and his wife, Pilar. It was as if royalty had just entered the room; I'd never seen movie stars in person before, and I was dazzled.

The next day while having lunch at La Concha, the beach club at Las Brisas, George Hamilton—tall, tanned, and gorgeous—walked in my direction. He looked like a Greek god in red bathing trunks, with a sun reflector tucked under his arm. I never in a million years thought I'd be this close to him. But he walked right past me, never even giving me a glance.

Aside from being ignored by my future husband, I met Francesco Scavullo on that trip. Francesco was one of the most successful, sought-after photographers in New York. He took one look at me and said, "Darling, you must come to see me." I'd had a lot of disappointments, so I didn't want to get my hopes up too high, but I couldn't help but feel that maybe this would be my big break.

Back in New York, my agents immediately called his studio and made an appointment. A lot of the important photographers usually had one of their assistants look at your book, but Francesco saw me himself. He was warm and friendly and happy to see me again. He looked through my photographs while I held my breath. He then politely thanked me, kissed me on both cheeks, and said good-bye. "Oh, well," I thought, "another dead end."

But the next morning my booker, Monique, called me very excited. "Scavullo just booked you for a shoot with *Harper's Bazaar* tomorrow!" I couldn't believe it. *Harper's Bazaar*! I was excited, overjoyed, and petrified.

I was so nervous as I stepped onto the set, remembering the terrible experience I'd had with Jérôme Ducrot. What if I got sent away again? Maybe Eileen would fire me, realizing I wasn't model material after all.

The music blasting, I started moving tentatively, as Francesco kept encouraging me. "Yes, yes. That's perfect, darling. Beautiful, beautiful!"

Francesco's approval was all I needed. Magically, something shifted inside me. I was no longer nervous. I literally felt like I was having an intimate love affair with the camera. At that moment I became a model, and I owe it all to Francesco, who became a good friend for years to come.

Eileen Ford and her husband, Jerry, often gave parties in their elegant townhouse. The first time I received an invitation I felt like I had truly arrived. No longer was I a little hick from Texas—I was an Eileen Ford model!

Among the glamorous guests were celebrities, ad executives, writers, and many of the power players from the financial world. And, of course, there was always a bevy of beautiful young models. There was nothing Eileen liked more than for one of her girls to meet and marry a wealthy man. She had a long and happy marriage herself, and she felt that should be every girl's ultimate goal.

At one of these parties I was standing in the corner of the room with my friend Yaffa Turner, a pretty Israeli girl who had started modeling at the same time as me, when Eileen came over with a short, balding, unattractive gnome of a man and introduced him to us.

"Girls, I'd like you to meet Bernie Cornfeld. Bernie's a very successful financier," she said, and walked on to another group at the party.

We made some small talk with Bernie, then he told us he was flying to Los Angeles for the weekend. "Would the two of you like to join me? There's a group of us going. We'll take my plane," he said.

We figured that because he was Eileen's good friend, he had to have been a nice guy. How wrong we were.

It was the middle of February, and though it was freezing in New York, Los Angeles was sunny and warm. The Bel Air house we stayed in was sprawling and impeccably decorated, with beautiful grounds and a fabulous pool.

Once we'd been shown to our rooms, Bernie checked in with us. "Is there anywhere you girls want to go? I have a driver waiting outside," he said. The idea of being chauffeur driven in a limousine to run errands was pretty exciting to us. So Bernie handed us both hundred dollar bills and told us to bring back some goodies for the house. That night we had a lovely dinner at the house, and Yaffa and I retired to our respective rooms.

I was sound asleep when suddenly I was awakened by someone crawling into my bed. It was Bernie! What could possibly make him think I'd even give him a second look, much less anything else? He grabbed me and attempted to kiss me. I pulled away and tried to push him off me. He became very forceful in a violent, scary way.

"No, stop! Please, please stop!" I pleaded.

"Shut up," he snapped coldly. He pinned down my arms and roughly began trying to force himself between my legs. All the visions of that terrible night in Houston came flooding back, and I started crying hysterically.

"Please don't. Please. You don't understand!" I somehow got him to stop and listen to me. I told him the story of the night I was raped through my tears.

Suddenly he became nice again. "I'm sorry," he said softly, and he left the room. I just lay there sobbing and shaking with fear and anger. I was so afraid he or someone else would come into my room, and there wasn't a lock on the door. I pushed a chair up against it and barely slept the rest of the night.

I avoided Bernie the rest of the weekend, and I didn't say a word to him during the flight back to New York. Whenever I ran into him anywhere afterward, I gave him the cold shoulder.

A few years later, when George and I were together, Bernie wanted to buy George's huge mansion in Beverly Hills. George was broke at the time and desperate to sell, and it was all I could do to be coolly polite to Bernie. Even worse, he kept inviting me and George places, and I just couldn't bring myself to tell George what had happened. I was too ashamed and embarrassed, so I was just polite to Bernie, but I could never forget it.

Back at work, Eileen decided to send me to Paris to learn the ropes. I flew over in coach on a crowded plane, crammed between an Indian man in a turban who smelled like curry and a skinny Afghan student with body odor. I stayed in a hotel on the left bank for $2.50 a night and shared a room with no bathroom with two other models.

What followed was a whirlwind of immersing myself in culture and taking modeling gigs throughout Europe. I got paid for modeling jobs in Italy and Germany and often in Paris with big stacks of bills. Also, a commercial I'd done before I left New York for Carnation Slender hit it big, and checks for thousands of dollars were pouring in. It seemed like things were really starting to turn around for me, but I still felt lonely and insecure much of the time.

I was still bulimic and eating as much French food and drinking as much red wine as I could. Then, on a photo shoot for Italian Vogue in Tunisia, I became terribly sick with stomach problems, from which I've suffered off and on ever since. I'm pretty sure the bulimia caused my stomach issues. You can't be throwing up all the time like that and not have it affect your health.

Years later, when I read Princess Diana's biography, I learned that she had bulimia for years and that it always resurfaced whenever she was feeling anxious or lost. I could definitely relate, as that had been my pattern as well.

By Christmas, I was feeling better, and I went home to Texas. Mother was still in and out of hospitals and mental institutions.

After Christmas, I escaped back to Acapulco. I was looking forward to spending time with Hugo again. One afternoon we ran into George Hamilton again, who was with his friends Tony Curtis and famed Los Angeles hairdresser Gene Shacove.

"George, meet Alana Collins," Gene said. "And Alana, I'm sure you know who George Hamilton is?"

"Hello," I said, politely, but said nothing else.

Later George told me he thought I was a snotty model, but I was just shy and had no idea what to say to a "movie star." Besides, I figured he was a smooth playboy, and I wasn't going to fawn all over him.

The next day my friend Carol Most invited me to come with her to Mexico City. She was friends with Tony, Gene, and George and was going to meet up with them there. When we arrived, I was disappointed to hear that George had gone back to Los Angeles to film a movie. Carol was also going back to LA and invited me to come. We all went out to The Factory, the hot night spot in LA, with Tony

Curtis, Gene Shacove, and Sonny and Cher. This was all pretty exciting to a little girl from Texas!

I went back to New York determined to buckle down and make a name for myself. I was starting to be booked a lot thanks to my *Harper's Bazaar* shoot and my work in Europe. I also started booking quite a few commercials, which was where the big money was. I flew back to Paris to do the collections, but this time I traveled with Eileen and we went first class, enjoying caviar and sipping champagne—a far cry from that cramped, smelly flight the last time! By now Eileen had taken me under her wing, and I was beginning to think of her as a second mother.

By June of 1968 it was "summer in the city." Work had slowed down for me, and I started suffering from dark depressions that would last several days at a time. As the summer dragged on, my outlook became more and more bleak.

Then, out of the blue, I got a letter from Mama telling me my birth father had died. He was only forty-six. His mother had written to Mama to let her know.

I felt a strange sense of sadness. I'd never known my father, but he had always been such a big question mark in my life. Why hadn't he ever reached out to me? Did he ever care about me? Now I would never know.

At twenty-one, I felt like my life was over, like I'd never work again, and that I'd never fall in love. I felt like something was wrong with me, that I'd never have feelings for anyone again. But all that was about to change.

Chapter 6

That summer I saw an astrologer whom another model had recommended in an attempt to try to understand why I was feeling so disconnected and unhappy. This was just the beginning of a long line of astrologers, psychics, soothsayers, and therapists that I consulted for years in a desperate attempt to find myself.

The astrologer recommended I see a therapist—not the warmest woman I'd ever met, to say the least. Whenever I saw her, I always felt like I was defending myself. Our conversations typically went like this:

She'd ask me something like, "Well, Alana, what did you do today?"

And I responded with something like, "I went shopping to find a pair of black heels."

Then she would ask, "Why?"

And I'd reply, "Because I needed them."

"You 'needed' them?"

"Well, yes, I don't have a pair of black heels to go with this black dress I have."

"Alana," she'd say, "you don't 'need' them. You 'want' them."

And I would argue, "No, I need them to go with my black dress."

Not surprisingly, I would always leave these sessions feeling depressed that I'd spent money I wasn't making for someone to argue with me about a damn pair of black shoes. I didn't see how she was leading me to explore why I thought I "needed" those shoes, as I hadn't yet gotten to the more introspective part of my life. That, thankfully, would come—though much later.

When I landed a Macleans toothpaste commercial that was going to shoot for three weeks in Europe, I was thrilled. Not only was I going to get paid well, but I'd also get residuals and a trip to Europe. I thought maybe, at last, my luck was changing! Then it changed back. Maud Adams, one of the biggest models in the business, had originally been booked to film another Macleans commercial for one day in New York, and because of a fever blister, they wanted to replace her with me. They were going to give me her commercial—and she would get mine. And my trip to Europe!

I had no idea that this was fate in disguise.

David Gilmour, a friend I occasionally had dinner with, invited me to Le Club, a very exclusive private dinner club on East 54th Street. David and I were dancing when he stopped to say hello to the man dancing with his date next to us, who just happened to be George Hamilton.

"George," David said, introducing me. "This is Alana Collins."

"Yes, of course. We met in Acapulco. So nice to see you again," he said, oozing charm.

"You too," I replied, smiling politely.

The next night I was out again with David at Le Club, and again we ran into George. We stopped and said hello, and he and David chatted briefly. I thought it was quite a coincidence we would run into him two nights in a row. I also thought he was just as handsome as when I had seen him in Acapulco.

The next day I flew out to Los Angeles for a modeling job. My first night there a few of us went to the Candy Store. I was dancing with a friend when someone pinched me on my rear end. I whirled around to find George standing there, with a big smile and a twinkle in his eye.

It had to be more than coincidence that we would run into each other three nights in a row—on different coasts! He got my number before I left, and I wondered if I'd actually hear from him.

George called and left a message the following afternoon. I waited a while to call him back because I didn't want to seem too eager. When I finally did, he said, "I didn't know if I was going to hear from you. I just made plans to see some friends, but I'll see if I can change them and call you back."

I was disappointed and wished I hadn't waited so long to return his phone call. I wondered if I'd see him after all.

He called back. "Okay, I was able to rearrange my plans. Would you like to join me and some friends at my place at nine, and we'll go out from there?"

"Sure," I said, now excited that I was actually going to be going out with George Hamilton. I carefully selected my wardrobe: hip-hugger pants from London, a silk shirt tied at the waist, and my favorite gold-chain belt that I'd bought in Saint Tropez the past summer. I followed the directions he gave me and drove through large iron gates, up a long driveway, and up to an imposing English stone mansion in my beat-up rented Corvair. I'd never seen a house like that, not even back in River Oaks. The house was called Grey Hall, and it was the second house built in Beverly Hills—in 1909, by Harry Lombard, Carole Lombard's godfather.

The house was enormous and impeccably decorated in priceless French antiques. It even had a ballroom! I couldn't believe people actually lived like this, though I tried not to act too impressed as he showed me around.

A friend of George's, Gould Morrison, and his date, a tall, exotic-looking model named Caroline, were also there. We all went to Candy Store.

George and I danced, then he danced a couple of times with Caroline. I would find out years later from George that Caroline was not Gould's date, but also George's! When he couldn't reach me, he had made a date with her. And when I called, he knew he wanted to see me but didn't want to break his date with her. So he brought Gould along and passed off the night as a "double date," with both Caroline and I thinking Gould was the other's date!

At one point while we danced, George leaned in and said, "I'm going to Europe next week. Would you like to come?"

As tempting as his offer was, there was no way I was going. "It sounds great," I said, "but I'm sorry. I just don't know you well enough to go on a trip with you."

He seemed disappointed, but after a few more dances we headed back to his house. "Would you like to have dinner tomorrow night?" he asked, as he walked me to my car.

"Sure," I replied, and I bid my polite goodnight. I could hardly wait to see him again.

The following evening George came to pick me up in a white Cadillac convertible. He was wearing a purple-and-white checked cowboy shirt—right out of "Your Cheatin' Heart." If that wasn't the way to a Texas gal's heart, I don't know what was! He told me years later that he carefully orchestrated the car and his attire.

George was not only handsome and charming; he was also smart, well read, and had a great sense of humor. I was definitely smitten but trying not to show it.

After dinner and a movie, we went back to his house and shared a joint in the ballroom. We kissed for a while, then he took my hand and led me upstairs to a huge bedroom suite, all decorated in red silk and beautiful antiques. There was a large canopied bed on a platform with steps. It looked like a bed a king would sleep in!

I was incredibly nervous because I was so inexperienced sexually, but the grass had certainly helped. We made love and eventually fell asleep. I didn't hear from him the next day and soon started to worry that I wasn't going to hear from him again.

Then fate stepped in. I got a call from Eileen Ford asking me if I wanted to go to London to do a modeling job, and I was thrilled. Later that day George called. I told him about going to London and said that I had to fly back to New York on the red-eye the next night.

"That's great!" he said. "Let's fly together. Come to dinner at my house tomorrow night and we'll go to the airport afterward." During dinner he told me he had to go to South America for a week before going on to Europe and asked if we might meet up in Saint Tropez. That sounded great to me.

The following night George's southern cook made us a fabulous meal—definitely the way to my heart. We ate informally in the kitchen, and during dinner George's mother, who lived with him, came down to meet me. She was very chic, dressed in a long flowing robe, with her jet-black hair pulled back in a chignon.

Ann "Teeny" Hamilton Spalding was straight out of Auntie Mame. She had been married four times (like my mother). Her last husband was Jesse Spalding, of the Spalding sporting goods fortune, although he, unfortunately, was disinherited. Ann had been married to several wealthy men, but somehow she ended up with no money, so George supported her and his half-brother, Bill, who was also very chic and very gay and just as much a character as their mother. Bill was also a very talented decorator and had done the entire house.

After dinner we flew together to New York. Just before we landed at JFK George headed to the restroom and changed his complete wardrobe! He then flew on to South America.

Two days later I left New York for London and a week of shooting there. I hadn't heard a word from George and was a nervous wreck I wouldn't hear from him. I had dinner with some friends in London who also knew George and who told me he was notoriously unreliable. Now I was really anxious I'd never hear from him again.

A friend had fixed me up on a date with Peter Sellers, and I was looking forward to it. I was feeling so down that I thought for sure this guy who was so funny in the movies would surely be a lot of laughs. But I was disappointed. He wasn't at all like the funny characters he played. In fact, he was actually sort of morose. He picked me up in his Rolls-Royce, and we went to dinner at Mr. Chow. Afterward he took me to Kensington Palace to meet his friend, Princess Margaret, and her husband, Lord Tony Snowdon.

When we arrived, Warren Beatty was playing the piano, with Princess Margaret sitting beside him. At this point in time, Bonnie and Clyde was a monster hit, and he was a huge star.

I was wearing a bracelet made out of elephant hair and gold, which was the new hot "must have" from Paris, and Princess Margaret's husband, Tony Snowdon, admired it. Peter took me aside and suggested I give it to him, and I did, though I wasn't really happy about it.

When it was time to leave, Warren asked if we could give him a ride back to the Dorchester Hotel, which we did. I was pretty impressed with this life I seemed to be living, but as always, I acted as if I was totally used to meeting royalty and movie stars.

When we dropped Warren off, Peter said, "Why don't we stop by my house and smoke a joint?"

"Oh God," I thought. "Is he going to try to kiss me?" I had no romantic interest in him at all. I was much too crazy about George.

"Okay," I said. "But I have to work early in the morning so I can't stay long." I had a couple of puffs with him, and when I said, "I really should leave now," he was a perfect gentleman and drove me back to the hotel.

Finally, the day I was supposed to leave for Saint Tropez I received a telegram from George telling me to meet him at the Byblos Hotel. I was overjoyed and nervously looking forward to seeing him.

Chapter 7

I've learned over the years that going on a trip with someone you've just started dating can either be a disaster or, which I think is probably rare, you just might fall madly in love. For us it was the latter. George and I had one of the most fun, romantic trips imaginable.

I'd been to Saint Tropez before with two model friends, but we stayed in an inexpensive pensione. Now I was experiencing it in a whole new light. The Byblos was a luxurious yet charming Mediterranean-style oasis in the middle of Saint Tropez, surrounded by flower-filled gardens and with a sparkling blue pool.

George arrived after me, along with his four large suitcases! This was my introduction to George's traveling habits. He also pulled up in a red Ferrari. He had just purchased the car from a friend from England, who hadn't told him that the steering wheel was on the right-hand side. I spent a fair amount of time on that trip hanging out the car window, helping navigate around the mountainous curves in the South of France.

We were invited to many glamorous events with beautiful, high-profile people during our stay. The first night there was a dinner party at the house of Countess Jacqueline de Ribes, a very prominent social doyenne from Paris. Valentino, the famous Italian designer, and his longtime partner, Jon Carlo, were among the guests. I had recently done my very first runway show for him in New York. He and Jon Carlo couldn't have been sweeter. They both remembered me and seemed impressed that I was dating George Hamilton.

But the next night almost ended our relationship. We went to a big party, and George, who had quite a few drinks, got up and started singing with the band—a big hit with everyone. When the party ended, I was tired and ready to go back to the hotel, but George was

53

still going strong. The band members encouraged him to come to a club with them where they could continue playing, so we all squeezed into his red Ferrari.

By the time we got into the club, I felt like George was ignoring me. He was completely caught up with his new friends in the band, and I had had enough. Without saying a word, I left and walked back to the hotel. I was fuming.

I crawled into bed, feeling hurt and angry, and finally I went to sleep. I woke up a couple hours later to the sound of his rummaging around in the living room. I got up and found him packing his suitcases.

"Where are you going?" I asked.

"Well, you left me at the club alone, so it seems it's just best for me to leave."

"You were acting as if I wasn't even there," I said. "You just waltzed off with the band, leaving me to straggle along behind you," I said.

"You left without even telling me," he replied.

I don't remember who said they were sorry first, but we ended up making love and making up.

I think almost ending our relationship over such a silly thing made us both realize how much we were beginning to care about each other. I think we also realized that we were both pretty stubborn and strong willed. George is a Leo and I'm a Taurus, and this means astrologically that although we were very attracted to each other, neither of us would easily back down in an argument.

The rest of the two-week trip was a romantic blur. We stayed at the Byblos a couple more days, sitting in the sun by the pool in the daytime or going to one of the trendy beach clubs for lunch. At night we'd have fabulous dinners and later head to Les Caves du Roy, the club in the Byblos, where the elite of Saint Tropez danced the night away. Then we drove down to Monte Carlo and stayed at the legendary Hotel de Paris.

One night we went to the Grand Casino and gambled until dawn. When we got back to the hotel, instead of going to bed, George said, "Let's take a drive to the Hotel du Cap. I want to take you to breakfast there."

We drove along the Corniche and arrived at the Hotel du Cap in about an hour. George had arranged a *framboise* (raspberry soufflé) and champagne breakfast, and I was just in heaven. Again, he knew exactly the way to win my heart! There was a slight ulterior motive, however. It seems George had left a suitcase of clothes the last time he'd stayed at the hotel and wanted to pick it up. As I was to learn later, George had clothes all over the world.

From Monte Carlo, we drove down the coast across the Italian border and stopped in Portofino for a couple of nights. We stayed at the incredibly romantic Splendido Hotel perched on the side of the mountain, overlooking the small town and the harbor and the amazingly blue Mediterranean. There was something magical about Portofino, and it was there that George first told me he loved me. I was already madly in love with him!

The second night we went to dinner at a lovely restaurant on the water. George loved to show off his command of languages, so he spoke to the waiter in Italian. I spoke a little Italian myself from having done some modeling in Italy, but George had the accent down so well that I thought he spoke it better than he actually did. Because he liked to do the ordering in Italian, I told him I'd have the fish.

"La signorina prende una pesca," said George to the waiter.

"Una pesca?" the waiter asked in surprise.

"Si," George answered emphatically. "La pesca."

"Si, Signore," the waiter shrugged. George gave him his order and the waiter left.

Later the waiter retuned with spaghetti for George and a peach, cut into sections, which he placed in front of me.

"What's this?" I asked.

"Il signore ha chiesto una pesca per lei," the waiter answered. It seems George had not ordered fish (pesce), but had gotten his words mixed up and ordered a peach (pesca) for me. By then the kitchen was closed, so I had to share George's spaghetti. We told that story for years, and we both still laugh about it.

The next day we drove to Rome. We shopped a lot in the daytime, had lovely lunches, and went out at night to wonderful dinners in charming Roman restaurants.

One day we were in Gucci near the Piazza di Spagna, and I noticed outside the store that about a hundred photographers and onlookers had gathered. I wondered what could be happening. When George and I came out the door, all hell broke loose. People were cheering and calling out George's name, and the paparazzi were snapping away. I hadn't realized that George was such a star in Italy and that our being in Rome created such a stir.

We had been invited to the island of Capri and the Mare Moda, which was a huge fashion event being held there. Capri was perhaps the most romantic of all the places we had been. One restaurant I will always remember was so charming, with the most delicious pasta and romantic Italian music. The owner asked to take a photo of George and me. I've never been back to Capri, but George was there several years ago and told me that the photo of us was still hanging on the wall.

When it was time for the trip to end, we returned to Rome for a night or two and then flew back to New York together. George went on to California because he had to get ready to head back to the South of France to film a new TV series, *The Survivors*. He'd made a fantastic deal and was getting paid more than any television actor had ever been paid; he was making even more than his costar, Lana Turner.

George said he would call when he got to France, but a couple weeks went by and I hadn't heard a word. I missed him desperately. I started to wonder, despite how much in love we both had seemed, that perhaps this was just a fling for him. I cried myself to sleep every night. When a friend invited me to a party being thrown by John Loeb Jr. (of Loeb and Loeb), I accepted, knowing it would be better for me than staying in my apartment being depressed over George.

The party guests were a glamorous group—New York society with a few movie people thrown in. I met Hugh O'Brian, star of the hit series *Wyatt Earp*, who asked me out. I also met Bob Evans, a very charming, handsome ladies' man who had gone from being a Seventh Avenue clothing manufacturer to a movie actor to the powerful head of Paramount Studios.

Bob admired the necklace I was wearing—a large, gold Edwardian-style cross with a ruby in the center, which hung from a long, heavy gold chain. I had found it in an antique store in London's Portobello Road, and it was my prized possession. But when I got home later that night, I realized that my cross was no longer hanging from the chain. I couldn't believe it.

The next morning, bright and early, the phone rang. It was Bob Evans.

"I hope you don't mind that I got your number," he said. "Did you enjoy the party last night?"

"I would have," I told him, "but I lost my beautiful necklace."

"Well," he said, "if you'll have dinner with me tonight, I will have your cross for you."

"That's impossible," I said. "I know it was on the chain when I left the party, and I must have lost it somewhere in the street."

"Come to dinner with me tonight, and I promise you that I'll have your cross," he said in his rather sexy, low voice.

Now I was really curious. How could I resist? I still hadn't heard from George, so I accepted.

Bob picked me up in a black, stretch limousine, and as I got into the car, he handed me a small box wrapped with a ribbon. I opened it, and there was my cross! Not a replica, but my exact cross. One side of it was a little smashed; it looked like it had been trampled or run over by a car.

"How on earth did you find it?" I asked, incredibly astonished that he could have produced it, as if out of thin air.

"I told you I would have it for you," he said smiling mysteriously. To this day I still don't know how he got it, but I was pretty amazed and very impressed.

Over dinner I told Bob I'd been going out with George, who happened to be a friend of his.

"You know, actors aren't so reliable," Bob said. "I think you need someone more stable"—obviously meaning himself.

In the limo on the way back to my apartment, Bob tried to talk me into going back to LA with him. Boy, these Hollywood men sure moved fast!

"Thank you for the lovely dinner," I told him, "but I have to work tomorrow."

The next morning several dozen roses arrived from Bob, and he called me from the airport to tell me how much he had enjoyed the evening. Then, the next day he called and offered me a part in a Paramount film and told me I could stay at his house for three weeks during the filming. I turned him down. Even though I found him attractive and charming, I was much too in love with George.

In the meantime a photograph of me and George in Rome ran in Time magazine and upped my stock in the modeling world. I was keeping busy but was still depressed I hadn't heard from George. I had almost given up on him when I received a telegram that he was coming to New York. I hadn't heard from him in over three weeks! I wanted to be cool about it, but I was ecstatic.

After spending a couple days together, he asked me to fly out to California with him. Our romance was definitely back on. When we arrived at his house late at night, sitting in the kitchen with his brother Bill was a friend of theirs from Memphis along with Troy Donahue! I'd had such a crush on Troy in high school. I was almost more impressed with meeting him than I had been meeting George!

Chapter 8

⁓

When I was growing up, the holidays were always my favorite time of the year. Even when the situation with Mother started to turn bad, she would at least still try to pull it together for Christmas dinner. Now, for the first time I was in love at Christmastime. I was going to do whatever I could to make it special.

I shopped all over New York for gifts for George—a cashmere scarf, a Cartier key chain, a beautiful antique pen. George said he hadn't had time to shop for me, but of course I thought this meant he was going to surprise me . . .

George was in Chicago for six weeks over the holidays doing *Barefoot in the Park* at the Drury Lane Theater and invited me to join him there. Because he only had a long weekend off for Christmas, he arranged for us to fly down to Caneel Bay in Saint John for three days.

George had rented the Rockefeller house, a charming wood-frame house right on the beach, but it was quite a distance away from the actual hotel at Caneel Bay. After flying all night, we arrived Christmas morning, and I excitedly gave him his presents. But . . . he actually hadn't bought me anything! If that wasn't bad enough, he was so exhausted from doing the eight performances a week that he slept for two days and I sat on the beach and cried.

I was lonely and miserable and so very hurt. I tried to hide that I was upset, but by the time we got to Miami to catch the flight back to Chicago, it was pretty obvious I was not happy.

We were at the bar at the Jockey Club, a famous Miami resort, when he asked why I was being so cold and distant.

Finally I told him, "I wouldn't have cared what the present was if you had just made the effort to get me some little thing, just to show you cared."

George apologized and explained that Christmas had never been a big deal in his family. At least I understood why we had such different points of view about the holidays, but when it happened again for my birthday when I was in New York, I was hurt and disappointed. George hadn't even called me. A wealthy young businessman who had been trying to date me had sent me flowers, so I decided to call George and rub it in.

When he answered, I gushed, "Thank you sooo much for the beautiful yellow roses. How did you know they were my favorite?"

There was silence on the phone. "Well . . . I'm glad you liked them," he finally replied. He never forgot my birthday or Christmas again!

After Christmas George was offered a movie with Peter Lawford that was filming in Yugoslavia. He didn't ask me to come, and I was very depressed, wondering how being apart for two months would affect our relationship. Once again luck intervened, and Eileen asked me if I wanted go to Paris and Milan to work. It was perfect—it meant I would be able to see George.

My first job was a trip to the Canary Islands with Italian Vogue, though there was nothing really beautiful about the Canary Islands that I could see. We stayed in a large, touristy hotel, we ate bad food, and the weather was terrible. To make matters worse, we were shooting in bathing suits and skimpy summer outfits and we were freezing. I was very vocal about my discomfort, but the other model, Agneta, who was more seasoned than me, gave me advice on how to be professional.

I found an old diary some years ago in which I'd written about the trip and talked about how I realized I needed to work on my tendency to be a prima donna. I learned later, after years of therapy, that people with low self-esteem can vacillate between grandiosity and feeling like the biggest loser on earth. Little wonder that I had these terrible depressions that would last for days at a time.

When George finally called, we met in Paris for a romantic get-away at the Lancaster Hotel before flying back to New York together. All it took was our being together and I was happy again.

We continued our long-distance romance several more months. I began staying longer periods in Los Angeles and getting modeling jobs through Eileen's associate, Nina Blanchard.

George's family, Teeny and Bill, liked me, but they also saw me as a threat: it was clear I wouldn't be as easy to manipulate as George was. I liked them both but saw how they took advantage of him.

George told me he would never get married because his mother had been married four times, and because the marriages had never worked, it had left him very commitment phobic. But we were in love, so I still believed that no matter what he said, we would eventually get married.

When *The Survivors* got canceled, ABC gave George a new show, *Paris 7000*, to finish out his contract. In it he played a charming young ambassador in the American embassy in Paris, and his agent at William Morris told me that the producers were looking for an actress to play George's secretary. He sent me to read for the producers without anyone knowing I was George's girlfriend. God only knows how, but I got the part.

I rehearsed my lines (and George's) until I knew them backward and forward. George continued to keep our relationship a secret on the set and pretended as though we'd just met so people wouldn't think he got me the part.

When we were ready to shoot, I delivered my line, perfectly memorized from the script, but he ad-libbed! I was completely thrown.

"George," I said, in an accusatory tone, "that's not your line!"

You could have heard a pin drop. Here was this young upstart actress admonishing the star of the series! George laughed it off and we went on shooting, but my part was cut from the show after that week.

It was really quite exciting going out in Hollywood and then seeing photographs of me and George in fan magazines and gossip columns. I was living a life I had never imagined.

George and I finally decided I should move to LA and live with him. Eileen thought it was a mistake. "He's a playboy and he will never marry you," she warned me, but she couldn't talk me out of it.

For better or worse, I followed my heart, leaving behind a blossoming career in modeling to begin a life of professional and romantic uncertainty in California.

Tension was mounting at the house, with Teeny and Bill spending George's money like it was going out of style, and we decided we needed our own space. We rented a small house in Palm Springs and spent weekends there. I loved when we were alone—no family, no staff. I cooked or we barbecued or went out to restaurants. We had a few friends with houses in the area and sometimes invited others to stay with us.

One August weekend in 1969, before George's birthday, we learned of the horrific murders of actress Sharon Tate, Jay Sebring, and Sharon's houseguests, Abigail Folger and Wojciech Frykowski. The atmosphere changed overnight in Hollywood. Everybody became paranoid, and people started hiring bodyguards and getting guns.

Jay had been a close friend of George's and was supposed to attend George's birthday party. We canceled the party immediately.

Sometime later friends of mine from New York came to visit, and I took them to the Candy Store. George had to work early the next morning, so he stayed home to work on his lines. A bearded man came over several times and asked me to dance. Each time I said firmly, "No, thank you," but he kept coming back. Brian Morris, who ran the Candy Store, came over to sit with us.

"I can't believe you turned him down when he asked you to dance," he told me. "I think he's in shock that any woman would do that."

"Why?" I asked. "Who is he, anyway?"

"Steve McQueen," he replied, surprised I hadn't recognized him.

A few minutes later Steve returned and asked me to dance again. This time I agreed, but I was quick to tell him that George was my boyfriend so he didn't get any ideas. He was married anyway, so at first I figured he was just being friendly.

The following week George and I were at a party where Steve and his then-wife, Neile, were also guests. Steve came over to say hello and continued to talk to me for a good part of the evening. I could tell that George was getting a little jealous. I was also terribly jealous when it came to George. When I found a letter in his briefcase from a woman he had gone out with when we were first dating, we had a terrible fight—he tried to turn it around on me, blaming me for snooping in his briefcase.

At this point in my life, I was a confusing mix of confidence and deep insecurity. I kept the insecurity on the inside, where no one ever saw it, but on the outside I displayed pure confidence. I was still occasionally bulimic, which, as I explained before, always got worse with anxiety, but I never let George know about it.

I was also strong willed and feisty. One night George and I were at the bar in El Morocco, a very fashionable, elite night club in New York, when a girl who had probably had one drink too many kept coming over and flirting with him. "Excuse me," I finally said. "We're together here and we're trying to talk."

She ignored me and kept talking to George. I too had probably had one drink too many. I grabbed her by the back of the hair, pushed her face down on the bar, and said, "I think you didn't understand me. This is my boyfriend and you need to go now!"

She left immediately. George thought it was just great and gleefully told the story for years (and still does). He chalked it up to my Cherokee heritage mixed with "firewater."

George and I had been going together for almost three years now, and I wanted to move forward in our relationship; he didn't seem to want to, which created one level of tension. Another level was the tension mounting between us and his family. Finally, I'd had enough, and we had an argument one night and broke up. He took off for Palm Springs, and I moved in with friends temporarily.

The following day I was driving down Beverly Drive, depressed and miserable. I was stopped at a traffic light and I could almost feel someone staring at me. I glanced over into the famous blue eyes that seemed to be boring into me: Steve McQueen. This time I recognized him—he was clean shaven and gorgeous. He smiled and waved; I smiled and waved back and went on my way. When I pulled over down the block and got out of my car, he suddenly roared up next to me in his black Porsche. He had made a swift U-turn in the middle of Beverly Drive.

"Do you want to grab a coffee?" he asked.

"Sure," I replied. He leaned across, opened the door for me, and I hopped in.

Steve had just separated from Neile, and when I told him that George and I had broken up, he asked me out for dinner that night and I accepted.

We went to a small restaurant near the beach, had a lot of white wine, and talked for hours. I felt horribly guilty, like I was cheating on George, but after all, we were broken up. Besides, I liked Steve; he was exciting and impulsive and so very attractive.

Steve and I had dinner a couple more times, and he invited me to his house in Palm Springs for the weekend. From there, we drove to Mexico for dinner, where we drank a lot of beer and tequila. It's a wonder we weren't killed driving back to Palm Springs in the middle of the night, especially at the speed Steve drove.

Steve and I had a great time together, but I soon realized that I really missed George. Finally George called, and we made up over dinner. We moved back in together, and that was the end of me and Steve—at least for the time being.

Chapter 9

By now George's mother and brother were starting to hate me because they blamed me for George not being their meal ticket anymore. George had put his house on the market. As tensions rose, he and Bill had a huge dramatic fight on the stairwell, and George and I moved out. We temporarily rented a guesthouse on Bedford, behind the famous house where Lana Turner had lived when her daughter Cheryl Crane supposedly killed Lana's lover, Johnny Stompanato.

George had bought a house in Palm Springs and wanted to live there. It was a charming old Spanish-style home with the main house perched on the side of the mountain and stairs leading past giant palm trees, fragrant rose gardens, and grapefruit trees to a large, Olympic-sized pool and a guesthouse covered in purple bougainvillea. The mini-estate was surrounded by a high stone wall and flowering olean der bushes. I loved the house and our time there but could only take so much of the boring desert. Besides, I needed to continue working in LA.

George and I had one more big breakup—still over his refusal to make a commitment. We always refer to it as the "green chair incident." We were in Palm Springs, and he was outside the guesthouse downstairs, attempting to re-cover the back of a bar stool. He was tacking on the green fabric with a hammer when I came storming down the stairs.

"George, this has gone on long enough. You want me down here with you all the time and not in LA working. We've been together almost four years. Either we get married or I have to move on with my life."

An argument ensued, and we broke up yet again.

George left for Europe and toured through the wine country with Leslie Bricusse. I moved in with Leslie's wife, Evie, as they had broken up as well.

I was so depressed and miserable that I stayed in my old blue chenille robe all day and ate sweets. Evie finally suggested we go down to their house in Acapulco.

My old friend Hugo Stiglitz was there, and one night when we were all going out, he took out a tab of acid. As there were five of us, he cut it into five pieces and gave us each one.

I was afraid. A little grass was one thing, but acid was a hallucinogenic drug. I might go over the edge and never come back. Hugo convinced me, though, and within minutes I started to feel an incredible sense of well-being. We went to Le Club and I danced with Hugo, feeling very carefree and very happy.

Then suddenly, anxiety hit. I began feeling flushed and started to panic. A friend told me I needed to take something to help bring me down right away and gave me half a Valium. I don't think it helped very much.

The next twenty-four hours were a nightmare; we were sitting outside by the pool and everyone seemed to be enjoying their trip but me. I thought for sure I was going crazy, like my mother, and would never come back to reality. My heart felt like it was pounding out of my chest, and I couldn't stop seeing fireworks across the bay that just weren't there. It truly was one of the most horrible experiences of my life.

Finally someone gave me another Valium, and eventually I went to sleep around six in the morning. When I finally woke up, I felt normal again and vowed never to take another hallucinogenic as long as I lived.

Meanwhile, George came back from Europe and asked me to have dinner with him so we could talk. "I missed you and I love you," he told me, "and if you want to get engaged, we'll get married within the next year, I promise."

He gave me a beautiful pear-shaped diamond engagement ring, and I was ecstatic.

A few months later we were in London at Tramps with our good friends Johnny Gold, the owner, and his wife, Jan, when I noticed a girl staring at George.

"Who's that blonde who keeps staring at us?" I finally asked Jan.

At first, she didn't want to tell me, but she finally spilled the beans. It was Britt Ekland, and while we had been broken up, George had had an affair with her in the South of France. Jan said he had left her there thinking that he was coming back to continue their affair but had instead come home and asked me to marry him.

At first I was taken aback, but then I realized it really didn't matter that much now. First of all, it was clearly over, and secondly, we were engaged. It was ironic that some years later I ended up marrying another man she had been living with for two and a half years: Rod Stewart.

For the next year George and I lived in Palm Springs most of the time. We had planned to get married on the QE2 that summer with Sammy Davis Jr. and his wife, Altovise, as our best man and matron of honor. Leslie and Evie Bricusse, who were back together, would also accompany us.

I felt like George was still trying to put it off for as long as he could, but I was also starting to get cold feet—after four years. We ended up canceling the QE2 and flew to London instead. George went off to Rome for a day to pick up some suits he'd had made. I decided to stay in London and went to Tramps that night to have dinner with Johnny and Jan.

Lord Patrick Lichfield came into the club with a couple of friends. He was a very well-known and successful photographer, as well as being cousin to the queen and descended from a long line of royals. He was young and handsome and was considered quite a catch. We were introduced, and he asked me to dance several times.

When I left the club, I got into the back of a taxi, and as we stopped at a light, Patrick pulled up beside us on his motorcycle and, smiling, gestured for me to get on the back. Impulsively, I paid the driver, got out of the cab, and jumped on the back of his bike. He was certainly handsome and charming, but I was engaged to George. When he asked me out to dinner, I told him I couldn't and the reason why. He gave me his number and said if I changed my mind, I should give him a call.

George returned the next day, and I was feeling distant and angry. I felt like he was stalling on the marriage, and frankly, I was not only starting to get fed up, but maybe, because of the resentment I'd built up, I was also feeling like perhaps we needed a little space from each other. We had an amicable but bittersweet split; we decided to take some time apart and revisit our relationship in a month or so. I don't think George had any idea that I would be dating anyone else so soon.

George took a disastrous excursion down the Amazon River in a dilapidated boat with his friend Peter Rittmaster while I went with Patrick on the Honorable Michael Pearson's boat, *The Hedonist*, for a fun, romantic trip from Saint Tropez to Sardinia.

We went back to London, where I got a flat with a girlfriend and started modeling. Patrick took some beautiful photographs of me, which helped me get plenty of work.

He invited me to Shugborough Hall, which had been in his family for many generations. It was a huge, sprawling estate in the Staffordshire countryside on acres and acres of beautiful rolling green grounds. We arrived at night, and I was shown to my own beautiful room with a huge canopied bed. I learned that all unmarried couples were given their own separate rooms—all very British and proper. And although one's boyfriend visited in the night, by the following morning everyone was back in their own room.

The next morning, when I woke up, I opened the curtains to look out over the beautiful English countryside and, much to my surprise, saw lines of tourists. "Good Lord," I thought. "What the heck are all those people doing here?"

Later I learned that the house had been given to the National Trust in lieu of paying the huge death taxes when Patrick's grandfather died and passed it on to him, so most of it was cordoned off for public tours, leaving only a large wing of the palatial mansion for the current Lord Lichfield and his guests.

I'd noticed before that Patrick drank quite a bit, but now I was noticing it even more. One night, when we were in a restaurant in London, he literally went to sleep at the table and fell forward into his soup. After my experiences with two alcoholic stepfathers, I was getting concerned.

Patrick was in love with me and wanted me to move to England permanently and move in with him. He was making plans to introduce me to his cousin, Queen Elizabeth, but in my heart I still missed and thought about George.

Patrick got a photographic assignment in Fiji, so we flew to Los Angeles together. I needed to get my clothes from the house in Palm Springs. We planned to fly back to London together when he finished his shoot.

Meanwhile, I called George and drove down to Palm Springs to get my clothes. Everything between us was warm and friendly, and I think it was clear that we had missed each other. We went to Colonel Parker's house for an early dinner. Colonel Parker was Elvis Presley's manager and was a kind of father figure to George. He was quite a character, with all his stories of his carnival days and his adventures before he became Elvis's manager.

George went outside to talk to the Colonel for a while. When he came inside, he told me "The Colonel has Elvis's plane waiting at the airport if you want to go to Las Vegas and get married. But you have to give me your answer right now."

Without even thinking, I said, "Yes!"

We were both wearing jeans and T-shirts. I grabbed some flowers from the Colonel's back garden and stuck them in my hair, and we flew to Vegas. The Colonel had already arranged for us to get married in the penthouse suite of the Las Vegas Hilton. It all happened so quickly that my head was spinning.

We returned to the small house on Cordell Mews that George was renting, and our marriage made all the newspapers—apparently in Fiji as well, because that's how Patrick found out. George and I were in the living room when his assistant came in. "Alana, Patrick Lichfield is on the phone for you."

George was glaring at me, and I took the coward's way out. "Just tell him I'm not here."

I felt terrible, but what could I have said with George standing there that would have made Patrick feel better? In the end I did nothing, but I felt guilty about hurting him.

Chapter 10

We headed to Greece, where George was filming *Medusa* with Luciana Paluzzi, former James Bond girl and Italian sex symbol. I was jealous at first because she'd be working closely with George for two months, but once I met her, we became instant friends. I even ended up with a small role in the movie.

During the filming I had long days with nothing to do; my old anxiety surfaced and my bulimia escalated again. It wasn't as bad as it had been years ago, but it was still happening, usually when I got anxious about my situation with George.

But we were married now—what did I have to be anxious about? There was something deep inside me that I didn't understand, some deep-seated fear, some ever-present low-level anxiety that remained no matter how good things seemed on the outside. I still hadn't delved into any of the demons from my earlier years. I always handled things the same way: keep moving, keep running. As long as I was busy, I was okay. But the minute life slowed down, instead of being able to relax, the anxiety returned, and I would use food to alleviate it. Then, as always, I felt sick and ashamed of myself.

As my marriage went on, this vague anxiety didn't get better; I just looked for more and more activities to fill that dark hole instead of looking within. But that was yet to come.

When George and I arrived back in the States, we decided to drive the new little Mercedes that George had bought in New York back to Los Angeles. We stopped in Nacogdoches along the way so Mama could meet my new husband. When we arrived, the visit was pleasant—until all the bad news came out.

Much to my horror, I learned that Mama was being treated for colon cancer. I wanted the best care for Mama and tried to convince her to let me take her to Houston where the doctors and facilities were more advanced.

"No, Lana Kaye," she told me. "I'm happy with the way things are. I don't need a fancy big city doctor."

I always felt guilty that I never insisted, but I knew Mama: she was stubborn as a mule, so I'd never be able to convince her. When George and I stopped by later to see Uncle Gene and his new wife, he assured me that Mama's doctor was very competent and they felt the treatment was going well, that she'd be in remission soon.

The other part of the bad news had to do with Mother, whom Mama had to commit to Rusk once again. I was so embarrassed about my mother and her problems that I told George as little as possible. Looking back, I find it strange that I wouldn't have turned to him for more support, but I felt such tremendous shame about it and kept it stuffed down inside of me with all the rest of my shameful secrets.

When Mother was released from Rusk, I flew down to Texas on my own and found her an apartment in nearby Dallas. For a brief while she was okay, but it wasn't long before she started the same old pattern. She was only forty-nine years old, but I had to put her into a nursing home. It was clear she couldn't take care of herself. But she kept getting kicked out of nursing homes because she would steal drugs from the other patients or from the office. It was a nightmare.

Finally, I had run out of options in Texas. I decided to bring her to Los Angeles where I could keep a closer eye on her. I called my stepfather, and as always he showed up to help me. It was all we could do to get her on the plane with me back to LA. She was so drugged that I'm surprised they let me bring her on board.

I took Mother straight to the Edgemont Psychiatric Hospital, where she stayed three weeks. When she was released, I rented her an apartment. I would take her each week to see the psychiatrist from

Edgemont. He said that getting anywhere with her was difficult because she refused to admit she had a problem with drugs. For my mother, it was always a virus, her back, her nerves that were the problems, and she continued to seek pills as an answer. I tried to take her shopping, buy her new clothes—anything to get her interested in life. I so desperately wanted a mother to have a relationship with, but it seemed that it was never going to happen.

George, too, was struggling; his trouble was debt. Because he wasn't being offered any good films, he returned to the well-paying Drury Lane Theater outside Chicago to do *Paisley Convertible*. The play had a second female leading role perfect for me, and I worked my butt off with an acting coach in LA before we arrived in Chicago.

Just before the play opened, George and I spent the weekend in New York. There we got a call from my Uncle Gene that my grandmother's colon cancer had come back. She was in the hospital in Nacogdoches and might only have a couple more days to live. I couldn't believe I was going to lose my grandmother. How had it gotten so bad so quickly? I was shocked and upset. Everyone had just assured me that everything would be fine. Had they been protecting me from the truth?

I wanted to head to Texas first thing the next morning, but George insisted he had to go back to Chicago first for an important interview he had committed to. He assured me we could leave right from there but also suggested I could go on my own.

I was angry at him for placing so much importance on a damn interview when I was losing the most important person in my life, but I couldn't face flying down to Texas alone, then driving three hours to Nacogdoches in the middle of the night and seeing my dying grandmother without his support. So I went back to Chicago and waited for him to finish the interview. I will forever regret that decision. When we finally arrived at the hospital the following evening, a male nurse was exiting her room.

"I'm sorry," he said, "but your grandmother just expired." Expired? I'd never heard that word used that way before. I looked past him and saw her figure covered with a white sheet.

I suppose I could have—should have—gone into the room to see her, but I think I went into shock. George took me gently in his arms and steered me out of the hospital.

The funeral was small. It was held in a tiny church on the edge of a wooded area on the outskirts of Nacogdoches. Mama was buried in the small cemetery next to her sister and her sister's husband. My uncles and their wives attended the funeral with my cousins, and we all hugged each other, though I hadn't seen them since they were small children. The only person missing was my mother. Sadly, she was in no shape to travel.

I was filled with guilt and sorrow. Why hadn't I visited her more? Why hadn't I written more, called more? Why hadn't I insisted on taking her to doctors in Houston to treat the cancer, even when she said she wanted to stay in Nacogdoches?

To this day I can't think of her death without crying. I don't know how I would have turned out without her influence in my life. I don't think I'll ever forgive myself for letting my busy life take precedence over spending more time with her and especially for not getting there in time to say good-bye to her. And I held resentment in my heart toward George for not making it a priority to get on the plane with me that night.

We left Texas and went on with our lives. The play was a success, and I even got some nice reviews. Once the play's run ended, George and I went to Palm Beach to spend Christmas with Bill and Teeny, with whom we had reconciled just after we got married. Afterward we were invited to the opening of a new resort in Haiti, and then, in freezing February, we headed to Ravenna, Ohio, just outside of Cleveland, for a six-week run of *Paisley Convertible*. We stayed in a little apartment overlooking a field, and it felt like we were staying in an army barracks. So much for glamorous show business!

The first day of rehearsal I was so nauseated I could barely get through the morning. I thought I had the flu. I went to a doctor, whose office was next door to the theater, and I learned I was pregnant!

I was so surprised. George and I were both happy and excited, but we hadn't planned on having children so soon. It was so unexpected; it didn't seem real.

For the next two and a half months I was nauseated constantly. It was overwhelming, but somehow I kept up with the show. Nothing made me feel better. I lived on saltine crackers, and my hormones were raging. One night George and I were arguing about something petty, and I threw a pizza at him. It splattered all over the wall; it looked like a Miró painting!

Back in LA, we bought a house on Tower Road from a probate court estate sale, a beautiful, old, Mediterranean-style house, built around an Olympic-sized swimming pool. However, it needed a lot of work before we could live there. George was away in Florida doing another play, and I was left to supervise the workmen while living in the small guesthouse in the back.

George's brother helped me decorate the house, but I wanted to do it my way; which was basically to never make a decision about anything, so that the house was half empty. George and I argued over every detail. He and Bill wanted to make it this glamorous Hollywood deco palace, and I wanted a more traditional, homey place now that we had a baby on the way.

When I was seven months pregnant, I went down to Clearwater Beach, Florida, where George was doing dinner theater, still trying to keep up the hefty house payments and the enormous construction expenses we were incurring every week.

George wasn't feeling well, but he wasn't sure why, and I had to fly back to Los Angeles to finish the house and the nursery in time for the baby's birth. When I got home, George called to tell me that he had been diagnosed with a severe case of hepatitis and that he was going to be kept in a Palm Beach hospital for two weeks. Because

I was so pregnant, my doctor wouldn't let me fly back and be with him.

When he finally came home, his doctors said he would probably have to stay in bed for a couple months. I was in a real panic now. We had no money at all, and the bills were pouring in. We had a Guatemalan maid who couldn't drive, cook, or speak English, so I was doing the shopping, cooking all George's meals, taking trays upstairs to him, all the while hoping I wouldn't catch hepatitis in my last month of pregnancy. Our financial situation frightened me so much that I would go to the grocery market every day so I could have a good cry in the car where George couldn't see me. I didn't want him to know how scared I was and feel even worse that he was sick and not working.

When George first came home, I called Gloria Swanson, an old friend of George's family, who was very into health cures. She sent me to an herbalist in Glendale, who gave me some herbal tea that he said would help heal George's liver. He took it regularly, and within a few weeks, much to his doctor's surprise, his liver tests were back to normal.

Chapter 11

When he recovered, George got a film offer and starting shooting in LA. I was already three days over my due date and starting to cramp on a day when he was on the set, so I drove myself to the doctor.

"You're starting to dilate," the doctor told me. "You better have someone drive you to the hospital right away."

I called George on set. "I can't leave yet," he told me. "We're in the middle of a scene and it may take a few more hours to finish. Is there someone else who can drive you?" I decided, screw it, I'll just drive myself to the damn hospital. It probably wasn't the smartest thing to do, but I couldn't waste time trying to find someone to take me.

This was all new for me, and I was scared. I had no idea what to expect. The doctor and nurses prepped me and explained they had to wait to administer the epidural, spinal block, until the labor pains had reached a certain stage. Then I had my first contraction. I'd never felt that kind of pain in my life. It felt like my insides were coming apart!

"Can you give me the epidural now?" I gasped.

"We really need to wait until you're in the next stage," the nurse said. "You won't know when to push otherwise."

"Give me the goddamned epidural now!" I snapped. "Just tell me when to push, and I'll push!" And push I did! There was no way I was going to experience any more of those excruciating pains!

Three hours later George Ashley Hamilton arrived—seven and a half pounds and twenty-one inches long, with a head of dark hair and the most beautiful blue eyes. As I held him in my arms, for the first time in my life I knew the meaning of unconditional love. My heart melted as I looked into the eyes of my beautiful baby boy. I'll never forget that moment as long as I live.

But still no George. Tina Sinatra, who had become my closest friend over the past couple years, was in the waiting room with a huge basket filled with baby gifts when George finally arrived.

"You have a son," she told him.

He was overjoyed and came right in to hold the baby. As happy as I was, I was a little resentful. He couldn't have told the producer that his wife was having a baby, that he needed to take her to the hospital? I never mentioned it again, but I didn't forget it.

Our first Christmas in our new house with our new baby was incredibly special. My mother even came. I begged her not to take any pills, and although she was mobile, she was definitely slow and a little shaky. When she held Ashley, I stood right there, nervous she would drop him. I was recently looking at the picture I took of her holding Ashley, and she looked absolutely stoned.

In the year that followed, George was traveling and working a lot. I'd finally given in to George and Bill's vision for the house. It had white carpets, white furniture, silver Mylar wallpaper, Lucite tables. Not exactly family-friendly or my taste, but at least I insisted on having a traditional country-style kitchen. It turned out to be quite a showplace in the end.

When Ash was a year old, *Town and Country* asked to do a spread on me and George in our house, and they wanted to shoot me for the cover! I was thrilled. It was a beautiful picture of me and the caption read, "Mrs. George Hamilton, Reviving Hollywood's Golden Glamour." Finally I was starting to feel as if I was somebody.

George and I decided to throw a housewarming party and invited all our friends. Johnny Carson, and his wife, Joanna, were among the guests, and he found it quite amusing that the birdcage with our parrot in it was covered in the same silver Mylar paper as the walls.

As the party began, I said to George, "What if somebody spills something on this white carpet?"

The words were barely out of my mouth when Liza Minnelli dropped a big glob of guacamole that was being passed with chips onto the white carpet. "Oops," she said, and quickly put her foot over the mess.

When the evening was finally over, David Janssen and his wife, Dani, were the last to leave. David turned as he was walking out the door and said in a loud voice and a wave of his hand, "Cut, print, and strike the set!" He'd gotten it right on the money. It looked exactly like an art deco movie set. And this was now our new home sweet home. I eventually ended up loving our glamorous house, even though it wasn't exactly the warm, cozy, family home I'd envisioned.

George was still having financial difficulty. He wasn't getting enough film offers coming in to pay bills. Also, he was not the most practical person in the world with money; he made it and spent it just as fast. It drove me crazy. We couldn't seem to get ahead. It may have looked to the world like we were this wealthy young Hollywood couple living a life of glamour and style, but I was counting every penny.

George was a wonderful husband and father even though he was away working so much. When he was home, he wanted to chill and stay home and relax, but I still craved action and excitement. I had everything I could possibly want—a husband, a baby, a beautiful home—but there was still this feeling of emptiness inside me that nothing seemed to fill. I couldn't put my finger on it.

The deeper part of this, I now know, was that I wasn't at peace with myself because I had too many demons I was still running from, and if I stayed still too long, the anxiety and depression started to rear its head.

All my life, I couldn't afford to feel because it would have been much too painful. I just stuffed everything down deep inside me; the drugs, drinking, and violence in my home, the early abandonment by my mother and father, the instability, not having a mother present to help me through my formative years, the rape. And, although, I put on a good front, always coming across as confident and in charge of my life, I was deeply insecure and had little real self-esteem.

I desperately wanted to feel valuable and important and I looked to outer things to make me feel worthwhile.

When George was out of town working, I spent a lot of time alone with Ashley, but he was still a baby and went to sleep at seven. I didn't want to go out every night, but on weekends I wanted to go out and party. Now I could drink again, and I could put away the bourbon and coke. George would want to go home by midnight, but I was just getting started.

Then George wanted to sell the Tower Road house. He said he could make a good profit and he needed the money. He was taking jobs like spokesperson gigs that he felt were demeaning to him. I felt bad for him, but I didn't want to sell our home. We had a child now, and this was my nest.

We were offered another play together in Chicago at the Drury Lane. It was a two-character play by Bob Randall, who had written *6 Rms Riv Vu*, a big Broadway hit. This new one hadn't been performed anywhere yet, and he wanted George and me to try it out.

I was excited about being in Chicago and doing another play. We took a two-bedroom suite at the Ambassador Hotel with Ashley and the Swedish au pair for the two months that we'd be there. The play was a success and got good reviews; people liked seeing us on stage together. One night in the legendary Pump Room of the Ambassador, George introduced me to Gore Vidal, who was an old friend of his. Gore joined us, and he and I bonded immediately over our Southern roots. We had quite a few rounds of drinks and became good friends. I have since had some wonderful times at his beautiful home in Ravello, Italy.

After the play we went to New York. Ann Turkel, one of my oldest friends from our modeling days, had married Richard Harris, the acclaimed British actor who was also a notorious carouser and drinker.

George and Richard had never met, so Ann and I arranged a dinner for the four of us. We started out at the famous 21 Club, where we had a lovely dinner. George and Richard took an instant liking to each other; both of them regaling us with stories of their escapades in the "old days" before me and Ann. Neither George nor Ann was drinking, and Richard was supposed to be on the wagon. After dinner we decided to go to Le Club to continue on with our evening. When we got there, I ordered a Vodka Stinger.

"What's a Vodka Stinger?" Richard asked curiously.

"Vodka and white crème de menthe," I said.

"That sounds yummy," Richard said, and ordered one as well.

Ann gave Richard a look, but he just said, in his most proper British accent, "Darling, please don't worry. I just want to try one. Just the one."

Well, you can only imagine what happened next. Richard and I had one Stinger, then two. I think we were on our third when Le Club was closing, much to the relief of George and Ann. Richard and I, however, had bonded and were having a fine old time.

"Let's not go home," I said, as we left Le Club. "Let's stop at P. J. Clarke's for burgers."

"Great!" roared Richard. "Let's go!"

So off we went to P. J. Clarke's, where we each had one of their famous hamburgers, and Richard and I had a couple of more Stingers. When P. J. Clarke's started to close down at 3 a.m., Richard and I were feeling no pain. We asked the bartender if he knew a good after-hours bar.

"There's one up on Second avenue and 94th Street," said the bartender. "It's up two flights of stairs, and as long as you don't look like a cop, they'll let you in."

"Great!" said Richard enthusiastically. "Let's go!" He and I hailed a taxi, with George and Ann reluctantly following us. We arrived at a sleazy-looking building and walked up the two flights of stairs to find a lively after-hours bar going full steam.

Richard and I ordered several more rounds of Stingers. Richard was a hit, reciting Dylan Thomas while standing on the bar. I was accompanying him, singing, "The Yellow Rose of Texas."

Meanwhile, George took Ann aside and suggested that because I seemed to be the instigator of this whole debacle, she should take me aside and get me to end the evening while Richard and I were still standing.

Richard noticed Ann pulling me aside. "What are you doing?" he bellowed. "Are you insulting Alana? Look, she's having a good time and you're insulting her!"

She certainly wasn't insulting me, but there was no reasoning with him by now. The "other" Richard reared his ugly head. Even in my state, I could see now why she didn't want him to drink.

He grabbed her by the arm, twisting it behind her back, as she cried out, "Richard, stop, you're hurting me!"

George, ever the gentleman, came to her rescue. "Richard, enough, let her go!"

That didn't go over so well. "Who the hell do you think you are? This is between me and my wife!"

With that, he took a swing at George, who barely missed being decked. Suddenly five burly men grabbed Richard, holding him back, while George grabbed me and Ann and pulled us out the door, down the two flights of steps, and into a taxi.

"But what about Richard?" Ann cried. "We can't just leave him there!"

"Oh, yes we can," said George. "Maybe you should come back with us. I'm worried about you going home and what will happen when he gets there."

"Oh, he'll be fine by that time," Ann reassured us. "I really want to go home."

So we dropped her off at their apartment and headed back to our hotel.

"Don't you ever ask me to go out with that maniac again!" George said. "He could have killed me if those guys hadn't held him down!"

"I guess he wasn't used to Stingers," I answered guiltily.

"Never again!" he said.

The next morning around eleven the phone rang and George answered it. It was Richard.

"Good morning, kids," he said cheerily. "Where are we going to lunch today? Tell you what, Annie and I will come by your hotel around twelve-thirty and we'll go from there. Meet you downstairs!" And he hung up.

George gave me a look that could kill. "I can't believe you got me into this. I'm not going out with that crazy man again!"

But despite all his protestations, we met Ann and Richard. Richard was cheery as could be, acting as if nothing out of the ordinary had happened; Ann's arm was in a sling!

"What happened?" I asked.

She brushed it off. "Oh, nothing much. Just when Richard grabbed my arm last night, it went into a funny position and it's sprained."

I felt terrible, like it was totally my fault, but I had no idea how Richard got when he drank. Never would I have imagined the evening would end with my friend getting hurt.

When we got back to California, George eventually sold the house. We moved into a small house that he had gotten possession of in a lawsuit; it was definitely a move down from the Tower Road house. An unassuming tract house with three small bedrooms, it had a tiny pool in back but a nice view of the city.

I was depressed, but I tried not to show it. Our marriage was not in the best of places. I was building up a lot of resentments, while George was very disapproving about me going out with my friends. I felt he was always critical of me, and we locked horns a lot. I started feeling like he was behaving more and more like the stern father and I was the rebellious daughter.

The saving grace in our relationship, though, was that we kept our senses of humor. George was so quick and witty that he constantly made me laugh. When we weren't at odds about something, we had such fun together. But it wasn't enough. Eventually the fact that we couldn't communicate on a deeper level was starting to unravel us.

George and I were both emotionally closed off. I think that, like me, he had a lot of suppressed emotions, and although he could easily psychoanalyze me, it wasn't so easy for him to look inside himself. I think as a result of where we came from and all the protective walls we had built in order to cope, we were both incapable of opening ourselves to a truly intimate relationship.

Richard and Ann recommended a therapist to me; I should have known he'd be crazy, and he was. He had George come in for a session with us together, and George couldn't stand him. I don't think he liked George very much either. In the end he really didn't help us resolve any of our issues, but he did help me see that I wasn't the only one causing the marriage to fail.

I guess it's true with any relationship that both parties are responsible, but at the time all my resentments started to surface—that I didn't get to see Mama before she died, that he wasn't there for Ashley's birth, that he sold our home, that he was always so critical of me.

Looking back, I wish I could have been a more supportive wife. I realize I wasn't as compassionate and understanding as I wish I had been—about his money problems, about him wanting to live a quiet life. But I guess at that time I just didn't know how. There were so many things I had never been taught.

But it was much deeper than that.

Because I was still running from my demons and hadn't really started to delve into what was underneath my need to be constantly moving, I always had this terrible feeling that something was missing. I loved George deeply, but I thought maybe I wasn't in love with him anymore. I would later learn that it wasn't up to another person to make you happy, that happiness needs to be an "inside job." But it would take a lot of time and a lot more heartache in my life before I got there.

My unraveling marriage wasn't the only strain I was feeling at this point. My mother's drug use had escalated, and she'd been kicked out of several apartments for her inappropriate behavior. I couldn't trust her with money, so I had to stock her food and even buy her cigarettes. I was doing everything I could to cut off her drug supply, but somehow she still managed to get them.

I dreaded going to see her. She slept most of the time, and if she was awake, she was stumbling around the dingy, messy apartment, slurring her words. It was excruciating for me to see her like that, and it brought up such rage and frustration because I felt so helpless. Sometimes I'd yell at her to stop taking the damn drugs and pull herself together. I didn't realize then that drug addiction doesn't work that way.

A part of me almost hated her. Sometimes, when I didn't know what to do anymore, I'd have a momentary wish that she would just die. I never meant it. I just wanted a mother—a normal mother. But I had a broken mother, and I didn't know how to fix her.

Then the worst happened.

Mother would often call the house at all hours of the night, saying she didn't feel well and needed to go to the hospital, or she would call her neighbors and have them call me.

To stop her from waking Ashley and George and disrupting the household, I changed our phone number. I would call her every day to check on her, and often she would shut off the phone so as not to be awakened, totally knocked out on pills. At this point I didn't even know how she was managing to get the drugs, but when it came to getting them, she could be amazingly resourceful.

At one point I had called her several days in a row and never got an answer. I know I should have gone over to check on her, but I couldn't bring myself to do it. I put off going for a couple days. Then, on Friday, March 6, 1976, around 6:00 p.m., the police called.

"Is this Alana Hamilton?"

"Yes," I replied.

"Mrs. Hamilton, I'm sorry to have to tell you this, but your mother is dead."

"Dead?" I tried to say, but I couldn't speak. The word got trapped in my throat.

"Her landlady called us today. She said she hadn't seen your mother in some time and asked us to come check it out."

"Oh my God . . . "

"We had to break in, and when we entered, well, we found her there. It looks like it might have been an overdose. I'm sorry," he said.

There was more to the conversation, but I stopped hearing the words. I could almost feel myself leaving my body and watching myself listening on the phone as he gave me the rest of the details.

I just stood there, numb. I don't know how much time had passed before George came home. I think the phone was still in my hand.

"Alana? Are you alright?" he asked.

I looked at him standing there; I hadn't even heard him come in. "My mother's gone," I said, and I cried in his arms.

For the next few days I was incapable of doing anything. I just wandered around the house in a daze. George made all the funeral arrangements. I had to go to Mother's apartment to find some clothes to bury her in. It was filthy and dark, and there were overturned bottles of pills everywhere—Darvon, Miltown, Librium, Chloral Hydrate, and too many others to remember. The pills were lying all over the floor, some of them even half-chewed. Once again in my life, it was as if I was in a bad dream and I couldn't wake up, but it was real and I was awake. The only way I knew how to cope was to distance what was going on from my reality.

The funeral was held in the little chapel at Forest Lawn. As we drove in, the skies were gray and it was lightly raining, unlike the normal sunny California days. I was so surprised to see that some of my friends had come to support me. I hadn't cried since I found out she was gone, but I broke down completely when the minister read this poem that I had found somewhere and given him about a mother.

Now my mother was gone, and I never got the chance to put my arms around her and tell her that I loved her. To this day I think of her dying by herself in that apartment, feeling alone and unloved, and it truly breaks my heart. I wish I had tried harder to help her, and I wish I'd gone over to her apartment a couple days sooner instead of making excuses to myself.

It took years of Al-Anon before I stopped feeling responsible for Mother's death. Even if I'd gone over and saved her that time, there would have been another time. I suddenly understand, in this moment, as I sit here with tears streaming down my face as I write this, that she was too damaged.

I wish I could tell her, "I'm sorry, Mother. I love you so much. I wish I'd known how to help you. Please forgive me for not understanding your pain. I forgive you for not being the mother I wanted you to be. You would have if you could have."

George had to make an appearance somewhere in the Midwest, and I couldn't believe he would leave me alone the night of my mother's funeral. Instead of trying to understand his position, I felt an icy curtain come down over my emotions, and I logged one more giant resentment toward my husband. Tina and Dani and David Janssen came over to be with me, and I got totally drunk while we looked through old photographs of my mother and me. But I don't think I truly grieved her death until years later. I just went into that numb, disassociated place and tried to move on with my life.

When George returned, I was still angry. I also think I was still in shock over my mother's death. A couple weeks later we took Ashley to the city zoo with friends. It was a long, hot, dusty day, and when we got home, I put Ashley down for his nap and lay down to take one myself. George chose this moment to want to make love, and somehow the phone at the side of the bed fell on my head. Out of nowhere, I jumped up and said, "I want a divorce!"

I couldn't believe the words had come out of my mouth. He looked at me in disbelief, hurt, surprise, and then just got up and walked out. I didn't hear from him for almost three weeks. I found out later that he had gone to some motel in the Marina and just hid out, wanting to think things through, before we talked again. I was worried sick and angry at him for disappearing like that when we had Ashley, and if I needed to reach him, I couldn't.

As sad as I felt, though, and as much as I missed him, I felt a little like that bird that had just been let out of the cage—kind of like I felt when I broke my engagement all those years ago in Texas. Except it wasn't that simple this time. Except now I felt like there was a huge part of myself missing. It was so confusing; I felt free, yes, but not whole.

Chapter 12

Although we were now living apart, George and I remained on good terms and were in no rush to divorce. I couldn't imagine my life without him. I felt a bit like a small boat adrift at sea without George. I was happy Ashley was with me. Being a mother grounded me and gave me a reason to make a stable home.

Some time later my good friend Marisa Berenson introduced me to Mick Flick, a tall, handsome German who was visiting Los Angeles. His family had owned Mercedes Benz, and he and his twin brother, both very eligible bachelors well known in the social circles of Europe, now lived in Zurich. Marisa arranged a dinner, and there was a definite attraction between Mick and me. We went out to dinner every night while he was in town. He also invited me to come to Europe, although I wouldn't commit to that yet. The night before he left, we went out and had a lot to drink, and I ended up staying at his bungalow at the Beverly Hills Hotel.

That evening I was making my famous Texas chili and cornbread for Tina, Suzanne Pleshette, her husband, Tommy Gallagher, and Dani and David Janssen, when the doorbell rang. I was busy in the kitchen, so Tina answered the door.

"I think you just got served," Tina said, handing me a packet of papers—divorce papers!

I called George in tears. "Why would you do this without even discussing it with me? I thought we'd agreed we weren't going to get a divorce."

"A very interesting thing happened this morning," he said. "I had a breakfast meeting at the Beverly Hills Hotel."

My heart felt like it dropped into my stomach.

He continued, "When I came out to get my car, the valet brought me yours instead. Since I didn't see you having breakfast, it's obvious you stayed the night with someone. That someone probably being Mr. Flick, since I hear you've been out with him the last couple of nights."

"George, I'm so sorry that happened. I really am. It's not what you're thinking," I told him. "I'd just had a little too much champagne and I fell asleep in the living room of his bungalow. Please don't go through with this," I pleaded. The next day, after much apologizing and groveling, George called his attorney and put the divorce on hold.

A couple months later, on a weekend that George had Ashley, I went into the drugstore downstairs at the Beverly Hills Hotel to pick up the newspapers.

"Mommy!" I heard a familiar voice call out. I turned around to see Ashley come running up to me, followed by a mutual friend of ours, Lisa, who also happened to be a beautiful model.

"Ashley, what are you doing here, sweetheart? Where's Daddy?" I looked at Lisa for the answer.

She looked sheepish as Ashley took her hand. "I was just bringing him here for some gum. We're having breakfast in the coffee shop with George."

So George was dating Lisa. That didn't sit well with me at all, and I wasn't pleased to have another woman with my son. It was too soon.

Sometime later I learned George was dating a blonde girl named Liz Treadwell, who also was seen taking Ashley around. This wasn't the way it was supposed to be. I didn't want other women in charge of my son.

In May Ashley went to stay with George for ten days while I went to Paris to visit my friend Florence Grinda. It felt strange to be going to Europe without George, and I knew I would really miss Ashley. But Florence had insisted I come stay with her in Paris and then come down to her house in the South of France for her annual Grand Prix party. It sounded like an exciting trip, and I felt like it would be silly to miss the opportunity. When Mick heard I was coming, we arranged to meet each other because he was also going down for the Grand Prix.

We spent a couple fun days and nights with Florence's friends in Paris before going to Saint Tropez to stay at her friend Ricky von Opel's beautiful house overlooking the water. A friend of Florence's, Helmut Berger, was also staying at the house. Helmut was the handsome, blonde, brooding German actor who had been discovered by Luchino Visconti and had become a star from several of the famed director's films, including *The Damned* and *Ludwig*. He had had a long-term intimate relationship with Visconti, and they were apparently still quite close. Helmut took an instant liking to me, and we became fast friends. I found him incredibly amusing with his sly wit and raucous humor.

From Saint Tropez, we all went on to Florence's family home in Biot, where she had a house full of guests for her big party. Mick had just arrived in Monte Carlo, and we made plans to meet that night at Regine's. Mick and I were very happy to see each other and were having a great time, drinking champagne and dancing, until I noticed Helmut and Mick speaking in German, seemingly having some kind of heated discussion. Mick left the club without even saying good night to me. I didn't have a clue why he had left so abruptly. I was puzzled and upset, and I drowned my sorrows in vodka before heading back to Florence's house with Helmut, Bianca Jagger, and the rest of her group.

Later I questioned Helmut about it. He just waved it off, saying, "Darling, he's not for you. He's a playboy. I was telling him that he should be a gentleman and treat you the way you deserved. That was all. I think he left to meet up with some other girl."

It still seemed strange to me. Mick and I had really had such a good time together, and I could tell he really liked me. I hoped he would call or we'd see each other so I could find out from him what had happened, but he left Monte Carlo the next day without getting in touch with me. Helmut invited me and my friend Susie Dyson to come to Rome and stay in his apartment. I still had a few days left before my ticket home, as Mick and I had planned to spend that time together, so we all went on to Rome.

It should have been fun to be in Rome, which had always been one of my favorite cities, but it brought back memories of all the times George and I had been there together, especially our first trip. I was depressed. And I missed Ashley.

A couple months later I saw Mick again. He had come back to Los Angeles for a few days, and a mutual friend of ours invited me to lunch with them. He was quite pleasant, but slightly cool. After lunch we walked out together and I asked him what had happened in Monte Carlo.

"Do you mean you don't know?" he asked, incredulously. He went on to explain to me that Helmut had told him in German that he (Helmut) and I were together (as in having an affair)—that I wasn't interested in seeing Mick anymore and that he should leave!

I couldn't believe it! Helmut? But he was gay! Apparently, he had this crush on me, however, and was very jealous of Mick. So he plotted a way to get him out of the picture. We'd never been anything but platonic friends, and although sometimes he would joke about being straight and me being his "girlfriend" to other people, it never occurred to me he could be serious.

After Mick and I cleared up the misunderstanding, we continued to see each other while he was in town, and he invited me to come to his birthday party in Germany. He arranged my transportation, and after the party, we spent a few days in Munich, celebrating the beginning of the famous German Oktoberfest. From there we flew to Mick's home in Zurich. By the time the week was over I was partied out. I liked Mick, but I realized that that this wasn't the life for me.

I was glad to get back home to Ashley, who had been staying with his dad. I had missed him so much and felt guilty for being away. Being a good mother was very important to me. Now I was a single mother, trying my best to be a good one but not sure I was always succeeding.

I did the best I knew how to do at the time, but looking back, I don't feel it was good enough. I think the most important thing you can do for a small child is provide stability, both physically and emotionally. I was able to provide a relatively stable home life, but I was still young and hadn't yet begun to heal my own emotional scars. I was still looking for the answers outside myself. I wish so badly that I had known then all that I know now.

I needed to restart my career and make some money. I started acting classes, got an agent, and began to focus on going back to work. I started booking some guest roles on a few television shows like *Love Boat* and *Bionic Woman*, and I even did a few modeling gigs.

George and I still saw each other occasionally and spent time with Ashley together. We were kind of stuck in limbo—not moving forward, yet not ready to call it quits.

I had met and become friends with Valerie Perrine, who was just beginning her rise as a full-fledged movie star. She was a gorgeous, zaftig ex-showgirl from Vegas—funny, uninhibited, and she loved to have a good time.

The two of us were invited to play in a tennis tournament in Palm Springs. The women were all actresses, and each of us was matched with a well-known tennis pro. One of the actresses playing in the tournament was Farrah Fawcett, who was just at the height of her *Charlie's Angels* and red-bathing-suit-poster fame. Farrah and I had seen each other occasionally at television commercial auditions when we both had just moved to Los Angeles, but we didn't really know each other. She was breathtakingly beautiful, but she also was just a really nice down-to-earth Texas girl.

Word had gotten around that Farrah was playing, and outside the clubhouse were hundreds of screaming fans, dying to get a close look or an autograph. This was all relatively new to her, and she seemed overwhelmed and flustered by the reaction of the crowd. She tried to be gracious, but it was evident she wanted to just escape the pandemonium.

I remember thinking how beautiful she was and how lucky she was to have suddenly become this huge star. It seemed to me that she had it all. I never could have guessed that our paths would cross again down the road and the part I would eventually play in her life—and she in mine.

Although Farrah was an excellent tennis player, Valerie and I were not. We'd been very upfront with the people putting on the tournament, but they had said this was all for fun and it wasn't necessary for us to be top notch. We had gone out shopping for tennis clothing and had bought the shortest shorts we could find, hoping to distract people's attention from our lack of tennis skills! Val and I were so terrible that we ended up being the comic relief of the event. Farrah easily won the tournament and the prize, a beautiful gold Rolex watch.

During this time I had introduced two very opposite friends of mine and George's who had, much to my surprise, fallen madly in love. Marisa Berenson was very European—stylish, glamorous, and sophisticated. Her mother was a countess, her father a diplomat, and her grandmother was the famous designer Elsa Schiaparelli. Jim Randall was a wealthy, tough-talking, funny, and totally unique character who owned an aircraft rivet manufacturing company in the City of Industry. George and I first met him when our old friend Carol Most brought him over to our house on Tower Road when I was pregnant with Ashley. He drank vodka on the rocks and talked a mile a minute, and I took an instant dislike to him because he wanted to buy "my nest."

In time, however, he grew on me and we became good friends. He bought a house on Greenway, which Debbie Reynolds and shoe magnate, Harry Karl, had owned, and started living a Hollywood lifestyle bigger than any Hollywood star. We jokingly called him "Gatsby."

Anyway, one night when Marisa was staying with me, we were going out to dinner, and I had to make a quick stop at Jim's. I didn't think they would get along and I suggested that Marisa wait in the car.

"No, I'll just come in with you," she answered.

I was praying he wouldn't say something offensive to her when I introduced them.

"Honey, what's up with all the kinky hair?" Jim said.

Oh God, just what I was afraid of. I was worried she'd be offended, but instead, she just laughed. "Well, you're certainly not one to talk," she said, noting his frizzy 'do.

The next thing I knew they were deep in conversation. To make a long story very short, Jim swept Marisa off her feet, and soon they were making plans to get married. Everything was going fine until just before the wedding, when they had a huge argument and Jim called it all off.

This argument of theirs would then spark an explosive fight between George and me. I called George because that's where Jim had ended up, and I insisted on coming over to speak with him. George tried to stop me. But there was no stopping me. When I arrived, Jim was three sheets to the wind.

"What are you doing?" I said. "Are you out of your mind? The wedding is tomorrow night!"

"I've had it," he slurred. "I'm outta here, babe. I'm going to Brazil!"

I launched into the many reasons Jim couldn't possibly do that, and at one point, George stepped in and said, "Why don't you stay out of this? Their argument is none of your business."

Now the argument became about George and me and our relationship. He got so angry at one point that he tried to kick me, but I moved quickly aside and he kicked a stone pot instead. He was hobbling around in pain, and we found out the next day his foot was broken. (To this day he swears that he purposely kicked the pot at the last second in order to miss me. Good try, George, but I never bought it and still don't!) Somehow everyone made up—including Jim and Marisa—and the wedding was back on.

After that night George and I decided to make an attempt to reconcile, believing that any two people who could get into such an argument must really still love each other. However, we both still had a lot of resentments toward each other and needed some help to work things out.

We went to see a therapist named Mason Rose that George had found who lived in a large wooden house on Hollywood Boulevard. Let me just note that he wasn't really a therapist at all (which I found out later) but rather a nutritionist who weighed about three hundred pounds (which might make one wonder about even his nutritional qualifications).

The "doctor" had George make a list of the things he needed me to do in order for us to reconcile. One was that I had to go to bed earlier and get up at seven with him. The other was that I wasn't allowed to talk to waiters. This had always been a bone of contention between me and George. He had been raised to be a perfect, old-fashioned southern gentleman and believed that a man should always do the ordering for the lady. He would have preferred it if I had just let him choose my food as well, but there was no way in hell that was going to happen.

We started out our reconciliation attempt by going out to a candlelit dinner at a gourmet restaurant that featured French food and an orchestra for dancing. I can't remember the name, but it was located on the top floor of the Hilton Hotel overlooking the city. When the waiter came over to take our order, George asked, "What would you like?"

After perusing the menu for some time, I said, demurely, "Sweetheart, could you please ask the waiter if there is any cream or dairy in the pea soup?"

George asked the waiter, "My wife would like to know if there is any cream or dairy in the pea soup?"

"No, sir," replied the waiter, looking at us both a little strangely.

"Hmmm, I can't decide between the soup and the artichoke salad. I wonder if the salad dressing has vinegar in it. Would you mind asking him, dear?"

"Madam would like to know if there is vinegar in the dressing," George asked the waiter, his smile starting to be just a little strained.

"Yes, sir, it does," replied the waiter.

"Thank you, sweetheart. I'll have the soup then. Would you mind asking him what's in the *poulet fricassée*?"

"My wife would like to know what's in the *poulet fricassée*," said George to the waiter, who by now was probably thinking we were a bit peculiar.

The waiter went through a long list of ingredients.

"Hmmm, how about the Dover sole? Would you ask him if it's sautéed or broiled?" I asked George sweetly.

George, still trying to maintain his cool, repeated my question to the waiter.

"However the lady would like it, sir," replied the waiter, getting testier by the minute and trying not to show it.

Finally, George was totally exasperated. "Oh, fuck it! Just order it yourself!" he said.

"Thank you, sweetheart. I think that's probably best." I smiled. I think I proved my point. That was the end of my not being allowed to speak directly to a waiter. The formal reconciliation attempt didn't work out in the end because we both had such definite ideas about how our marriage should work. But we continued to see each other off and on and I still thought that we would probably end up together.

In April of 1977, after selling the Devlin House, I decided to rent a small, inexpensive house on Carbon Beach. Ash loved being at the beach. We took long walks and built sand castles. The only drawback was that it took a lot of driving back and forth for me when I had to go into town for auditions, work, or acting classes.

In May I went to New York for my friend Bianca Jagger's birthday. Bianca and I had met several times and hadn't really hit it off. She had come to a party at my house with Sue Mengers when George and I were married. At the time I had thought she was breathtakingly beautiful but rather stuck up. Later, when I got to know her better, I found out she was just reserved.

Sometime later Wendy Stark had brought Bianca and Andy Warhol over. This time we really hit it off. We ended up becoming the best of friends and still are. Andy and I also ended up being good friends.

When I arrived in New York, Bianca and Halston took me to Pearl's, a fashionable Chinese restaurant on the West Side where everyone went to dinner on Sunday nights. During dinner they told me about this new club that had just opened called Studio 54. We decided to check it out.

The owner, Steve Rubell, greeted and ushered us downstairs to the private VIP room, where we all sat and talked and drank until late. When Steve heard Bianca's birthday was in a few days, he insisted on giving her a huge birthday party. Halston offered to do a smaller birthday dinner for some close friends before and would co-host the party afterward with Steve.

After a lovely dinner at Halston's we all headed to 54, except for Bianca, who arrived after us. She made an entrance, seated on the back of a white horse looking absolutely stunning in a beautiful red Halston gown.

The party was packed with fashion people, tycoons, rock stars, tennis players, and more. Photos of Mick and Bianca, Jacqueline Bisset, Margaux Hemingway, Calvin Klein, Reinaldo and Carolina Herrera, Mikhail Baryshnikov, among scores of beautiful New York people, appeared in newspapers and magazines, including a picture of me, Bianca, Mick, and Baryshnikov in *Newsweek*. We drank and danced until dawn. The party put Studio 54 and Steve Rubell on the map, and it remained the hottest place to go for quite a few years.

Once back in California, Ashley and I enjoyed the summer. On weekends some of my girlfriends would come down, and we'd sit on the deck in the sun. There was no man in my life—I wasn't even dating—but fortunately I had a group of friends who lived at the beach, so I wasn't completely isolated from any kind of social life.

Linda Evans lived down the beach with her husband, realtor Stan Herman, and David and Dani Janssen had a house next door to them. Linda was stunningly beautiful as well as a fabulous cook, and I still remember her chili-cheese casserole and many of the other delicious dishes. We always had great lunches and dinners together.

One of the fun parties that summer was Allan Carr's alphabet party at his beach house in Malibu. The first night, August 12, were guests with last names A through L. It was also George's birthday, and we were going together, so Allan had a big birthday cake for George.

During the party I found George talking to Britt Ekland (who had been living with Rod Stewart for the past several years). When he mentioned to her about how ironic it was that his ex-girlfriend, Liz Treadwell, was now going out with her ex-boyfriend, Rod Stewart, she was shocked. She and Rod were still living together and she had no idea about his dalliance with Ms. Treadwell until George spilled the beans.

Who could have known then what was in my future? The last person in the world I would ever have thought about dating was Rod Stewart. If I'd made a list of fifty men I thought were interesting, he wouldn't have been on it.

Later that month I got a phone call from George, who was in Europe with Ashley (and, as I found out later, some random temporary girlfriend). He told me that he had some rather shocking news to tell me. Our divorce, which had been put on hold all this time, had, because of some legal technicality, gone through.

I was devastated! Our still being married gave me a sense of a safety net; I could have my freedom with George still in my life. I felt lost without him. I fell apart. I got into my bed sobbing and wouldn't get out. Tina was so worried about me that she called David Janssen, who lived down the beach.

When David appeared at my door, he said, "Get up, Tex. We're going to the liquor store."

David, who was known to have a fondness for drinking, was certain this would be the best cure for me. And he was probably right, at least for a temporary measure. He got me out of bed and took me to the liquor store. "What do you feel like drinking?"

I wasn't a daytime drinker, but I remembered being in New Orleans and having Ramos Gin Fizzes for brunch at Brennan's. For some reason, that appealed to me. We drank Ramos Gin Fizzes all afternoon, and David had me laughing, smashed, and cheered up. I didn't get over the divorce in one drunken afternoon, but it sure helped get me back on track.

Around this time Steve McQueen and Ali McGraw had also broken up. He called and came by the beach house on his motorcycle with a six-pack of beer. I was shocked at his appearance; he'd become quite overweight and was fully bearded. We talked for a while, catching up on our lives over the past few years. Things hadn't worked out in the end between him and Ali, and they were divorcing. Ali wasn't a close friend, but we'd known each other for years, and out of respect for her, I didn't really want to get involved with Steve. And he just wasn't the Steve I'd known from before; he'd gotten extremely paranoid and liked to hide out in his suite at the Beverly Wilshire, smoking pot and drinking beer.

In September I moved from the beach house to another rented house in Bel Air on Stone Canyon Road. It was a lovely, small, two-story traditional house, and I loved it. I felt less isolated than I did at the beach, and Ashley was going to be starting nursery school, so it was much better for us to be back in town.

One night I was going to dinner with my friend Ronnie Wood from the Rolling Stones, who was in town from London. He suggested we go to dinner with Rod Stewart and Liz Treadwell. Rod and Britt had broken up after she found out about his affair with Liz, and now he and Liz were openly dating. Ronnie said he wanted to torture Rod because I was just his type—a tall, pretty blonde.

We met Rod and Liz at Ma Maison, a hot restaurant in town. We had a fun dinner, with Ronnie and Rod reminiscing about some of their escapades during the time they were in a band together called the Faces. They had remained close friends and took great pleasure "taking the piss" out of one another.

After dinner Rod suggested we head to his place for a drink. When we got to his large, gated Mediterranean house on North Carolwood Drive in Holmby Hills, Rod discovered he'd forgotten his keys. He looked to Liz to see if she had them, but no luck. He climbed over the gate, but finally Tony Toon, his flamboyantly gay British assistant, showed up and let us in.

We entered a high-ceilinged marble hallway that led into the living room. It was decorated in art nouveau style, with red velvet drapes and furniture and vases of peacock feathers everywhere. I joked to Ronnie later that it looked like a bordello.

The living room led into another marble hallway leading to the bar, which was decorated all in black with mirrored walls and a jukebox and pool table. Rod made us drinks, and we hung out for a while. I'd had an enjoyable evening, but I can't say there was any attraction between me and Rod. He seemed nice enough but definitely wasn't my type. Famous last words.

Yet somehow Rod Stewart's name kept popping up in my life. I was in a comedy workshop taught by Harvey Lembeck, an older but well-known comedic actor, and always sat next to Carole Mallory, a girlfriend of mine from my early modeling days. One morning she came into class and whispered to me, "I went out with Rod Stewart last night. He's really sexy, don't you think?"

"Actually, he's just not my type." I still just didn't get the big deal about Rod.

Just before Christmas my friend Maggie Abbot dragged me to a party at the Playboy Club that Hugh Hefner was giving for Rod

Stewart. We had just left a dinner party at a friend's house, and I really didn't want to go anywhere else, but I agreed to stop by with her for just a few minutes on our way home. While we were there Rod came over to our table. He took off his bow tie and tied it around my wrist. I thought he was kind of cute and charming but didn't think much more about it. When I got home that night, I took the bow tie off my wrist and for some reason put it into one of my closet drawers.

I still have that bow tie.

PART III

Rock 'n' Roll Royalty

Chapter 13

It was New Year's Eve, the end of 1977, and I was alone and depressed. I wasn't dating anyone. In fact, I hadn't found anyone who really interested me in the year and a half since George and I had broken up. I also wasn't working and my money was running out. I was so down in the dumps that I called my psychic, Jacquie Eastlund, hoping she would have something encouraging to tell me.

"It's all going to be fine, Alana," she told me. "Things are going to be looking up for you in the coming year."

"How?" I asked her.

"For one, your financial situation will improve, but you're also going to meet a new man the week of March 13 who's going to change your life."

I started to feel somewhat better. But it wasn't all roses. "Whatever you do," she warned, "stay out of a red or maroon sports car. I see danger around it."

Things *did* begin to turn around soon after the New Year began. I got a guest spot on *Fantasy Island*. Shortly thereafter I got a call from my old friend Ann Turkel. She and Richard Harris were doing a big Warner Brothers film called *The Ravagers*, and the producers were looking for someone to play Richard's wife. Ann and Richard thought I'd be perfect.

When my agent couldn't get me in for a reading, I contacted Tina Sinatra, who was now working as an agent. "I've known the producer for years," she said. "I'll call him." That's what I love about Tina—there's nothing she can't do. I got an audition with the director, Richard Compton, that evening at six, and I went over to Ann and Richard's to work on the part with him.

When I did my reading, I felt like it had gone well, but Carole Horn, who had recently been nominated for an Oscar, was also up for the part, so I figured I probably didn't have a shot.

The following morning Tina called at 9:00 a.m. beyond excited. "You got it!" she said. We both started screaming and jumping up and down.

"I can't believe it!"

"Well, believe it," she said. "You leave for Alabama on March twentieth," she said. "But that's not all. They want to sign you for a three-picture deal."

Jacquie had been right. Everything was turning around. And I'd already forgotten about the man I was supposed to meet the week of March 13 . . .

Noted Hollywood agent Irving Lazar and his wife, Mary, invited me to one of their parties, and Tina and I made plans to attend together. We also asked George to escort us. Even with our divorce finalized, George and I had remained close.

We were seated at a table with the Countess Marina Cicogna; her amore, Florinda Balkin, the beautiful Brazilian actress; and Rod Stewart, who had brought his assistant, Tony Toon. I noticed Rod staring at me, though I pretended I didn't.

After dinner George and Tina headed home, and I decided to join a group of friends at the Daisy, where everyone was drinking champagne, dancing, and having a great time. Rod was also there, and he asked me to dance. I was surprised, but I accepted. He was a great dancer, and we danced in perfect rhythm together. For the first time I started to think of him as kind of sexy.

The next day Tony called. "Rod would really like to go out with you," he told me.

"Really?" I replied. "Well doesn't he know how to use the phone here in America?" Tony thought that was really funny. He told me later that he went back and said to Rod, "I think you've met your match with this one."

I still hadn't heard from Rod when Maggie Abbot invited me to a small dinner at music producer Robert Stigwood's house.

"You know, Rod and Tony will also be there," she said. "Rod invited us to swing by his house for a drink first."

Was she now trying to fix me up with Rod?

I agreed anyway, and we had a drink with Rod and Tony before heading to dinner. When we were getting ready to leave, Tony steered me toward Rod's red Lamborghini. I had totally forgotten the psychic's warning about not getting into a red or maroon sports car.

I didn't talk to Rod that much over dinner, but afterward we headed back to his house with Maggie and Tony for more drinks. Rod brought out some cocaine and offered it to me; I took a tiny bit.

We danced, drank, and talked until all hours. As disinterested as I was in him before, I was now starting to get his charm. He had a cute, boyish way about him, and I definitely found him attractive. At 6:00 the sun started coming up, and I jumped up to leave. I never stayed out that late!

"You've had a lot to drink," Rod said. "Maybe you should sleep here."

I laughed. "Yeah, right!" I said. Did he think I was going to sleep with him on our first "sort of" date?

"No," he said. "I mean you could just sleep here. No funny business," he said, and added, sincerely, "I promise."

The offer was tempting. I was exhausted and had definitely had a lot to drink. Ashley was at George's house for the weekend, so there wasn't anything to rush home for—or so I justified it in my mind.

I followed Rod upstairs and crawled into his bed with everything on but my shoes. He slid into bed next to me and we talked some more.

"Do you want me to massage your neck?" he asked.

"Oh, God," I thought. "This is where I need to get up and go home to my own bed." What was I thinking? I know I should have said, "No thanks," but my neck did feel awfully stiff, so I instead I said, "Okay, but just my neck." The rest, as they say, is history!

When we woke up around noon, we looked at each other and started to giggle. He jumped up, left the room, and came back with a tray of toast and tea. He couldn't have been sweeter. I didn't feel at all uncomfortable, although I was a little annoyed at myself. I didn't want to be like all the other girls who probably just jumped into bed with him. But it was too late for that now.

He asked me to dinner that night, but I already had plans.

"The old brush off, huh?" he said jokingly.

"I'm free tomorrow night," I said, smiling sweetly.

So the next night we went out with a group of Rod's band and football friends—Rod's only friends in Los Angeles. He wanted me to spend the night, but I had an early meeting the next day with George as well as the writers and producers of a show ABC had of-fered us, and I also wanted to get home for Ashley. Rod then asked me out for the weekend, but I also already had plans to go to Puerto Vallarta with Jim Randall, Allan Carr, and possibly George, if he finished shooting in time. (George ended up getting caught up with work and didn't make it.)

The night I came home Rod took me to a dinner party, and he was aloof and cool the whole night. When I pressed him, he told me he was pissed that I had gone off with another man.

"Jim and I are just friends, and Allan is gay," I told him. "Anyway, I'm a free woman and I don't have to answer to anyone."

I thought this might be our last date, but things worked themselves out by the end of the night. He wanted me to stay with him, but I had a screen test early the next morning for the female lead in *Love at First Bite*, a movie George was doing with our friend Stan Dragoti.

He finally convinced me to let him come back to my house. As I was following Rod in my car on Beverly Glen, I watched in horror as his Lamborghini slid out on a curve, spun out of control, and ca-reened right through a hedge and tennis court. Thankfully, he was unhurt, but the side of the car where I would have been sitting if

I had ridden with him was completely demolished. It was only then that I remembered the psychic's warning to stay out of a red or maroon sports car.

By the time we got back to my house, it was after 3 a.m.; I had to be at the studio at 8:00 a.m., and I arrived hungover and underslept. I could tell it wasn't going well. The next day I saw the test, and I looked like I'd taken a sleeping pill before doing the scene. I was really disappointed and angry at myself. The part was tailor-made for me, and both George and Stan were in my corner. It was a perfect example of how I let the man in my life take precedence over my career. George was not happy at all—about me blowing the opportunity or dating Rod.

The next night I took Rod to a party at Polly Bergen's house. I was having a great time—talking to everyone, laughing, flirting—but again, when we got into the car to go home, Rod got quiet. I pulled up at his house, and he got out of the car, said goodnight, and walked right into the house.

Driving away, I had no idea what I had done. Maybe I didn't pay enough attention to him at the party? I decided to just let it go. I was definitely attracted to him, but he seemed moody and possessive. Luckily I was about to get very busy, and I didn't have the time to focus too much on it; it was almost time for me to leave for shooting in Alabama.

I didn't hear from him for two days. I felt a little depressed. I wasn't even sure why. Then Tony called and suggested I call Rod in the studio. I didn't. Shortly afterward the phone rang and it was Rod.

"I'm depressed," he said.

"Me too," I answered.

"Let's have dinner at Ma Maison," he said.

It was the turning point of our relationship. After a couple of drinks Rod took my hand. "You know, I've really missed you," he told me.

"I've missed you too," I said, realizing it was true. We finished dinner and went back to his house, where we had champagne and half a quaalude. That night something had changed radically in our love-making. The other couple times it had been okay but not memorable. Suddenly, it was as if we were both completely free. It was unbelievably sexy and romantic. He told me he loved me. I realized at that moment that I loved him too, and that's why I'd been so miserable and depressed the past couple days.

From that moment on we were so madly in love and obsessed with each other; we couldn't bear to be apart.

Ashley had never really seen me with another man up to this point. The first morning Rod stayed over, I woke Ash, gave him his breakfast, and let him know Rod was in the house. Ash was excited and wanted to see him. When we got upstairs, Rod was blow-drying his hair upside down, and Ashley, who was three at the time, thought it was hysterical to see Rod like that.

Rod was funny and adorable with Ashley, and Ash really seemed to like him. This was a huge relief for me. I couldn't be with a man who wasn't accepting and loving to my son.

Suddenly it was time to leave for Alabama. Although I was excited about doing the movie, I was really sad to leave Rod. He and Tony headed to his new house in Spain, where he had no phone.

The three weeks of shooting seemed like it went on forever. I was missing Rod and anxious because there was no way for us to talk to each other. Finally, I got a telegram that he was on his way back to Los Angeles. I returned to LA to find him standing at the gate at the airport, two dozen red roses in his arms. We picked up our romance just where we had left off.

In May Rod wanted me to go to Europe with him. I could only manage to get away for ten days because I had to be back to start the show with George and I didn't want to leave Ashley for too long.

We had a wonderful time in Paris. There's nothing more exciting and romantic than being in Paris when you're in the beginning throes of love and passion. Rod loved shopping for clothes for me. He wanted me to liven up my classic style of dressing and picked out leopard-skin stretch pants and miniskirts. Most of the time, I paid for his choices, not him.

Rod and I got along great. We'd never had a serious argument or disagreement during the past couple months, and we were together all the time. I noticed, however, that occasionally he could be moody for no apparent reason. For example, I had gone to the salon in the hotel one afternoon for an hour. When I came back to the room, Rod was sulking and barely speaking to me. I couldn't imagine what was wrong. His dark mood continued until later at dinner that night. After a few drinks I finally got him to tell me what was wrong.

"I was upset because I wanted to spend the afternoon making love and you decided to get a manicure instead," he told me, petulantly.

How was I supposed to know that's what he wanted? I wasn't used to a man being so possessive; it never occurred to me that leaving him for an hour would bother him.

Rod got tremendous attention everywhere we went, and I started to realize just how famous he was. I wasn't that familiar with his music. I was country girl at heart and loved Willie Nelson and Waylon Jennings. But he had just had three huge hit albums in a row; "You're in My Heart" was his latest hit. I had to admit that all the attention was exciting.

Our next stop was London, where throngs of paparazzi lay in wait to get a look at Rod's new girlfriend. We stayed at Elton John's fabulous estate in Windsor, about forty-five minutes outside of London, in the beautiful English countryside.

Elton was wonderful, warm, and very funny. He and I hit it off right away.

Every morning we had big English breakfasts. We'd take long walks on the beautiful grounds and dine at a new restaurant every night. Rod and Elton had a running competition ever since they'd become friends, and it was good-natured most of the time. Elton called Rod "Phyllis" and Rod called Elton "Sharon," and they had a lot of fun at each other's expense.

The few days at Elton's were heaven, and it seemed with each passing day Rod and I fell more deeply in love.

One night after a romantic dinner at Mirabelle, a trendy restaurant in London, Rod, who had had a lot to drink, joked, "I bet you wouldn't marry me if I asked you."

"You're much too young to think about marriage," I teased him back.

Then Rod slipped into one of his sullen moods. "A relationship has to go somewhere. It doesn't work if it has nowhere to go."

He then told me how much he wanted me to have his baby.

"We have plenty of time to think about it," I told him.

I realized later that Rod wanted something all the more if he wasn't sure he could have it. If I'd thrown myself into his arms and said, "Oh darling, I want desperately to marry you," he probably would have backed off immediately.

When it was time to go home, I couldn't bear to leave Rod, and I pretended to lose my passport so I could have two more days with him. Looking back now, I can't believe I was so unprofessional.

Rod was extremely jealous of George, whom he called "the old man," and he resented that I was working with him. I felt very torn. I was in love with Rod and didn't want anything to come between us, but I also had to retain my independence and focus on my career. I had no money coming in except what I made and a small amount of child support for Ashley. For the next few weeks it was a delicate balancing act of keeping Rod happy and showing up for work, as well as being there for Ashley.

Around this time I had to move out of the house on Stone Canyon because the owner had sold it.

"You and Ashley can move in with me," Rod offered, but I couldn't move my three-year-old son in with a man I'd only been dating for two months. And I didn't intend to live with anyone unless I was married.

Me at fourteen months. Clearly not happy to have my picture taken.

Me (age 3) with Mother (age 23) on one of her visits to see me in Nacogdoches. To me, she was the most glamorous woman in the world.

Living the good life? Me (age 2) with Uncle Gene and my great-grandmother "Granny" in our backyard. Granny was half Cherokee.

My first-grade school photo.
Nacogdoches, Texas.

Twelve years old at the house of my Grandma and Grandpa Ahrens (my stepfather's parents) in Pennsylvania. I look like a poster child for the NRA!

Me (age 20) in Houston just before I left for New York to try my luck at modeling. I won first runner-up at the Miss International Airline Stewardess competition.

Me (age 21) visiting Grandma and Grandpa Ahrens.

One of my first fashion shoots for *Glamour* magazine.

"She is learning to put herself back together from the scattered bits and pieces recent generations have made of her"

Alana Collins is the new Southern Renaissance girl, free, honest, gallant, a young model from Texas, now living in New York. Hair by Angela of the Kenneth salon. Fashion and beauty details, page 166

STUPAKOFF

My first shoot for *Glamour* magazine—one of my favorite photos.

PAGE FROM *GLAMOUR* MAGAZINE, COURTESY OF THE AUTHOR.

My first big modeling break—with Francesco Scavullo for *Harper's Bazaar*.
PAGE FROM *HARPER'S BAZAAR* MAGAZINE, COURTESY OF THE AUTHOR.

Choisissez directement un maillot Rasurel. Il faut si peu de choses pour rater des vacances.

RASUREL ß

A French ad shot in Paris by renowned French photographer, Jeanloup Sieff.

TOWN & COUNTRY

ESTABLISHED 1846

MAY 1975

Mrs. George Hamilton:
Reviving
Hollywood's
Golden
Glamour

An Entire Issue On
THE HAPPY CALIFORNIANS
And Their Pleasure-Seeking Life Styles
PLUS:
A Hedonist's Guide to San Francisco
Love & Marriage in Los Angeles
Who's Who in Palm Springs
Bohemian Grove's Billion-Dollar Barbecue
The Most Fascinating People to Know,
Sights to See, Things to Do

Town & Country cover.
TOWN & COUNTRY MAGAZINE, MAY 1975, COURTESY OF THE AUTHOR.

George and me in Capri
soon after we met.

George and me early in our
courtship, in Acapulco—
one of our favorite getaways.

Our spur-of-the-moment wedding in Las Vegas. A few hours before, we'd been riding motor-
cycles in Palm Springs, 1972.

George, me, and infant Ashley in front of our pool. Lord Patrick Lichfield had come from London to photograph us for a magazine and, as a favor, snapped this shot with my camera.

George and Ashley (with four new teeth).

George and me in our new home on Tower Road in Beverly Hills, for a spread in *Town & Country*.

Ashley (age 16), George, and me. Christmas in Brentwood, 1990.

A publicity still for "The George and Alana Show."

Our wedding at Tina Sinatra's house in Beverly Hills, April 6, 1979.

Tina Sinatra helping me put flowers in my hair for my wedding. She was my maid of honor. Jane Bachelor, my friend and Ashley's nanny, is in the background.

Rod and me on our honeymoon in Spain, 1979.

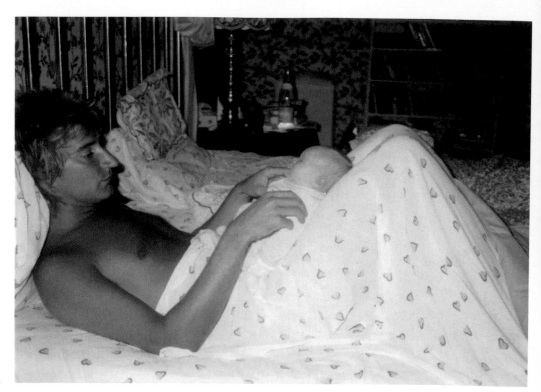

Rod and baby Kimberly.

At the pool with baby Kimberly.

Also, as far as our having a baby went, I still had my old-fashioned Texas values—again, not going to happen unless I was married.

I found another house to rent on Loma Vista in Truesdale, and Ash and I moved in there. Rod was in the studio finishing an album, and he would come to my house when he finished late at night. I'd have something ready for him to eat, and we would spend the night there.

In late June Rod finished laying the music tracks and wanted us to go to his house in Spain so he could write the lyrics. Rod's house was an hour from Marbella, outside the tiny town of Estepona. The house sat on a cliff overlooking the ocean with views of the island of Gibraltar in the distance. It was a new house that had been built just before Rod bought it, and although it was nice enough, it felt like it was in the middle of nowhere.

I never loved the house in Spain because it was on a windy bluff, and I've always hated wind, but in those days I was happy being anywhere as long as we were together. And Ashley loved it even though there wasn't a lot for him to do other than swim in the pool and collect shells on the beach.

Rod wrote a song for me called "The Best Days of My Life." I sometimes felt like this was some kind of a fairy tale I had fallen into. How had this all happened? And so quickly?

When we returned to Los Angles, Rod went back into the studio to finish his *Blondes Have More Fun* album. We continued our normal routine until August, when he wanted to go to Hawaii to finish the lyrics. He had trouble writing unless he was on an airplane or somewhere there were no distractions. Also, as I was learning, Rod got bored very easily and always had to have something to occupy him; he had to keep moving.

Rod had to go to Toronto in September to finish laying down his vocals. I couldn't go with him because Ashley was starting prekindergarten. I felt such emptiness when Rod left, and he wasn't happy that I couldn't go.

The second day he developed a throat problem and couldn't sing. He was restless and depressed and called me. "Please come, just for a couple of days," he begged.

I couldn't say no to him. "Okay," I said. "But I can't make it until Saturday."

The night before, my friend Wendy Stark had a party for Princess Margaret at her father's house in Holmby Hills. It was a fun gathering of movie stars, musicians, and the social elite of Hollywood. Afterward a few friends came up to my house on Loma Vista for drinks— Wendy, James Caan, Mick Jagger and Jerry Hall, and a few others.

The phone rang, and as a joke, Mick picked it up: "Hello, Alana's house."

Mick and Rod exchanged pleasantries, and Mick handed me the phone. Rod was furious that Mick had answered my phone. I excused myself and went into my bedroom to talk to him. I felt sick to my stomach and guilty, as if I'd done something wrong.

"What is he doing there?" Rod demanded. Although Rod was always cordial, even friendly, to Mick when they saw each other, Rod didn't like him.

"They came by for a drink after Wendy's party with a couple of other friends," I told him. "That's all."

"Well tell them to leave now. I don't want him at your house," he said.

I couldn't believe it. "How can I tell them to leave? They just got here!"

"Just tell them you have to go to bed!" he ordered. "And call me back when they're gone!"

I didn't know what to do. I didn't want to fight with Rod, and yet I couldn't be rude and tell my friends to leave. In the end, I was in the bedroom on the phone for so long that they all were leaving anyway when I came back into the bar. I apologized and said good night. I called Rod back, who was still sulking, and tried my best to appease him.

A pattern was emerging, one I didn't see at the time. I had always been outgoing and friendly, and it was my nature to flirt, but Rod was so jealous and possessive that I started to be quieter and more subdued when we went out. I had a lot of men friends who were just platonic buddies, nothing else. But if I talked to another man at a party, Rod would demand to know if I'd ever slept with him.

Some of my friends—George was the most vocal about it—told me that I had lost my personality around Rod. I felt that perhaps they were right, but as I've said, I was so in love with him that I didn't want to argue or, worse, have him be cold and angry and not talk to me, so I just went along with it. In some way I was even flattered by his possessiveness because, although I covered it well, deep inside I was so insecure that it made me feel more loved. This was before I understood codependency.

Codependents often suffer from low self-esteem and tend to be attracted to narcissists. That probably is a pretty succinct description of the dynamic of our relationship, but at the time I had no idea of the deeper significance of what was happening to me.

In Toronto Rod picked me up at the airport, and we had a romantic dinner. We stayed up most of the night talking and making love. Rod told me how much he had missed me and that we must never be apart again. Then he surprised me. "I think you should stop using birth control," he said.

"I wouldn't even think about having a child if we're not married," I told him.

"That goes without saying," he said. "We just have to find a break in the tour when we can get married."

"Are you really sure you want to do this?" I asked. "Because if I get pregnant, it will be too late to change our minds." Rod convinced me that he wanted me to have his baby more than anything, and I felt for the first time that we were in this for the long haul together, that our commitment to each other was strong and solid, and that we had a future together.

Rod had to leave in October for Europe, and as the time came closer for him to go, I was worried sick about what would happen to us. He wanted me to go with him, but there was no way I could leave Ashley. Finally, he talked me into coming with him while Ashley went to stay with George for a month. Then Ash and our nanny, Jane, would fly over to London, where Rod's manager had rented a house for us. Fortunately, George was going to be in town and was more than happy to have the time with Ashley; I breathed a sigh of relief, and off we went.

We left the end of October for England and a few days at Elton's house, where Rod got the stomach flu and Elton and I spent our time doctoring him. Elton would come sweeping into the room in his robe, armed with a bottle of some disgusting British remedy and a spoon, which he took great pleasure giving to Rod.

"Come now, Phyllis, open up. This is good for you, dear!"

Rod would practically gag. "What is this ghastly concoction? Are you trying to kill me, Sharon?"

They kept me laughing constantly. Elton loved teasing Rod because he complained about everything. He told me that Rod once called him complaining that the sheets at the Dorchester were too stiff and they scratched his elbows!

From there we went to the incredibly beautiful Ashford Castle on the west coast of Ireland so Rod could rest before starting the tour.

The first day we were at the castle I came down with the stomach flu, which I had obviously caught from Rod. I was so weak from throwing up all night that I could barely get out of bed, much less even look at food. I decided to order some soup for dinner and asked Rod what he would like.

"Nothing," he said sullenly. I kept asking him what was the matter, but he sat sulking in the living room of the suite while I miserably ate my soup in bed. Any time Rod turned on his cold, silent treatment, I felt like the world was coming to an end. Finally, I got so frustrated that I said I was leaving if he didn't tell me what was wrong.

"You knew I wanted to go downstairs and have a nice dinner and some wine," he said. "I hate eating in the room."

Rod's first performance was in Paris. The two days before the concert were spent doing photographs and interviews for all the British newspapers, who clamored for pictures of the two of us together. The headline of the *Sun* (London) read, "I want Alana to have my baby, says Rod." I was a little embarrassed but at the same time flattered that he had made his love for me so public.

I'd never seen Rod onstage before. He was the most amazing performer; I couldn't even believe this was the man I was in love with. Everything he was in person was magnified a thousand-fold; he was rowdy, sexy, raucous, and charismatic, and the energetic way he danced and moved all over the stage had the audience in the palm of his hand.

Just before the show was over his manager escorted me backstage, and the minute Rod finished we were rushed into a waiting limousine and out of the arena. Rod never stayed afterward at his concerts because he wanted to escape before the fans got out. His dresser had wrapped a blanket around him, as he was soaking wet with perspiration. I wasn't sure what to say. I was still kind of in shock over seeing the man I'd been involved with for seven months transform into one of the world's biggest rock stars.

We went back to the hotel, where Rod showered and changed so we could go to the party the promoters were giving for him. He was strangely silent and cold to me. When I asked him what was wrong, he said, "You haven't said much of anything to me about the show. You're the person whose opinion matters most to me, and you haven't said if you even liked it!"

"I'm sorry," I said. "I never saw you perform before. You were just so amazing that I guess I was kind of speechless."

I learned that night that all performers are insecure and need reassurance that they were great. They can never get too much adoration. I never made that mistake again.

After Paris we flew to Oslo. While we were there we got the news that Rod's "Do You Think I'm Sexy" had gone to number one on the charts in America and Britain. Rod was overjoyed. The album became a huge hit all over the world and was a huge disco favorite, but the critics took a dim view of it. Some of the reviews were scathing, and they accused Rod of selling out and making a disco record.

When George and I had traveled, we just got on a plane and went; Rod had a huge entourage of people who looked after him. We were escorted on planes, never having to think about tickets or baggage, and whisked off into a waiting limousine and straight to the hotel. The wardrobe girl arrived at each hotel before us with our luggage, which she unpacked for us before putting up black-out drapes in the bedroom of the suite. Rod was always up late after the performance and liked to sleep very late. He didn't eat before going onstage, so afterward we would go out to eat with the band.

Sometimes the promoters would throw a party for Rod after the concerts. By the time we ate, partied, went back to the hotel, made love, and went to sleep, it was easily 3:00 or 4:00 a.m. We'd sleep until noon, get up, have breakfast, and then go out for a walk or a little shopping before Rod had to go to the sound check. By then it was time to get ready and leave for the concert.

It was all kind of exciting and new in the beginning, but the touring got old very quickly. Every night it was the same, just in a different city. I'd hang out backstage in Rod's dressing room with him or in the green room. Then he would have me escorted to the lighting stage in the middle of the venue, where he liked me to sit during his performance. Although I loved watching him perform, there were times I'd get restless watching the same show every night, so I'd sneak into the green room and kill some time there for a while; however, I could never let Rod know I hadn't seen every moment of the show.

I had to fly back to London for two days for some meetings my agents in LA had set up for me. Rod arranged for me to stay at Elton's house in Windsor and for a car and driver to take me back and forth into London.

The second day, I had dinner at the home of Rod's manager, Billy Gaff, in London. I called Rod when I arrived, and he wasn't pleased about my being there. I had to describe the six other guests, but when Rod heard they were all gays and women, he was okay with it. But then he called back before I even finished dinner.

"Make sure you go straight back to Elton's," he said, "and call me the minute you get in."

Bianca was in town, and I had promised to stop by and see her on my way home. I conveniently didn't mention that to Rod. I spent an hour at Bianca's with her and an old friend of ours, Arnaud de Rosnay. Bianca, who had recently filed for divorce from Mick, staged a mock ceremony of crowning me "the new Queen of Rock and Roll," and we all collapsed in fits of giggles. She and Arnaud teased me because I was so nervous about getting back.

"I can't believe this is the same Alana I knew," Bianca said. "What have you done with my independent, fun-loving friend?" she half-joked.

Nevertheless, I said good night and was driven back to Windsor, feeling slightly guilty.

When I arrived, I called Rod immediately, but there was no answer in his room. It was a little after midnight, so I waited half an hour and called again. Still no answer. Now I was pissed off. Why had I rushed back to call him if he wasn't even there? I called several more times before going to bed. I felt sick and panicky. Where could he be? What if he was with someone else? I finally fell into a restless sleep.

As soon as I woke up the next morning I called him. I was upset and angry. "Where were you? I kept calling your room and you weren't there!"

"I went to dinner with the band and came back and went to bed," he said. "The operator must have been ringing the wrong room. I was upset you hadn't called. You went straight home, didn't you?"

"Of course," I lied. I decided to drop the whole thing while I was ahead.

"Are you sure you're telling me the truth?" he asked suspiciously when I arrived back in Stockholm that evening. "You know, if you ever lie to me or if you're ever unfaithful, I'll be able to look in your eyes and know. If you don't tell me and I find out, it'll ruin our relationship."

I felt sick every time he brought up the subject, but I knew deep in my heart not to tell him the truth or he'd hold it against me forever. This kind of questioning went on long after we were married. I should have put my foot down in the beginning, but unfortunately, I hadn't.

I was thrilled when we got back to London and moved into the house on Chester Square for the British part of the tour. The house that his manager had found for us was a magnificent four-story home in Chester Square, across from a beautiful sixteenth-century church.

I often still felt like I was living in a fairy tale. Rod and I were still in the throes of romance and passion, and we were seldom apart for even an hour. If he watched television, he wanted me with him. If he took a nap, I'd take one with him. At times I felt claustrophobic, but I never let on.

In November Jane brought Ashley over. I had missed him so much, and I was so happy and excited to see him. I couldn't wait to show him around London and take him to some of Rod's concerts. Rod was really sweet and inclusive with Ashley, and Ashley idolized Rod. I felt like I had everything in my life that could make me happy.

At one point during the tour Rod came down with a terrible cold and bronchitis. The doctor told him that he must quit drinking for a week or so until he got better. Rod only drank in the evening, but his routine was pretty much the same every night. If he was performing, he'd have several rum and cokes before going onstage and then continue on after the show, always having a bottle of very good wine with dinner, often followed by a cognac or two. When he wasn't performing, he'd start with a sherry around 6:00 p.m., perhaps having a stronger drink or two before dinner, and, as always, wine with dinner. If we were going out to a club or party afterward, he'd continue on with rum and cokes. If it was a very late night and we were with the band or other friends, some cocaine would come out and the occasional quaalude.

I didn't really think anything about it or that it was even a problem. My only experience with alcoholism had been with my two stepfathers, both of whom drank until they passed out at night and then started again in the morning. To me, that was an alcoholic. Actually, Rod was always more fun and much more affectionate and loving when he'd had a couple of drinks. Sometimes, the next day, however, he'd be moody and quiet until time for his evening cocktail.

In any case, for a few days he tried to stop drinking after the doctor's warning. He couldn't do it. After a day of feeling miserable and shaky, he said, "Sod it, I'm having me drink."

Christmas was fast approaching, and because Rod was in the middle of the British tour, many of our evenings were spent in Manchester or Brighton or Birmingham. We got a big Christmas tree and decorated the house beautifully. I took Ashley to Harrods to see all the Christmas decorations and toys.

We had a wonderful Christmas together, one of the best I could remember. Rod gave me a beautiful pearl and diamond deco bracelet and a fabulous pair of pearl and diamond earrings, and I gave him the new Cartier tank watch I had bought for him when we were in Paris. There were lots of toys under the tree for Ashley; Rod had bought him an electric car that Ashley loved.

I cooked Christmas dinner myself—an old-fashioned Texas turkey. I cooked a few traditional English dishes as well. Elton and Bob Halley joined us for Christmas dinner, and Elton gave Rod a beautiful antique platinum pocket watch. He gave me a delicate Cartier gold, diamond, and emerald bracelet. I couldn't believe it when I unwrapped the box. He was and still is one of the most generous people I've ever known.

As a joke, Rod and I gave Elton a toaster because he hadn't had one in Windsor when we were there. His real present was a beautiful Galle vase that I had talked Rod into buying.

Chapter 14

Christmas was over, and it was the week of the last concerts at Olympia. I was feeling a little under the weather, and the doctor said I had the stomach flu. Three days later the doctor came to the house again. Now my period was three days late.

"I think I need a pregnancy test," I said, nervous about what the result might be.

"Sure," he said. "I can do one now."

The doctor disappeared into the bathroom with a urine specimen. He came out a few minutes later.

"Congratulations!" he said. "You're pregnant."

Rod and I were both sitting up in bed, and we just looked at each other. We'd talked about it so many times, and suddenly it was a reality. I think we were both kind of in shock. We hadn't expected it to happen so quickly.

The doctor left, and Rod was still quiet.

"Are you sure you want this baby?" I asked him, thinking it was a little late now to change his mind.

"Of course I want it," he said. "It'll just take me a little time to get used to it."

That night was his last concert in London, and I'd assumed we'd have a romantic little dinner to celebrate the happy news. Instead, Rod invited the band to join us and hardly paid any attention to me at all. I sulked most of the evening and later told him why I was upset.

"It was the last concert, Poop [our nicknames for each other]. We had to celebrate with the band," he said. "We'll have plenty of time to be alone."

The following night was New Year's Eve, and we were going out on the town with Elton. It had snowed the night before, and the streets

123

were covered in ice. Rod had more and more to drink, and he was acting as if I was hardly there. He'd jump out of the car and head for the next club, leaving Elton to help me make my way across the icy sidewalks in my high heels.

As we headed down Jermyn Street, Tony Toon suggested we have a drink at a trendy club called Monkberry's. We sat down at a table with Keith Richards and Ron Wood and ordered champagne. I was barely sipping mine because I didn't want to drink alcohol now that I was pregnant. Tony had conveniently forgotten to mention that Britt Ekland was there. She had obviously been drinking all evening, and the minute she spotted Rod, she made her way straight over and plopped herself down on his lap, totally ignoring me. She began talking to Rod and planting kisses on his face, as he turned beet red in embarrassment. At first I thought his predicament was amusing, but she didn't stop, and finally, I'd had enough.

I turned to Ron Wood and said, with a wink, "I think Britt needs a little cooling off." I poured my entire glass of champagne down her bare back.

She squealed and jumped up. Then one of the club managers came over and led her back to her table. A number of people had been watching, wondering how I would handle the spectacle she was making of herself. "Well done!" several of them said.

Rod, Woody, and I were giggling like little kids. A writer from the *Daily Express* had witnessed the incident, and it was all over the newspapers the next day. Fortunately, I came out the heroine, good-naturedly defending my territory.

We proceeded to the Ritz Hotel, where Keith and Woody were staying. Rod once again jumped out of the car and hurried into the hotel, leaving me to struggle along behind him. It was close to 4:00 a.m., and I was exhausted and wanted to go home, but Rod was oblivious.

I ended up pouring my heart out to Elton, telling him I was pregnant and that I couldn't understand Rod's behavior.

"You have to understand that when he gets around the 'boys' and drinks and does drugs, he becomes a different person. He doesn't mean to be inconsiderate. He's just unaware of anyone else," said Elton, trying to explain Rod's unacceptable behavior.

We didn't get home until around 6:00 a.m., and I was feeling really weak. The next morning I noticed I was bleeding slightly. I called my doctor in California, concerned.

"You're in danger of miscarrying," he told me. "You need to stay in bed and stay off your feet. And please abstain from sex for a while," he said.

"For how long?" I asked.

"At least until you make it through your first trimester," he said.

I was frightened. This couldn't be happening, I thought. Terrible nausea set in as well, and just as with Ashley, it never subsided.

Being bedridden complicated everything; I couldn't do anything with Ashley, nor could Rod and I go out, so he was going stir-crazy.

I hated being confined and was feeling not only sick and worried about losing my baby but also depressed because Rod's attitude toward me was different. We couldn't make love, either, which had been such a huge part of our relationship.

We took the Concorde to New York and checked into the Carlyle. I had to go straight to bed and stay there because I was still bleeding. Rod did a show, which I couldn't attend, on January 10, his birthday. Afterward we went to Elaine's with Billy and the band. I looked pale and drawn so I told everyone I'd had the flu.

Rod didn't seem loving and understanding. Not only couldn't I drink and keep up with him, but now I had to stay in bed all the time. I began to feel like it was more an inconvenience for him than anything else.

From the moment we arrived back in LA there were torrential rains that never let up, and Rod was bored and restless. I was about two months pregnant by now, still feeling sick all the time and forced to stay in bed to prevent a miscarriage.

Finally, I had enough. "Rod, I can't take your attitude anymore. You're the one who talked me into not using birth control so I could get pregnant, and now you act like you don't want this baby. If that's the case, I think it would be best to tell me now before it's too late. As devastating as it would be, I don't want to bring a baby into the world unless you want it."

"You know I want this baby," he assured me. "You just have to let me get used to the idea of a baby and getting married. I promise you, it'll all work out." He held me in his arms. I felt somewhat convinced, but I knew I wouldn't rest easy until we were husband and wife.

After that, Rod became a little more sensitive about my condition and looked after me in his own way. For instance, he bought me Elton's white Rolls Corniche convertible so I wouldn't have to drive my stick shift Porsche while I was pregnant.

Things were looking up. I knew Rod was nervous about getting married and the responsibility of being a father so soon, but I also knew he loved me and wanted this baby.

Rod had to leave for the Australian leg of the tour, but I couldn't travel that far yet so I stayed behind. Finally, the bleeding stopped. I was still horribly nauseated all the time, but at least I could move around. Rod and I talked several times a day on the phone. We had talked before about buying a house in Acapulco, so he suggested that I take Ashley and Jane and go down there with Gail, his secretary, and look for one while I rested and soaked up some sun. Later on, when I could travel further, I would meet him in Australia.

While we were in Acapulco, Jack Martin, a journalist for the *New York Post*, somehow tracked me down. Just as I was wondering why he was calling me, he dropped the bomb on me.

"So what do you make of all these rumors about Rod and Belinda Green in Australia?" he asked.

I was stunned. "What rumors? And who is Belinda Green?" I asked, trying to sound casual.

"You mean you haven't heard? Belinda Green is the former Miss World, and the Australian press is having a field day that Rod is having an affair with her."

I knew that he was looking for a reaction, so I forced myself to stay composed.

"I never believe any of those silly rumors. Rod and I talk every day; everything is fine, and I'll be going down to join him soon," I said calmly.

My heart was pounding out of my chest. I wasn't sure what day or what time it was in Australia, but I tried to get through to Rod, which was no easy task from Mexico.

"Who is Belinda Green?" I asked him, getting straight to the point.

Rod was taken aback. "She's just a journalist who interviewed me when I first got here," he explained.

"You mean, you've only met her once?" I questioned.

"Well, she came on a boat with us one day," he admitted. "Somehow the press got a photo of the two of us and tried to make a big thing out of it. There's nothing to it," he assured me.

I didn't believe him. It just sounded too fishy to me.

"I've had it," I said sobbing hysterically. "It's over."

Rod had a way of turning things around. "I promise you, nothing happened. This wouldn't have happened if you were here. I don't want to lose you or the baby. Please get on a plane and come here right away," he pleaded. "We'll work everything out."

We flew back to LA the next day, and I went to get my doctor's permission to leave for Australia. I arranged for Jane and Ashley to stay with George and meet us in Hawaii in two weeks, as Rod had suggested. He was seeming much sweeter and more loving, so I started to believe there really was nothing to the rumors. He arranged to have Gail accompany me because he didn't want me to travel alone.

When we arrived at the Sydney airport, an onslaught of photographers and journalists swarmed around me as Gail pushed me into the waiting car. I wasn't sure what all the fuss was about until one reporter shouted out, "What do you think about Belinda Green?"

"Never heard of her," I said, smiling sweetly, as I slammed the door.

When I arrived at Rod's hotel, he was waiting downstairs for me. We rushed into each other's arms and he kissed me passionately. He grabbed my hand and took me straight up to our suite, where we spent the rest of the afternoon making love. He was tender and loving and seemed like my Rod again.

That night, after the concert, we went out to dinner with some Australian record executives. Rod and I held hands the whole time and couldn't get enough of each other. The next morning the newspapers all had front-page pictures of my arrival along with stories about Rod's week of encounters with Belinda Green. It seemed she had showed up everywhere he was, even in Perth, which was a five-hour flight away. Just a coincidence? I thought not, but Rod tried to explain it all away by saying it was just the Australian papers trying to make something out of nothing.

"I swear to you, I didn't do anything with her. I couldn't do something like that, knowing you were home carrying my baby."

I believed him; the truth is that even though there was a nagging doubt, I desperately wanted to believe him. Though I would find out some years later that the rumors had actually been true . . .

The next day Rod and I went out on a boat with the band. Afterward we ended up having an argument because I thought he was being inconsiderate and he thought I was being touchy and sensitive. With all my pregnancy hormones raging, I probably was.

"I wish I'd never gotten pregnant with your child!" I blurted out angrily. We didn't speak for the rest of the evening, and Rod continued to have one drink after another.

When we got back to the room, he was terribly cruel to me. "I don't want to get married," he said coldly. "I never wanted to get married!"

I don't even remember what else he said, but I started crying hysterically. He seemed to be taking pleasure in hurting me. Eventually he retired to the bedroom and went to sleep, and I cried on the living room sofa all night long.

I didn't know how much more stress I could take. I'd been reduced to a nervous, crying wreck. I'd never felt more insecure or alone in my life, and I was concerned that all this stress was going to affect the baby.

The next morning I was sure it was over between us, and I was ready to head back to Los Angeles to have my baby on my own when Rod came out of the bedroom and found me still crying. He put his arms around me and held me close.

"I'm so sorry," he said. "You know I didn't mean any of it. Of course we're getting married as soon as we get home."

The next few days were more peaceful, although Rod continued to have late, rowdy nights with the band. He didn't seem to realize how exhausted I was. Once he started drinking with the band, he forgot everything else.

We arrived in Honolulu to begin the American portion of the tour, which would continue until mid-April. Ashley and Jane joined us there. When I told Ashley that Rod and I were going to get married, he started to cry.

"I thought you liked Rod," I said, holding him in my arms.

"I do," he said, tearfully. "But if you marry him, I won't have a mommy anymore."

"No, baby, I'll always be your mommy," I assured him. "Now you'll have a stepfather too, and you'll live with us and visit your dad whenever you want, just like always."

Looking back, I wish I had spent more time alone with Ashley when he was so young. Years later, when I got into Al-Anon, I wrote Ashley a letter telling him how sorry I was that I hadn't been the mother I wish I had been, and I asked for his forgiveness. I've tried

129

to make up for what I didn't do in his younger years by being there for him now in every way I can, but I've still never been able to forgive myself completely.

We arrived back in Los Angeles and began making arrangements for the wedding. On the day we were to get our blood tests, Rod decided instead to go to Long Beach to buy a new car. I was furious that he could nonchalantly cancel something he knew was so important.

Then I was informed that I would have to sign a prenuptial agreement before the wedding. I tried to be understanding about it. Britt Ekland had gone after Rod for $11 million dollars in her palimony suit, and I knew that Rod was very distrustful about women and his money. But deep down, I was hurt by his lack of trust in me. I felt he should know by now that I wasn't that kind of person.

Tina sent me to see Mickey Rudin, who was her father Frank Sinatra's attorney. He looked over the agreement and said it was unfair and demeaning. His letter reads, "The agreement you submitted simply constitutes a waiver by Alana of any rights that she may have as a wife. I could not possibly put my name to such an agreement. I think such agreements are unfair, unconscionable, and under the circumstances of the parties probably unenforceable." The agreement stated that if Rod and I were to break up at any time in the future, I would get a settlement of $100,000.

"You can't possibly sign a prenuptial agreement without doing discovery of his assets and without the amount of the settlement increasing during the period you're married," he told me. "I can't possibly represent you if you insist on signing this agreement as it's written."

Rod's manager sent me to another attorney, who asked me if I understood what I was signing. At this point I didn't care that much about any of it. I was not in a very rational frame of mind; I just wanted to sign the damned thing and get it over with. I wanted Rod to know I loved him and had no interest in his money. I told Rod that I knew in my heart that if anything ever happened with us, he would take care of me and the baby, and he assured me that he would but that it would never be an issue because our marriage would be forever.

We decided the wedding ceremony would be private, but we planned a large celebration dinner at L'Hermitage, a French restaurant that we loved. Our friends were told it was a party to celebrate the beginning of the American tour, so no one would suspect we were getting married. Rod was adamant about no one knowing because he didn't want our wedding to become a zoo.

Rod and I picked out wedding rings, and he bought me a beautiful diamond deco ring at Francis Klein, a prestigious jewelry store in Beverly Hills.

Finally, the big day came. I wore a cream-colored lace-and-chiffon off-the-shoulder dress that I had found at a shop in Beverly Hills, and Rod matched me perfectly in a cream-colored suit with a pink tie and pink suede shoes—for a little rock-and-roll touch.

A white limousine arrived to take us, along with Ashley, Jane, and Tony, to Tina Sinatra's house a little after 7:00. Tina had a beautiful bridal bouquet for me made of pink and lavender flowers, and we pinned baby's breath all through my hair.

When I walked down the stairs and Rod and I looked into each other's eyes, my heart welled up with happiness. He looked so adorable and nervous and vulnerable, as he downed his Bacardi and Coke.

At 7:45 we took our places in the living room. Jacquie Eastland had become a dear friend and because she was an ordained minister, she performed the ceremony. Ashley stood next to Rod, who put his arm around my small son and pulled him close.

The ceremony was so beautiful that I cried all the way through it. I noticed that Rod's eyes were misty too. When Jacquie pronounced us husband and wife, we kissed tenderly.

"Would you like some champagne, Mrs. Stewart?" asked Rod. That was music to my ears! We had some champagne and caviar, finally relaxing enough to enjoy it, until it was time to leave for the party.

When our limousine pulled up in front of L'Hermitage, I was shocked to see the number of photographers and television cameras. Sheer pandemonium erupted when we stepped out of the car. By this time Rod didn't mind at all and we posed, smiling ecstatically, before several bodyguards hired for the evening ushered us into the restaurant through the throng.

It was a wonderful, warm evening with a fabulous five-course meal, ending with lots of speeches wishing us well. Rod stood up and toasted "his bride," and I was overcome with tears of happiness. We ended the evening at Tina's with a little more champagne, and by now it was 3:00 a.m.

We had reserved a large suite at the Bel Air Hotel for our "honeymoon" night, but Rod looked at me and said, "Wouldn't you rather just spend the night at home?" I was exhausted and couldn't think of anything I'd rather do.

Chapter 15

We were going to continue living between Rod's house in the day-time and my house at night because Rod was building a new master bedroom suite upstairs, a garden room, and a ballroom. How funny that both of my husbands had ballrooms. I would have never guessed, growing up in Nacogdoches without an indoor toilet, that I would one day live in not one but two houses with ballrooms.

The tour resumed with dates in Vancouver and the Northwest. Rod chartered a Lear jet so he could fly home and be with me every night after the concert, even though it was a two-and-a-half-hour flight.

From the moment we got married, Rod did a complete about-face. He had never been so loving and attentive.

"I've always been so frightened of marriage, but I can't believe how happy I am," he told me. "I never dreamed belonging to one person could be so wonderful."

It felt like we had the perfect life. We never had a cross word, and the only thing I ever felt uncomfortable about was the subject of money. I hated asking for anything, but I was still paying the rent on my house, which we were living in half of the time. He didn't hesi-tate for a minute to pay for it. Then Tony presented me with my own Gold American Express card that he'd instructed Rod's office to order.

If anything, I was eventually the one who tried to curb Rod's spending. He was terribly extravagant when it came to buying lamps, furniture, or cars that he wanted. However, he could be very penuri-ous over the smallest of things. He hated paying bills, so after the of-fice sent them up for him to sign personally, which he would insist on, he would stash them away somewhere and sometimes end up misplacing them altogether. He was always sure he was being ripped off, even if it was fifteen dollars for a petunia plant that the gardener couldn't account for. It drove me crazy. I tried to convince him that people needed to be paid on time for their services, and eventually he turned the check signing over to me.

When we decided to buy a beach house, Rod sent me and Billy Gaff out to look for one while he was touring in the Midwest. I found the perfect one, but Billy was the one who made the deal.

Then Rod's attorney drew up an agreement for me to sign saying that I would forego any ownership in the house. I was shocked and hurt that Rod would ask me to do such a thing. But instead of voicing my feelings, I just signed the papers. In those days it still wasn't easy for me to talk about my feelings, so I just stuffed them inside and tried to forget about them and get on with our lives.

Rod took a break during the tour in May so we could go to London for the annual Scotland-England match. No matter what Rod was doing, this was a game he never missed. It's a good thing the baby wasn't due then. It would have been a tough decision for him! When we arrived at the airport in London, the press was there in full force because word had gotten out that I was expecting. I was almost six months pregnant by now and definitely starting to show it.

At the end of June Rod finished the tour with six nights at the Forum. Rod was in great form, and all of our friends turned out to see him. It was fascinating to see Gregory Peck, Fred Astaire, and Irving Lazar, apart from all our younger friends, enjoying this wild rock concert with half-clothed girls screaming hysterically.

On the night of the final concert we had a party at my house on Loma Vista. When Keith Richards and Ron Wood showed up, I knew it was going to be a very late night. The band was there as well, and Rod was ready to party all night. On nights like these I'd often give him a kiss and sneak off to bed because, being so pregnant, I couldn't handle the late hours. He'd try to persuade me to wait for him and then promise to come to bed soon. I'd be awakened when he crept into bed, because God forbid a night should go by without us making love.

As soon as the tour ended, Rod sank into a deep depression, which he said always happened at the end of a tour. I could understand what an adjustment it must have been for him to go from thousands of screaming fans every night to being at home with nothing much to do.

I was in my eighth month now, and the doctor had said no more traveling. Rod, I suppose without meaning to, made me feel terribly guilty that he was stuck at home. I didn't realize it was his inability to be at peace with himself that drove him to stay constantly busy. I felt like his restlessness was my fault and that somehow I wasn't making him happy.

It's hard to believe that I was not only so insecure but that I felt so responsible for his happiness. As I said, I hadn't yet learned about codependency.

Several nights before Kimberly's birth we went to a Blondie concert at the Greek Theater. Rod had always been an admirer of Debbie Harry, and this was at the height of her popularity. He thought she was very sexy, so of course, I attempted to hide my jealousy as she danced and sang onstage in a tight minidress while I was wearing a tent. I was happy to see that at least she was short!

When we were invited to a party at Carlos and Charlie's for the band, Rod jumped at the chance and I wasn't one bit pleased. What on earth did I think was going to happen? I was married to him, about to have his baby any minute. Did I think he was going to leave me for some singer he'd never met? What on earth had happened to me? As it was, her band showed up, but she never did. Rod was disappointed, but I was secretly thrilled.

The next day I started having contractions, and the following day I went into labor. Rod drove me to the hospital. The labor pains had begun full force, and I was cursing like a sailor. Rod was allowed to stay with me; he made quite a picture in a green paper shower cap kind of thing, a mask, and a green hospital gown with his leopard skin boots sticking out underneath. A short time later my baby was born.

"It's a girl," the doctor announced and handed her to Rod, whose eyes were filled with tears. It was an incredibly touching moment, watching him hold his tiny daughter. Then he gave her to me, and for the second time in my life I felt that incredibly protective, overwhelming, and unconditional love that only a mother can feel at that moment.

On the third day we took Kimberly home. I was worried about Ashley feeling jealous of the new baby in the house, so I made sure that I spent as much time with him as possible. Even though he was curious about his new baby sister, it was hard for him not to resent all the attention a new baby gets. When people would come to visit and bring her presents, I knew he was jealous, so I'd try to make sure he got something special as well. He still had a hard time with it and would continue to harbor a little resentment toward her for a long time to come.

Chapter 16

When Kimberly was six weeks old, Rod and I left for London on the QE2 with our new daughter. He wanted to spend three months there working with the band on a new album, so we arranged to rent the same house in Chester Square where Kimberly had been conceived.

Ashley stayed behind with George because he was in kindergarten now, so he would join us after we got settled and I had found a school for him in London. He really wanted to come with us on the boat, and I felt terribly guilty leaving him so soon after Kimberly's birth. I knew it wasn't easy for him, having a new stepfather and a new sister in such a short period of time, but I was torn between my feelings of guilt about leaving my son and my desire to please Rod by not altering his plans.

Looking back, I wish I had just brought Ashley with us, school or no school. Missing a month of kindergarten couldn't have made that much difference, and it would have helped him feel more a part of this new family.

Pulling out of New York Harbor with my husband and new baby was one of the most thrilling moments of my life. The sun was sparkling on the water as we slowly made our way up the Hudson River and past the Statue of Liberty. I was taking pictures of everything and asking other passengers to take pictures of us. But when I opened the camera later, I found that I had stupidly forgotten to put film in it!

Everything seemed so perfect in our lives. Still, I had this vague, underlying feeling of anxiety. Even though I had everything I ever dreamed of, I couldn't ever fully appreciate it because there was always that unconscious fear that "the other shoe would fall" and once again, like it always had in my childhood, my dreams would be shattered.

I never mentioned my anxiety to Rod, and as I had learned to do early on, I tried to ignore it and just get on with my life. And that's just what we did.

We arrived in Southhampton five days later, embarking into a sea of photographers all vying to get the first shot of baby Kimberly. I covered the baby and held her really tight so the flashing lights and clamoring paparazzi wouldn't scare her. Rod got very pissed off and was really rude to the press. I almost felt like I had to pinch myself to believe this was all actually happening to me, the little barefoot girl from the one-room shack in Nacogdoches, Texas.

We moved into the beautiful four-story house in Chester Square, and Rod started working right away on the new album. He arranged to work with the band in the daytime so we could have the nights to ourselves. When he came home, we'd get dressed and go out for dinner and sometimes to a club or a party afterward. I was still breast-feeding Kimberly, so I'd often have to run home and feed her and rush back out to meet Rod. Our relationship was still incredibly passionate and romantic, and we couldn't bear to spend more than a few hours apart.

I soon came down with what I thought was a terrible flu. It lingered on for over a week. When I finally went to see Rod's doctor, he insisted on doing some blood tests. A couple days later he called me back into the office.

"It appears you have a case of glandular fever," Dr. Cooper told me.

"What's that?" I asked. It sounded terrifying.

"In the States you call it mononucleosis," he said, which sounded equally terrifying. I'd vaguely heard of mono before, but I'd thought it was a disease that college kids sometimes got—the "kissing disease."

"Is there a cure?" I asked him.

The doctor shook his head. "Not really," he said. "All you can do is get a lot of rest and wait it out."

"For how long?" I asked.

"It could take several months," he said.

I guess trying to keep up with Rod had just been too much for me so soon after giving birth. Little did I know that this was the beginning of ongoing health problems that would plague me for years to come.

I was so exhausted all the time, and yet I just couldn't stay in bed. I had a new baby, a very active husband, Ashley had just arrived, and the holidays were approaching.

Rod didn't understand how sick I was. He still wanted to go out to dinner every night, and I was determined not to disappoint him. But I was so tired all the time—not just tired, but a heavy exhaustion, the likes of which I'd never experienced before. Sometimes it seemed an effort just to lift my arm.

I finally ended up in Dr. Cooper's office, sobbing uncontrollably.

"I just can't do it anymore," I told him through my tears. "It's just too much. And Rod seems to think I'm making it up. I don't know what to do."

Dr. Cooper called Rod right away. "You need to understand how important it is that Alana rest now," he told him. "And that means staying in bed! Not running around London and staying out all night."

I got through the holidays by sheer willpower, and in January we went back to Los Angeles. The Carolwood house was under construction, so we moved into our new beach house.

I went to my doctor for follow-up blood tests, and boy, was I ever in for some news. Not only was mononucleosis still very active in my system, but I was also pregnant!

We were absolutely floored. I thought it wasn't possible to get pregnant while I was breastfeeding. Did I ever prove that old wives' tale wrong! Although the pregnancy surprised both of us, we were happy about it. I only wished my health were better.

Rod went right into the studio to finish recording the new album, but he was generally home every night by midnight. One night he called around 10:30 to tell me he'd be home within the hour. By midnight, I was starting to worry. When I called the studio, I learned he'd left hours ago. When he still hadn't appeared by 2 a.m., I was practically hysterical. I had visions of him crashed in a ditch somewhere on the dangerous Pacific Coast Highway.

I had just called the Highway Patrol for a second time to see if he'd been in an accident when he walked through the door, absolutely wasted.

"I went to see Muddy Waters with the guys," he sheepishly tried to explain. "One drink led to another, and I guess time got away from me."

I was livid. "You didn't think to call?"

"I didn't want to wake you," he said.

Admittedly, my hormones were making me insane. But I started to feel like Rod didn't love me as much anymore. We had lived in each others' pockets for so long now that I felt threatened if he wanted to do something apart from me. It tapped into my deepest fear, that of being abandoned, as I'd so often been as a child. We ended up having a huge fight. I had somehow become as jealous and possessive of Rod as he had been with me in the beginning of our relationship.

We were coming up on our one-year wedding anniversary in April, and because the Carolwood house would be finished by then, we decided to have a big party to celebrate. We planned an incredibly lavish black-tie party in the new ballroom, and it was a truly fabulous evening.

It started with a sit-down dinner for one hundred people, beginning with caviar and champagne, followed by a fabulous four-course meal served impeccably by Chasen's. We danced and drank (well, I had one glass of champagne) all night, and everyone thoroughly enjoyed themselves.

It was a perfect evening. When they served a very special Château d'Yquem that we had chosen with dessert, Freddie de Cordova, the producer of *The Tonight Show*, stood up and toasted us.

"This is the best Hollywood party I've ever been to!" he said. I felt like we were truly the golden couple.

We hadn't told anyone that I was pregnant again, but that night, as I was standing with Sue Mengers and Farrah, Sue quipped to me, "You are the luckiest woman alive."

There was something about that moment that made me feel like sharing. So I told Sue, whom I was close with, and Farrah, whom I was beginning to feel a special bond with, about the new baby on the way. That was the start of a deep and lasting friendship.

Chapter 17

This was a very special time in our lives, and Rod and I often talked about how lucky we were. We really did have everything two people could possibly want, and we were still so very much in love. Our friends would often comment about how wonderful it was to see two people who were so crazy about each other. We always had our arms around each other or held hands. Even at dinner parties Rod insisted we sit next to one another.

When I was four months pregnant with Sean, we took a brief trip to England. We were still very possessive and jealous of one another as well, and I resented anything or anyone who took his attention away from me. This was one of the reasons I wasn't so fond of the time we spent in England. Rod always wanted to spend a lot of time with his family, and I secretly resented it, but I didn't dare say anything. I dreaded the evenings when they would have a family "do," and everyone would be dancing, drinking, and singing old songs I'd never heard of until all hours. I thought it was all silly. Because I'd never had a close-knit family, I guess there was a part of me that was jealous of Rod's attachment to his.

Another source of irritation was spending time with Rod's band. Again, I tried not to show it, but I dreaded going out to dinner with the boys and their wives. They were always very rowdy; no matter how elegant the restaurant, the evening would usually end up with them putting their napkins on their heads, acting loud and silly, and throwing food. The other customers didn't appreciate it, and I often wanted to crawl under the table in embarrassment. I'm sure my disapproval was pretty obvious, although I still didn't say anything because I didn't want to start an argument with Rod.

When we got back to LA, Rod went back into the studio to finish the tracks of the new album. He was often there until very late at night. Occasionally he would stay out drinking with the band, and I resented it. I wanted him to come straight home to me like he used to. I felt like he wasn't quite as attentive and loving as he'd been in the past. I wasn't completely happy, and I didn't know why.

I started seeing a therapist, but as I didn't want Rod to think I was unhappy, I described her as more of a "spiritual healer."

At my first visit she told me, "Alana, you need to prepare yourself that your life might change by starting therapy."

"But I don't want my life to change," I told her. "I love my husband and my children. I just don't feel completely happy, but I certainly don't want anything to happen to my marriage."

I think she realized that she had panicked me.

"No," she said. "I didn't mean to imply that your marriage would break up. Only that through therapy, you may start to see certain things in your life differently."

I had no idea at the time the kind of doors therapy would open for me, for better or worse. I just felt better about having someone to talk to.

Until therapy, I never realized that Rod and I never talked about our deepest feelings. Rod was prone to deep depressions, but he never really examined what might be causing them. He could go around all day with a miserable face and in such a dark mood that it affected everyone around him. His spirits would usually lift after his first drink in the evening.

Most of the time I didn't mind Rod's drinking. The only time I really hated it was when he would get drunk with the band, which might lead to doing cocaine and staying out until all hours. As I said, we really never discussed our feelings, so instead of telling him that it worried me and made me feel alone and scared, I'd just be angry when he got home and we'd end up in an argument. Then we'd both sulk and not speak until one of us—usually me—took the first step toward making up.

The end of August came, and my due date with Sean was a little over a month away. I was really tired all the time and having trouble gaining weight. I would eat a pint of ice cream at least once a day, on top of regular meals, but I didn't gain an ounce. My doctor insisted I stay home now and try to rest.

On Sunday night, August 31, we were at the beach house when I started having contractions. The doctor told me to head to the hospital. By the time Rod and I got dressed and got into the car, the contractions were getting really strong and much closer together. We were almost an hour away from the hospital, and Rod was driving like a bat out of hell.

We were flying down the freeway when we heard the siren behind us. I was doubled over in the midst of an excruciating contraction when Rod pulled over to the side of the road, leaped out of the car, and ran toward the police car. I watched in horror as two policemen jumped from their car, with guns drawn, pointed them at my husband, and shouted, "Stop where you are!"

He stopped, thank God, and they recognized him just as he was shouting, "My wife's having a baby!" They came over to my side of the car to assess the situation.

"Don't worry, lady," one of the officers said. "We'll call an ambulance to take you to the hospital."

I was in the middle of another contraction, and now they were coming really close together. "There's no time to wait for an ambulance!" I gasped.

"Oh, it's much too dangerous to allow you to drive that fast. It puts other motorists in jeopardy. Besides, I've delivered a few babies in my time," one of the policemen said.

Well, I went crazy. "Listen, you asshole, you're not laying a finger on me or my baby, and I'm going to get to that hospital if I have to drive this car myself! You'll have to shoot me to stop me!"

I guess they figured I meant it, so they reluctantly agreed to escort us.

So with sirens screaming and lights flashing, we arrived at the Cedars Sinai emergency entrance. They pushed me into a wheelchair and into the corridor, where an orderly tried to stop us, insisting we fill out medical forms before we could go upstairs. "Listen, I'm about to drop this baby on this floor. I'm not filling out any papers, so you get me upstairs now or I'll get up and walk!" He wheeled me up there fast, with Rod running along beside us, not knowing quite what to do. He'd never seen me in such a state.

My doctor was waiting in the delivery room. After examining me, he told me the baby was breeched and he was going to do a Cesarean section immediately. He asked me if I wanted to be awake or out completely. There was no time to think about it.

"Out completely," I said quickly.

The anesthesiologist put the needle in my arm, and the next thing I knew, my doctor was leaning over me saying, "You have a baby boy and he's just fine."

Rod was holding Sean in his arms and brought him over to me. He was so perfectly beautiful, and again, for the third time, that amazing feeling of unconditional love washed over me.

When we were finally allowed to leave the hospital, it was still so painful to walk that I couldn't stand up straight. When we arrived home, with Sean in my arms, Kimberly, who had just turned one, wouldn't come near me or the new baby. When I tried to take her in my arms, she pulled away, giving me a dirty look. She continued to be distant and cool toward me for the next couple weeks. It took her a while to accept her new little brother. Ashley, who still felt Kimberly was the intruder, seemed to have no problem with Sean.

Rod went to the studio to work, and I wasn't very happy that he hadn't arranged to be home my first night back from the hospital. I could hardly make it from the bed to the bathroom by myself. He said he would be home around 10.00, so when he hadn't arrived by

1:30, I called the studio. They said he'd just left, so I assumed he'd walk in the door any minute.

As usual, I couldn't go to sleep when I was waiting for him to come home. I turned and tossed and worried and fretted. As the hours passed, I became more frantic. I just knew something terrible had happened. I had just finished breastfeeding Sean when he finally walked in at 6:00 a.m., drunk and disheveled. He looked very surprised when he saw me at the top of the stairs. Now that I could see that he was alive and well, I was furious.

"Where the hell have you been?" I demanded, angrily.

He sheepishly explained, "I went out with the boys and had a few drinks to celebrate the birth of me son."

"How could you stay out drinking all night? I just got home from the hospital."

"Aw, please don't be mad, Poop." He looked like such a contrite little boy that I couldn't help but forgive him, even though I was hurt that he hadn't shown more concern for me.

I guess it was at about this point in our relationship that I started resenting the rock-and-roll lifestyle. It was the typical scenario of a woman falling in love with a man and then wanting to change him.

Also, I was changing. I now had three children to look after, and I was exhausted all the time. My life was so wrapped up in Rod and the kids that I had practically lost touch with all of my friends. I started feeling sort of strange and disconnected if I went out into Beverly Hills alone. I only felt secure and whole if I was with Rod.

Chapter 18

When Sean was five weeks old, Rod left for his European tour. Three weeks later the kids and I checked into a three-bedroom suite at the Dorchester and set up house. Rod would charter a plane and fly to see us as often as possible.

The second night Sean came down with a temperature of 104, and I spent the whole night walking with him as he cried in my arms and bathing him in tepid water. Finally, his temperature went down slightly, and he fell into an exhausted sleep.

I had been calling Rod all night at his hotel in Stockholm, and he wasn't there. He finally answered the phone around 5 a.m., and I was practically hysterical. He told me he'd been out at a party that the record company had given him.

We had a terrible argument. "If you're going to behave like you're single, I don't want to be married to you," I told him. We both hung up angrily, and I felt sick inside. I really thought that our marriage was over, and I wanted to die. I was so irrational that it didn't even occur to me that people can have an argument without it being the end of the world.

Around 11:00 that morning, three dozen yellow roses and an adorable apologetic note arrived from Rod.

I felt so relieved that the whole horrible mess was over and that my husband still loved me. For the rest of the tour Rod flew back to London every time he had a day off, or I would join him for a few days, leaving the kids with the nanny.

Fortunately, the British press had taken a liking to me and were always very complimentary, much to Rod's delight. He liked that they described me as the "Yellow Rose of Texas who tamed the Tartan Terror."

In most of Rod's interviews his marriage and fatherhood took precedence over his music. "I know I used to be a bit of a Don Juan, but I was searching for the perfect woman. I was looking for true love and I found it with Alana," he said in one interview. In another: "The freedom that I've lost I didn't want anymore. I was getting tired of it. There comes a time when you want one good friend, one companion, and Alana's it. The amazing thing is, I don't know what I did with my life before I had children."

They all painted a rosy picture except one article that ran in the *Daily Mail*. The writer, Simon Kennersly, had been in Stockholm with Rod and apparently had picked up on the argument we were having:

"At 35, Rod Stewart is confronted by the greatest dilemma of his life. He is married with two children and has to face up to the responsibilities of being a father. Yet he is trapped in an industry in which youthfulness is all important and machismo an obsession. When he is touring, he has an image to maintain and nurture—that of the rock star who drinks hard on late nights surrounded by beautiful women, and remains not merely young but juvenile. The moment it is over he has to slip quietly into being a mature family man."

The article went on to describe how Rod was out at a nightclub drinking port and brandy in an attempt to be his old flamboyant self and although dozens of beautiful women were vying for his attention, he left to go back to the hotel and phone me. It ended by pointing out that "this double life was something faced by almost every major rock star who has chosen to get married. The outcome is usually a sad mess like Mick and Bianca Jagger."

That article was probably the most insightful of them all, but we refused to believe that anything could ever come between us.

The tour ended a week before Christmas, and I was so happy to be going home to Los Angeles for the holidays. Two months of living in a hotel suite with three children was quite enough.

I hadn't regained my strength after Sean's birth and was hoping that being at home would bring a change for the better. It was still such an effort to keep up with Rod, but I forced myself to maintain that pace rather than stay home and rest. It's as if I was afraid that if he was out of my sight, I'd lose him. I didn't totally trust him. Was it a kind of sixth sense or my terrible insecurity? Perhaps it was a little of both.

Rod was a workaholic, and once a tour was over, he went right into the studio to record another album. As time went on I began to resent how little of his time the kids and I were getting, and I felt subtle changes happening in our relationship. Our disagreements were usually about the same things—soccer and drinking with the boys.

Even though he had the weekends off from the studio, he always played soccer on Sundays and was gone most of the day. The game itself was only a couple hours, but afterward they all went to the pub for a few hours more. I always cooked leg of lamb on Sunday nights, and he was always late, coming home to a cold dinner and a colder wife. I hated that we could never be together as a family on Sundays.

Rod left for a tour of Japan and the Far East in the middle of April. It would be five weeks before we'd see each other, and we'd never been apart for such a long time. We missed each other terribly and spent hours talking on the phone every day. It was one of the few times I wasn't jealous or anxious about Rod being on tour. There certainly weren't any tall pretty blondes in Japan, I told myself, and short dark-haired women had never been the least bit interesting to him.

After the tour I took the kids to meet Rod in London, and it was as if we'd been apart for a year. Rod was loving and attentive, and we made up for the weeks of love-making we'd missed. Being apart had seemed to refresh our relationship, at least momentarily.

When we returned to Los Angeles in the beginning of June, Rod went back into the studio to finish the album, which I dreaded. He seemed to be staying out drinking with the boys more often, and we were having more and more arguments about it. One night I was so upset with him that I picked up the portable cassette machine he'd been carrying and threw it at him. Fortunately, it didn't hit him, but he gave me a black look and went into his bathroom to get ready for bed. Then he got into bed, turned his back to me, and went to sleep.

I was miserable and hardly slept at all. The next morning, when I finally got up, Rod was in the garden lying in the sun. Ashley was with him. When they saw me, Rod said jokingly to Ash, "Your mom's mad at me. She tried to kill me with my tape machine."

I was still furious and continued to be cold and withdrawn. It was my way of punishing him for hurting me. The sad part was that I couldn't seem to communicate my feelings to him and tell him how deeply his behavior hurt me. I covered my vulnerability with coldness and anger.

My hormones were still out of whack at this time, and I was in a very irrational state emotionally. Each one of these episodes left me feeling shaken and out of control. Each time I was sure it was the end. I was beginning to feel helpless to control my own emotions. Then Rod and I would make up and I'd feel like my world was back together again.

I've learned since then that many women from my kind of unstable background end up in relationships that give them a feeling of constantly being on an emotional roller coaster. Growing up, I never knew what was going to happen next, and now I felt the same terror and lack of control in my marriage. I lived in constant fear it would fall apart, and ironically, I behaved in such a way to ensure its demise.

Rod seemed to be pulling away, and the more he wanted some freedom in our relationship, the more tightly I held on. The more I demanded he behave in a more responsible way as a husband and father, the more rebellious he became.

I think the state of my health affected my emotions strongly. I'd never really recovered after Sean's birth. I kept getting ill constantly with sore throats, swollen glands, and extreme fatigue. I couldn't remember what it felt like to be healthy and energetic.

I was still in therapy and convinced Rod to go as well. I was only able to get him to agree by persuading him that it would help his creativity.

For his last couple of albums, Rod had agonized over writing the lyrics. He was afraid he was losing his ability to write, and I honestly felt therapy would help him and, hopefully, help our relationship at the same time. He grudgingly went but was not very receptive to it.

It was a tense period, and Rod was under a lot of pressure. He didn't make me feel very included in his life, and I wasn't very understanding at all. I took everything he did as a personal slight instead of seeing that he was very distracted and could have used my support.

One night he and the band had gone up to the top of Mulholland to have the photo for the album cover taken. We had planned to have a romantic dinner alone afterward, which I was really looking forward to. I got dressed and waited to hear from him. Around 9:30 he had one of the roadies call me to tell me that he was at the Rainbow having a drink with the boys after the session. Well, I absolutely saw red. How could he dare leave me just sitting at home waiting, not having eaten anything, and then not call me himself? To me it just verified how inconsiderate he'd become and how little he valued my feelings.

I got in the car and drove in a fury up Sunset Boulevard to the Rainbow, went marching in, and found him sitting at a huge table with all the boys in the band and the rest of his entourage. I knew I was doing something really stupid, but I couldn't seem to stop myself. I confronted him. He'd obviously been drinking for quite a while. I should have kept my mouth shut, but I didn't.

"Rod, I've been waiting for you for hours. What were you thinking?"

"Well, you're here, aren't you?" he nonchalantly replied. That only infuriated me more, and soon we were shouting back and forth at each other. I got so enraged at one point that I threw a glass of red wine in his face.

He looked at me so coldly that I was frozen on the spot. Everyone else at the table was dumbstruck and didn't know what to do. I was horrified at what I had done.

If I could have taken it all back, I would have in a second, but it was too late. I knew I had gone too far this time, no matter how inconsiderate he had been. Eventually, we made up, but there was a very cold atmosphere in the house for the next few days.

This was such a crazy time not only in our marriage but also in my life. I was out of control and I knew I was. I knew the state of my health and the hormones had something to do with it, but I just kept falling further down the rabbit hole of being an angry, controlling wife. I could see myself destroying my marriage, but I couldn't seem to stop myself.

I was actually kind of relieved when Rod left in November to start the American tour. I thought perhaps the time apart might ease some of the friction in our relationship as it had done the last time we had spent some time apart. As usual, I'd fly to meet him whenever I could.

The most humiliating fight of our marriage happened just before Christmas. Rod was performing at the Forum in Los Angeles for six nights, and he'd invited his parents and his brothers and sisters over from London to stay with us for the concerts and on through Christmas.

The band members had persuaded Rod to hire a double-decker London bus to transport them to and from the Forum. Usually there were several limousines for the band members and their wives and one for me and Rod, but they had convinced him that being with the band was better for their morale. Rod told me to go ahead in our limousine and he would come with me in it after the concert.

When the concert was over, I was waiting outside in the limo, but when the band came out, Rod rushed onto the bus. I got out of the car, boarded the bus, and confronted Rod just as the bus was pulling away.

"What were you going to do? Just leave me sitting in the car alone while you left with the band?"

I don't even remember what he said. It all happened so fast. We were both filled with adrenaline—him from the show, and me from my anger—and the next thing I knew, I pushed him and he pushed me back. Then all hell broke loose. We were pushing and shoving each other, and the boys in the band had to separate us.

I ran to the front door of the bus, and before anyone could stop me, I made the driver open the door. I jumped down to the ground and ran away, crying hysterically. I guess I thought they would stop and come back for me, but they didn't, and I was left alone on the deserted street, sobbing my heart out.

The Forum was in one of the worst neighborhoods in Los Angeles with a crime rate second only to Watts. And here I was, in a short sweater-dress, boots, and an armful of gold and diamond bangles. And I had no purse and no money to even make a phone call!

Starting to panic, I saw an open 7-Eleven and hurried inside to ask for help. The cashier behind the counter and several customers, all young black men, looked at me with such open hostility that I stopped in the middle of my explanation. Two of them started to move toward me menacingly, and I turned and ran out of the store and down the street.

A truck pulled up beside me, and the driver, a white male, said, "Lady, I saw you back at that store and you can't be wandering around alone in this neighborhood. You're in serious danger. Get in and I'll take you where you need to go." I sized up my choices. Get in this truck with a strange man or stay on the street and take my chances?

I continued to run down the street, still sobbing hysterically, ignoring all the catcalls and sexual comments coming from men on house porches and from passing cars. One car filled with black youths stopped next to me, and I ran into another convenience store with a pay phone booth. I was trying to call someone, collect, to help me when a police car pulled up next to me. I've never been so happy to see the cops in my whole life.

"We just got a call from a man who said there was a white woman alone who was in danger. He said he tried to help you but you ran off," one of the officers said. "I don't know what you're doing in this neighborhood, Miss, but you're not safe here. A woman just got raped down the street an hour ago."

Still sobbing, I told them what had happened. They put me into their car and took me back to the Forum, where Rod's brothers picked me up.

There was a lot of tension in the house for the next couple days, but by Christmas Rod and I made up. Rod's brothers gave us a pair of boxing gloves as a joke.

We may have been able to have a laugh about that insane night, but the crack in our marriage was definitely widening.

In late January of 1982 Rod was in Miami doing several concerts. On one of the nights I decided to try calling him before I went to bed to say good night, but he hadn't returned to his room yet. It was three o'clock in the morning in Miami.

I couldn't go to sleep, so I tried calling again, but still no answer. I figured they'd gone to a nightclub and told myself just to go to sleep and stop worrying about nothing. I still couldn't sleep, however, so I continued to call. I had this funny feeling that something wasn't quite right. The nightclubs had closed, so where could he possibly be? At 5:30 a.m., he finally picked up the phone.

"Where have you been? I've been calling you for hours," I asked, accusingly.

"The boys and I were on this boat that one of their friends had and we ended up drinking and doing some drugs and just hanging out," he explained, sounding defensive.

I should have known better than to pursue it when he was completely loaded, and we ended up having an argument. I was crying and accusing; he was cold and cruel. I finally couldn't take it anymore. I told him, "I feel like you just don't love me anymore."

I can't remember exactly what mean-spirited thing he said to me next, but what I do know is that it set me into a tailspin. Again, I was at a point in all of this that I was really out of control, and I said to him, "I may as well take a handful of sleeping pills and kill myself!" And then I hung up the phone.

Oh, it was such a terrible night. Too much emotion compounded by lack of sleep, a flood of hormones, and a feeling I just couldn't shake of not being able to trust my husband. I took two more Valium and two quaaludes and cried myself to sleep.

Rod didn't call back to try to stop my threatened suicide attempt. He probably thought I was being overly dramatic, which, of course, I was. Yet somehow, in my unreasonable state of mind, I rationalized that if I scared Rod enough, he'd rush home and assure me that he really did love me.

I had locked my door and shut off the phone before going to sleep. I woke up to the sound of a knock on my door, but I didn't respond. I knew it was Gail, and I could see from the lights on my phone that she had someone on hold. I knew it was Rod or else she wouldn't be trying to wake me.

Soon there was more knocking, louder and louder. Still I said nothing. I wanted to make them worry, but even as I lay there, pretending to be unconscious or dead, I couldn't believe what I was doing. I was horrified at myself, but I couldn't stop myself from wanting to punish Rod by making him worry.

I heard Gail walk away, and now I started to think I'd carried things too far. A short time later, I heard a male voice at the door: "We'd better break it down."

"Oh no," I thought. "What am I going to do now?" I certainly didn't want my beautiful art deco door broken into smithereens. So I staggered sleepily to the door and opened it.

I found our doctor standing there with Gail, and they both looked pretty concerned. Now I really felt terrible, but I was backed into a corner and had to continue my charade.

"Are you all right?" the doctor asked. "We've all been very worried about you. What did you take?"

"I just took a few Valium and a couple of quaaludes," I answered, purposely slurring my words.

"Are you sure that's all?" He looked at me sternly.

"Yes, I'm sure," I said, starting to cry. I was no longer acting. I really just wanted to crawl into a hole and die.

"Leave us alone for a few minutes, please," he said to Gail. He sat me down and asked gently, "Now, what's going on with you?"

Sobbing on his shoulder, I told him that Rod and I had had this terrible fight and that I was so unhappy. "Well, you must never do anything like this again," he chided me. "Nothing is worth harming yourself. Promise me you won't ever do this again."

I promised him and I meant it. At that moment, Gail reappeared. She said that Rod was on the phone and wanted to talk to me.

Rod was angry. "Why did you do such a silly thing? We were worried sick about you."

"Because I thought you didn't love me anymore. Please don't be angry," I said, as I choked back my tears. How I wished I'd never started this whole stupid mess.

"You know I love you and you must never do anything so stupid again," he said.

We talked a few minutes more. After we hung up, I wondered how I could have let myself get into such an emotionally unstable state. We never really spoke about it again.

Chapter 19

Just as this horrible divide kept growing between Rod and me, something happened outside our marriage that actually helped repair it— at least temporarily. Rod's tour was in terrible financial distress, and after a big blowup Rod fired his manager. It was stunning and complicated, and Rod didn't know who he could trust—that is, except for me. Rod needed me now and looked to me to help and advise him. I loved feeling needed and wanted to be there to support him fully. I got on the case, helping him find the right legal and financial advisers to sort out each new discovery.

The next blow was finding out we were practically broke! It seemed inconceivable that this could happen to someone who made the kind of money Rod did, but he hadn't paid attention to the way his affairs had been handled. As performers often do, he'd left it up to others and wound up with a lot to regret. Tina Sinatra helped us to find new attorneys, and they were able to make arrangements for a loan from Warner Brothers Records to tide us over temporarily.

Apart from the financial drama, 1982 became the year of the "Rod Stewart Exposés." Several people who had worked for Rod started selling stories to the tabloids.

One of the most prominent was Tony Toon's three-part tell-all. We had fired Tony, and the story he told was exactly what we'd expected— full of lies and exaggerations. What really upset me, though, was what Tony had to say about Rod and other women, especially on the Japan tour. Tony talked about how I'd thought that Rod would have no interest in Japanese women, but there had been a contingent of American models who had joined the band on the tour. He also spilled the beans about Belinda Green in Australia all those years ago—and there was more!

Rod denied it all, and I chose to believe him. However, I had a terribly uneasy feeling that amidst all this "smoke" just might be some "fire," and this created a great deal of tension between us.

In the midst of all this Rod got robbed while he was with Gail and Kimberly, who was only three years old at the time. Around this time Rod had been talking about moving back to England, and this incident only made him want to go back more. It started to become an issue between us. He argued that he was homesick. I liked the idea of having a place in England to spend several months in the summer, but I didn't want to live there. In any case, we were in no position to buy another home.

That year Rod and I decided to take a little trip to the South of France with my friend Liza Minnelli and her husband, Mark Gero. It should have been a marvelous, happy time for us. We wandered around the hills of Saint Paul de Vence and had lovely, long lunches and dinners in the surrounding villages.

I wasn't feeling well on the trip. I tried playing tennis in the daytime with Rod, but afterward I was so weak and shaky that I could hardly stand up. I began to get frightened that something was really wrong with me. For days after the tennis match I remained so weak and exhausted that I could barely drag myself around. I felt depressed and unable to think clearly. To make matters worse, I felt that something was missing between me and Rod. Maybe it was just the way I was feeling physically, but I had no desire for him sexually. I loved him, but I didn't feel any of the magic that I used to feel when we made love.

Sex had always been one of the strong points of our relationship, the glue that held our marriage together in the tough times, so I didn't tell him how I was feeling.

Back in Los Angeles, I saw my doctor, who recommended a specialist. After a battery of tests, I learned I had Epstein-Barr, a recently discovered virus that was a chronic form of mononucleosis.

Rod was back in the studio, and we were not getting along very well. He felt I'd become a "stick in the mud" because I didn't want to go out with him and his friends in the band. He didn't seem to realize that I was so sick. I knew that when we went out with them, between the alcohol and the drugs, it would be an endless night of carousing, and I just didn't have the energy or the strength.

Then on top of everything else, I found out I was pregnant. My doctor insisted I was in no shape physically or emotionally to have another baby, but I was torn. I desperately wanted to have the baby, but I knew in my heart he was right. After agonizing over it, I finally decided to have an abortion. If I had it to do over again, though, I would have had that baby, no matter what. I still regret it.

I checked into the hospital the evening before, as the procedure was scheduled for very early the next morning. Rod was in the studio, as usual, and when I spoke to him, he said he'd invited some of the boys over for a barbecue later that evening. He clearly hadn't planned to come to see me. I desperately needed his support. I knew in my heart that, no matter how hard I tried, I wouldn't be able to forgive him for that.

PART IV

The Unraveling

Chapter 20

The situation between Rod and his former manager was finally resolved around November, and Rod and I seemed to have been brought closer together again, as we always were whenever Rod needed my help and support. But as the holidays arrived, he became more remote. On Christmas Eve, after we got the kids into bed and all their toys under the tree, we went to a party at Nancy Sinatra Sr.'s house. Rod hadn't really wanted to go, but I insisted.

He was so cold to me all night that finally I broke down and cried my heart out to Tina in the bathroom. "I don't know what's wrong," I sobbed. "He just doesn't act like he cares anymore, and I'm so unhappy."

Meanwhile, Arnold Stiefel, who had been my agent for some time and who was now representing Rod, took him aside. Rod confessed to him that he was terribly unhappy as well. Arnold told us about a therapist he'd been seeing named Robert Lorenze and suggested we go to see him after the holidays.

We began seeing Dr. Robert Lorenze together. We'd each built up a lot of resentment toward the other over the last few years, and we were both very disillusioned with the way things were going. What could have happened so quickly to those two people who were so madly in love with each other and who had everything in the world to be thankful for?

When Robert took me aside and asked me if I'd like to come in alone to work on some of my issues, I told him, "I don't have any issues. If Rod would just stop partying with the band all night, and stop spending his entire Sunday playing soccer and going to the pub until dinner was ruined, and spend some time with me and the kids, everything would be fine."

I went on to say that I felt like I was raising the kids on my own with a husband who just wasn't present physically or emotionally. And on and on I went with my personal laundry list of all the things Rod wasn't doing right. I only focused on him and where he was at fault, not even realizing or acknowledging that I played a huge part in our problems.

My close friend Allan Carr, was remaking *Where the Boys Are* (George had actually starred in the original), and when he asked me to be in it, I was thrilled. Rod was leaving for a European tour, though, and I wouldn't be able to bring the kids and accompany him as we had planned. I did, however, fly to London to spend my birthday with Rod. He hadn't gotten me a birthday present—even though Elton had given me three beautiful Cartier rings!

When I got home, it was time to head to Florida. Ash stayed with George to finish out his school year, and I took Kimberly, Sean, and Nancy Whittle, our Irish nanny, with me for six weeks for the filming.

I was excited to be working again. For the first time in years I felt kind of like my old self again. I was doing something for myself and it felt great, even if I still wasn't feeling up to par. For so long I hadn't been getting any kind of positive reinforcement in my life. My self-esteem, especially lately, had been bruised by Rod's indifference.

Rod was unbelievably jealous of whom I might meet while away doing the movie; he'd heard enough Hollywood scandals in his life to know that romances do sometimes spring up on location.

So he called me every morning at six to make sure I'd slept in my bed. He kept constant tabs on me. I came to believe much later that Rod's jealousy was probably due to his own shenanigans. He was afraid I might be doing what he already was doing.

When the filming ended, we all headed to London. We'd rented a great house for the summer in Chelsea, and the kids and I would stay there while Rod finished touring in Europe. I was actually really looking forward to seeing him, hoping the time apart could have helped our relationship.

I met Rod in Rome for his concert there, excited we'd be there together for the first time in a while. We stayed at my favorite hotel, The Grand, but what was meant to be a romantic time turned out to be miserable. Rod had a bad throat and had to cancel the concert, and he was cold and distant most of the time. I couldn't understand what I was doing wrong. Finally I chalked it up to him being sick.

After Rome we flew to London to pick up the kids and then headed to Tel Aviv for the concerts there. I'd been to Israel before with George and was excited to see it again with Rod, who had never been there.

The first night we went to dinner, just the two of us. He seemed to warm up to me again, but later, back in the room, when he wanted to make love, I was clearly just going through the motions.

"I don't think you're as attracted to me as you used to be," he said plaintively, wanting me to reassure him otherwise. Suddenly I knew I couldn't continue on like this.

As hard as it was, I had to tell him how I was feeling. "I guess I'm not . . . ," I said, haltingly. "But it's because things aren't right between us. All the fighting has made me feel cut off sexually. I still love you very much," I went on, "but I think when we get home, we really need to work on our marriage. I know the physical part will come back, but we need to communicate honestly and try to sort out our differences."

Rod was silent. I could tell he was hurt. As I said earlier, sex was the glue that had held our marriage together, no matter what we went through. I'll always believe that my honesty that night was the nail in the coffin on our marriage.

The kids and I left to go back to London while Rod went on with the band to South Africa. Elton was flying down to see Rod and wanted me to come with him as a surprise, but I just wasn't up for a fourteen-hour trip and leaving the children. It's just as well I didn't go. Later I would find out that Rod had a girl with him.

During this time I came close to having my own affair. London in August was quiet and boring. Everyone was away on holiday, and I was feeling terribly lonely. Rod and I talked every day, but he was cold and distant.

One night when I was in Tramp's having dinner with the owner, Johnny Gold, and his wife, Jan, George Best walked in. George was one of the most famous soccer players of all time—one of Rod's heroes in fact—who also had a reputation as a big drinker and quite the ladies' man. He was also very attractive.

Johnny ordered a bottle of champagne, and by the time we'd finished it, it was closing time. George leaned over to me and whispered, "I know a place that's open all night. Would you like to have a night cap?"

The champagne and my loneliness got the better of me, and he whisked me upstairs and out the door into a waiting cab, which he directed to some godforsaken part of London, but he couldn't find the after-hours club.

"Let's go back to my hotel for a drink," he said, and against what was left of my judgment, I did. We went up to his room, where he opened a bottle of champagne, and we talked for a while. Then he kissed me, and before I knew it we were lying on his bed making out like two teenagers. A voice in my head kept saying, "You can't do this. You can't do this to Rod, to your marriage."

"I'm sorry, but I have to go!" I said, and I jumped up. He tried to convince me to stay, but I knew I had to leave. He walked me downstairs, and before putting me into a cab, made me promise to have brunch with him the next morning before he left.

The next morning I met him in the bar of his hotel, where he was drinking Bloody Marys. I had a big English-style breakfast while he drank, and I could see that his drinking was beginning to show on him. He tried to get me to come back to his room, but in the light of day, it was much easier to keep my wits about me. I knew there was no way I would see him again.

Meanwhile, Elton had returned from South Africa. When I asked about the trip, he seemed strangely vague and said only, "It's just as well you didn't come. It was such a long flight."

When Rod returned, he seemed angry and aloof. I couldn't wait to get back to LA, where I hoped we could go to therapy immediately and try to repair our relationship, but the atmosphere didn't change much once we got back home.

After spending some time with us, together and alone, Robert made a suggestion that rocked my world. He told me and Rod that we should separate for a month. I tearfully protested, but Robert explained that it was just so we could each have a little space. At the end of the month Rod would move back home.

I was crying my eyes out when we left, and Rod finally softened and put his arms around me and held me. "It's just temporary," he said. "I just need a little space."

"But we've been away from each other the better part of two months. You've had plenty of space," I argued. He didn't seem to have an answer for that, but it wasn't going to change his mind.

I since have developed this theory that whenever a man tells a woman he needs a little space, there is always another woman in the picture. Whenever one of my friends tells me that her husband says he needs "space," I immediately wonder whom he's having an affair with.

We went down to the beach with the children. The idea that we were going to separate seemed to lighten Rod's mood, and he was much nicer and even more loving. I was almost lulled into a false sense of security when, later that day, he told me, "I'm going to London for a week."

"But you just came from London!" I tried to dissuade him in vain.

Kimberly, who was four at the time, picked just the wrong moment to come into the room, and she saw me in tears.

"What's wrong, Mama?" she asked.

"Your father is leaving us!" I told her. I wanted to hurt Rod and make him see how he was tearing our family apart, but when she started to cry, I felt beyond horrible. I felt so terribly guilty for doing that. I know how seeing my own mother and my stepfather fighting affected me, and the last thing I ever wanted to do was put my children through that kind of emotional stress.

Rod held Kimberly and assured her that he was just going for a few days and would be back shortly.

While Rod was in London, he stayed at Elton's house. Every time I called I was always told he was "unavailable." This was so new to me. Rod and I typically talked several times a day while he was away; now I was lucky to catch him at all.

He took the Concorde to New York. I wanted to know why he wasn't coming straight back to Los Angeles, but he gave me some excuse that pacified me temporarily.

Meanwhile, someone called me early the next morning and told me there was a piece on Page Six in the *New York Post* that said Rod had been on the Concorde with a tall, blonde model.

My heart was pounding out of my chest as I called Rod's room at the Mayfair. He had a "Do Not Disturb" on the room, and when the operator refused to override it, I insisted on being put through to Arnold. He also had a "Do Not Disturb," but I guess the operator knew she'd better come up with something.

He answered groggily, and without any pleasantries I demanded, "Arnold, what's going on?"

"I don't know what you're talking about," he said, not very convincingly. Looking back, I realize he was caught between a rock and a hard place. I was his close friend, and he was now Rod's manager, thanks to me, and obviously felt he couldn't betray Rod's confidence.

Now I was sure something was going on. I figured if something was in the *New York Post* today, it was surely in the English papers by the next morning. I called our publicist in London and tried to sound casual. "Can you read me the story in the paper today?"

There was a stunned silence on the other end. Finally, she asked, "Which one?"

"The worst one," I said.

The poor woman was almost in tears as she read me the headline and the accompanying story, which said that Rod Stewart had traveled on the Concorde from London to New York, and although he denied it, there was a young woman on the plane, and her ticket had apparently been paid for by Rod's company. I could barely get the words out, but I thanked her and hung up, in shock.

It was Sunday, and Rod was coming home that night to Carolwood. I was waiting by the door when the limo with Arnold and him pulled up. Rod got out of the car with a dark, angry look on his face. What the hell did he have to be angry about?

"We need to talk," I said tersely. We went into the bar, where I had opened a bottle of red wine, and I poured each of us a glass. He continued with the angry attitude, as if it was me that had done something wrong.

When I questioned him about the story, he was defensive. "There was some reporter on the plane who made up this story that I was with this young, blonde woman who was also on the plane. It's all a lie," he defiantly protested his innocence. It didn't seem reasonable to me that this intricate lie had just been fabricated, but he was so outraged that I doubted his faithfulness that I started to believe him—or rather I wanted to believe him.

The next day when I got up, I went downstairs to look for Rod. He was lying glumly on the lavender silk sofa in the garden room. I tried to engage him in conversation.

"Please let's try to work this out. I don't want to lose you."

"That's because you still love me," he said flatly.

"Are you saying you don't love me anymore?" I asked in disbelief.

He looked at me so coldly that my heart froze. "Yes," he said.

At that moment my world turned upside down. I ran out of the room sobbing. I ran to our bedroom and threw myself on the bed, crying uncontrollably. I couldn't stop. The one thing I'd never doubted was that Rod loved me. His words cut me to my very core.

I sobbed hysterically the rest of the day.

Hours later Rod finally came in and tenderly took me into his arms. "I didn't mean it," he said. "I don't know what's going on with me."

He suggested we go out to dinner, so we went to a Japanese restaurant, where we sat in a back booth and drank sake. There, he talked more about his childhood and his father than we had ever done in all the time I'd known him. He told me his father had never hugged him or showed him affection. It brought us closer than we had been in a long time. After dinner we went back home and made love.

In hindsight it seems crazy I never knew these kinds of things about his childhood and that he, my husband, never really knew anything about mine. Both my grandmother and my mother were gone long before Rod came into my life.

Crazily, of course, the secrets I kept deep within myself, those things I shut away inside me, were a real catalyst to the end of my relationship with Rod—and also with George. I was so shut off emotionally. Rod was so shut off emotionally . . . we never talked about our childhoods—we never talked about anything except in the most superficial ways.

After dinner I really felt like we'd turned a corner and maybe everything would be alright again.

Well, of course, I couldn't have been more wrong. The next day he surprised me again.

"I'm going to Dallas for a couple days to a car show," he told me. A car show? I'd never known Rod to go to a car show in his life.

I felt once again like my world was exploding out of my control. I tried to hold myself together and be there for the kids, but it was difficult. My every waking moment was spent obsessing about Rod—where he was, what he was doing. None of it made sense to me.

Then I spoke to my astrologer in Florida.

"Who is this other woman in his chart?" she asked me.

"What other woman?"

"A woman is showing up in his chart, and it's part of the disruption and confusion he's going through." As shocked as I was at actually hearing this, there was a part of me that had already known it. That would certainly explain all this odd behavior.

I called Rod's hotel, but the desk clerk informed me that he'd just checked out. I told the clerk I was his assistant and was trying to get an important message to the young lady in their group. "Oh," he said. "They've all checked out. I believe they're on the way to the airport."

I confronted Rod the minute he arrived. He not only denied that there was a woman with him, but he did it so convincingly that he managed to make me feel like I was being gaslighted. Then he told me he had rented a house nearby and was going to move into it for a month. We were going to be officially separated.

I sat Kimberly, Sean, and Ash down on the front steps of Carolwood and told them that Rod was moving into another house for a month. Kim and Sean had just turned four and three, respectively, and they didn't understand. They started to cry and so did I.

I took them into my arms. "Don't cry, don't cry," I said, trying to soothe them and myself. I told them all the things I'd heard you were supposed to tell children to reassure them when their parents were splitting up.

"Mommy and Daddy are just having a little trouble getting along right now. It won't be forever. Just for a little while. And Daddy will see you every day." As I spoke, I hoped Rod would not make a liar of me. "Daddy loves you very much, and so do I, and what's going on between him and Mommy will never change that. Please know that none of this is your fault. Everything will be fine."

Ash was older and had been through it before, but it still wasn't easy for him. He loved Rod and thought of him as a second father.

That was in September. The following two months were a blur of ups and downs. One Saturday afternoon I was sitting in the nursery playing with Kim and Sean when Rod came walking in. He came to the house any time he wanted, which was fine with me. I wanted him to spend as much time with the kids as possible.

I had stopped being cold and angry to Rod and decided to try to be neutral—nice and not accusatory. When I smiled warmly and asked how he was, he sat down, put his head on my shoulder and started to cry. "I don't know what I'm doing. I'm so miserable. I'm not happy and I feel terrible not being with you and the kids. This is where I belong."

Oh God, how I'd longed to hear him say that. We went to dinner that night, we made love, and it was wonderful. Although I had totally turned off Rod sexually during the past year because of all our arguing, now that I was possibly losing him, all the passion came back. It was like when we'd first met, but with more deep feelings.

He told me he loved me and wanted to come back. Then, a few days later, he told me it would be another month before he moved back home. I didn't know what to believe anymore. I consulted every astrologer, soothsayer, and psychic I could find. I always had to look to someone to reassure me that I'd be alright; I didn't yet have that resource myself. They all said Rod and I would be back together, and I wanted to believe them wholeheartedly.

Rod was spending a lot of time at Carolwood with me and the kids. We were going out to dinner often and were communicating more than we ever had in our marriage.

It was nearing the end of October, and Rod was planning to move back in shortly. He was busy in the studio recording, and I decided to go to New York for a few days to get away from the stress. I was having dinner with Marisa Berenson one night, who asked, "What are all these rumors about Rod and Kelly Emberg?"

There was a moment of stunned silence.

"What rumors?" I asked, my heart in my mouth.

"It was all over the newspapers in New York that they've been having an affair," Marisa explained. I felt like I'd been hit in my stomach with a baseball bat.

"Who is she?" I asked.

"A model here in New York. From Texas." I tried to finish my dinner, but couldn't. I made an excuse to leave as soon as I could. I needed to get to the hotel and call Rod. My hands were shaking so much that I could barely dial the phone. "Who's Kelly Emberg?" I blurted out when he answered.

"I've never heard of her," he said.

I pressed him. "Rod, if we're going to have a fresh start with our marriage, you have to be honest with me. Just tell me the truth."

There was silence on the other end of the phone. I'd expected and almost hoped for a vehement denial.

"Come home and I'll tell you everything," he said quietly.

I didn't dare ask any more on the phone. I didn't want to know anything that would devastate me while I was there in a hotel room alone. I couldn't have coped with it. I couldn't sleep all night and was an anxious wreck the whole five-hour trip home.

When I arrived, I put the kids to bed, and then we went down to dinner in the beautiful red art-nouveau dining room. He opened a bottle of red wine and poured us both large glasses.

"I have to tell you the truth," he told me.

"Okay," I said, and took a sip of wine that nearly finished what I had in my glass.

He took a long sip of his wine. "I met her in New York. I've been seeing her for a while," he said.

I had that old familiar "detaching myself from my body" feeling.

"Are you in love with her?" I asked. I was praying to God that he'd say no.

"I'm not sure," he said. "I'm very confused. I love you and I don't want to ruin our marriage, but I definitely have feelings for her."

I hadn't expected this. I'd been expecting him to tell me it was over and ask my forgiveness, and then he'd come home and we'd live happily ever after. I went around in a haze of pain and uncertainty the next few days.

Then Rod took a sudden trip to New York, obviously to see Kelly. When he returned, he left several frantic messages. I called him back and he started to cry. "I don't want to do this anymore. I'm so torn apart and confused, but I want to come home."

This time I needed him to prove it—if he was, in fact, serious. I couldn't keep on like this. "Are you going to tell her it's over?" I asked.

"Yes," he said. "I'm supposed to meet her in Acapulco this week-end, and I'll tell her then."

"You're going to go to Acapulco to tell her it's over?" I asked him, incredulous. "How about doing it over the phone?"

"I owe it to her to do it in person," he told me. "You have to trust me."

I couldn't talk him out of it, so I rationalized, Just let it go. The end result is that you want him to end it with her, and if that's the way he needs to do it, then just accept it.

I resisted the urge to call him every day and say, "Have you done it yet?" When he called home, I asked him if he'd told her.

"Tonight," he said. "I'll tell her tonight."

"Why don't you just tell her now and come home?"

"I promised I would stay another day and go to a party with her."

Well, that incensed me, but I held my temper. I wanted my husband back, and I didn't want to rock the boat. But was I being smart? Or was I being a doormat?

When I called Arnold for advice, he said, "Just hang in there. I think he'll come home after this."

Then a picture appeared in the early edition of *People* of Rod and Kelly dancing at a party in Mexico. I was livid. How could he do this to me? Couldn't he at least have some sense of decency? Now I had the press from everywhere trying to track me down for a comment. I just laid low and avoided going anywhere.

When he finally arrived home, the first thing I asked him was "Did you tell her?"

"Yes," he replied sullenly.

The lease on his house was up, and I was expecting him to move back in, but lo and behold, he extended it another month. His reasoning was that he wanted us to go to London for the Christmas holidays and get a fresh start there. Then he'd come back home with us and we'd start all over.

In the past I would have resisted spending the holidays in London, but I wanted to show Rod that I was going to do everything in my power to please him and make our marriage work. And I truly meant it.

Chapter 21

Two weeks before the holidays I was offered the guest lead in an episode of *Masquerade*, a weekly television series starring Kirstie Alley. My part wouldn't shoot until just before Christmas. I didn't want to turn down work, although taking it would throw a wrench into our plans. Rod wanted to go on ahead to London with the kids, and I would join them as soon as the shooting wrapped. As it turned out, we ran two days over, and I made it to London Christmas Eve morning.

Everyone was still sleeping when I arrived, and I woke Rod up by creeping into bed beside him. It felt so warm and wonderful to be under the covers cuddled up next to my husband. We made love and talked until we heard the children waking up. I was so happy to be back with my family, and I dared to hope that the excruciating bad dream was finally over.

We spent the morning with the kids, and then Rod and I were going to go Christmas shopping. Just before leaving the house I'd found a fashion magazine in the bedroom closet with a photo layout of her in it. I felt like a knife went through my stomach. Why would he buy a magazine with her pictures in it and then leave it in the house where I surely would see it?

I finally summoned up the courage to ask Rod about it at lunch.

"I found the magazine."

"Oh, that," he brushed it off. "I sent Malcolm [his roadie/assistant/gopher] to buy some magazines for me at the airport. That one just happened to be among them."

Harper's Bazaar was hardly a magazine that Malcolm would have chosen, but I let it drop. I desperately wanted to believe that Rod was telling me the truth. After all, I thought, I'm here with him at

Rod, me, and ten-month-old Kimberly on QE2. I was four months pregnant with Sean.

Celebrating Kimberly's first birthday. Kim had just put her hand in the cake, and Rod was restraining Ashley from doing the same.

Rod and Sean, wearing Daddy's hat.

Joking around in boxing gloves after our famous fight on the tour bus. Christmas Day, 1982.

Rod showed up to surprise Sean on his birthday. Sean was so happy, he cried.

Rod with Kim and Sean just before leaving for the "Tonight I'm Yours" tour.

With Kimberly and Sean at their birthday party, 1984.

On our way to Dani Janssen and Hal Needham's wedding on the back lot of Universal (obviously a Western theme).

Me, James Caan, and Michelle Phillips in 1977.

Me and Elton (as a blond).

Farrah, Joan Collins, Michelle Phillips, and me at one of my Trivial Pursuit parties in the 1980s.

The Three Musketeers, Farrah, Tina Sinatra, and me, at a Christmas gathering at my house in the late 1980s.

At super-agent Irving Lazar's house for a party, 1980s. Farrah, Cybill Shepherd, Jackie Collins, and me.

Ryan and his "girls."

Farrah and me in Harbor Island, Bahamas, before she became ill.

At my birthday party in the early 1990s, thrown by my good friend, Suzanne de Passe. With Michael Douglas and my dear, departed friend, Don Simpson.

With Liz Taylor and Carole Bayer Sager at my birthday party given by Carole.

To Alana Stewart
With Best Wishes, Bill Clinton

With President Clinton in the Oval Office, 1996. George and I were in DC for our talk show, and his old friend, Lynda Johnson Robb, gave us a personal tour of the White House.

Mother's Day, 1997, with Sean (age 16), Ashley (age 22), and Kim (age 17).

My two sons on Sean's birthday, 2009.

Me and Kim just before she gave birth to Delilah.

Grammy with Delilah, my first grandchild, 2011.

Christmas and she isn't. He made his choice, and it was to keep our family together.

We had a wonderful Christmas Day with the kids, and everything seemed back to normal. Then, the following day, the pendulum swung, and Rod was back to being distant and remote. Early that evening he told me he was going to his parents' house on his own.

"I thought the whole point of this trip was for us to be together," I said, but I could feel Rod closing down. The more I pressed, the more distant he became.

Finally, he said, "Look, I can't seem to stop thinking about her. I'm just not happy."

He might as well have put a dagger through my heart. "If that's how you feel, I'm taking the kids and going home and you can just go back to her."

I dragged my suitcases out of the closet and began furiously throwing my clothes into them. Rod watched me for a moment and then turned and left the house without saying a word. I threw myself down on the bed, sobbing so hard that I could barely breathe. I couldn't believe this was happening again.

When Rod came back later, he said, "Maybe this is the best thing for me now. I love you, but I need to get this girl out of my system."

It was late when he came to bed. I was still sobbing, and he reached for me and held me in his arms, and then we made love as tenderly and passionately as ever. He didn't seem like a man who wanted to end his marriage. It was all very confusing.

Rod's calm acceptance that I was leaving was unbelievable to me. When he told Kimberly and Sean he wasn't coming back with us, they both started to cry, and my heart broke for them. Rod left for his parents' house, and I stumbled through the rest of the day in a haze, packing and trying not to think or feel.

That night when he came home, he asked me to have dinner with him, but before we left we got into a huge argument. All the rage I'd been suppressing came out with a vengeance, and I grabbed a bottle of Campari from the bar and tried to hit him over the head with it. At that moment I really wanted to kill him for what he was doing to me, to our family. Rod grabbed it away from me just before it connected with his skull and wrestled me to the floor. He was really shaken by my attack.

"I'm not staying in the same house with you. You're crazy," he said, heading toward the door. I was lying on the floor, crying uncontrollably. Then suddenly, he stopped, turned back, and came over to help me up.

"Come on," he said. "Let's go eat and forget what happened." Eating was the last thing on my mind, but I didn't want him to leave me alone, so I dried my tears, pulled myself together, and off we went.

I'll never forget that dinner as long as I live. We sat at a table for two in the very elegant formal dining room of the Ritz, one of London's oldest and grandest hotels. While violinists played in the background, we ordered our food and a bottle of Rod's favorite red wine. Here we were, going through the motions of having dinner as if everything was perfectly normal, and yet my world was crashing down around me.

Everything seemed surreal. I couldn't swallow my food, but I drank glass after glass of wine, trying to numb the pain inside me. Finally, I excused myself to go to the ladies' room, just as the violinists began playing "Lara's Theme" from *Dr. Zhivago*.

Somewhere my love, there will be songs to sing. Hearing those lyrics, the emotions I'd been trying to numb with the wine overcame me. I ran into the bathroom and cried and cried until there were no more tears left inside me. Then I washed my face and went back to the table.

We talked about everything but the fact that our marriage was ending. Rod suggested we go by Tramp's for a drink. Anything not to face going home alone together.

The rest of the evening was a blur. When we got home and got into bed, Rod even tried to make love to me, but that I couldn't do. I curled up in a tight little ball and tried not to cry anymore.

The next morning Rod left early to see his parents. That evening he would be leaving for New York—and her. I resented that he was choosing to spend yet another day at his parents' house instead of being with Kimberly and Sean.

Rod still hadn't returned by the time the car came to take the children and me to the airport, so we left without any good-byes. I couldn't believe he could be so heartless.

Just as we arrived in the passenger lounge, a British Airways representative approached me.

"Mrs. Stewart? Your husband's on the phone for you," she said and motioned for me to follow her.

The words just hung in the air. "Your husband" . . . For the rest of the world I guess he still was my husband, but the idea of that seemed so foreign to me at that moment, traveling back home with my children while the man who vowed to be with me till death do us part was off to meet another woman.

I picked up the phone; Rod was frantic. "I rushed back to the house to stop you from leaving, but you were already gone," he said. How convenient, I thought. "I love you," he continued. "I know somehow this will all work out."

As we were about to board the plane, a group of reporters and photographers descended upon us, wanting to know where Rod was. Unable to contain my hurt and my rage, the words just popped out of my mouth. "Rod prefers the company of blond bimbos over his family," I snapped.

Apparently, that made the front pages of the London papers the next day. The vindictive part of me was glad. I wanted the whole world to know how despicably he was behaving and how he was destroying our family. But the sane part of me—if there was one left—felt embarrassed and humiliated that I had made such a public statement about something that should have been a very private affair.

When Rod came back to LA after his New York trip he moved into another rented house. Once again, he started talking about reconciliation.

Whenever Rod thought I might be going out with anyone, he got incredibly jealous. One night I went to a party with my good friend Jim Randall. Jim had a few too many, and I dropped him off at his house and drove myself home in his car. I was soundly sleeping when Rod came charging into the bedroom early the next morning.

"What are you doing here?" I asked groggily.

"I was on my way to play soccer. Whose car is that?" he asked, looking around suspiciously. He'd seen Jim's Mercedes parked outside the door and thought I had a man in my bed.

Another time he went through the drawers by the side of my bed and found a scrap of paper with the name and phone number of an actor I'd run into at a party. It was nothing—some guy gave me his phone number and I tossed it into a drawer and forgot about it. I couldn't believe Rod had the nerve to question me about my activities when he had left me for another woman.

Speaking of the "other woman," I hated her with a passion like I'd never felt in my life. How could she be so callous and heartless as to break up someone's home and family? It was easier, somehow, for me to put more of the blame on her than on Rod. Just like when he used to stay out all night doing drugs with the boys in the band, I blamed them for being the bad influences on Rod instead of holding him accountable for his choices.

Interestingly, a number of years after Kelly and Rod broke up, she and I ended up becoming quite friendly, and I got the real story of what happened. Rod had tried to go out with her, and when she questioned him about being married, he told her that we were separated and that we were in the process of divorcing. By time I knew

Kelly well enough to know that she was an incredibly nice woman and was telling the absolute truth. But back then, I hated her guts.

Then, to my great surprise, I found out Rod was planning a trip to Hawaii with Kelly to finish writing the lyrics for his new album. What happened to the reconciliation we'd been talking about? This was the last straw for me.

"If you go, I'm filing for divorce," I told him. It was an ultimatum, yes, but I was so unsettled by all the back and forth, all the tenderness and talk about getting back together, that I really believed that he would cancel the trip. Much to my great shock, he left the next day.

On February 3, 1984, the day Rod and Kelly Emberg left for Hawaii, I filed for divorce. I watched in a daze that night, as it was all over the news. It was bad enough to be going through heartbreak, but to have the rest of the world seeing and reading about it made it even more unbearable.

The drama, however, was still not over. Rod came back from Hawaii and straight to Carolwood from the airport. I was lying on the bed, watching television, when he walked into the bedroom. Again, he broke down in tears.

I found myself comforting him instead of the other way around. He had destroyed our family, and I was comforting him? I was that confused.

Deep down, I still loved Rod and wished we could work things out, but now something in me had changed. I was no longer willing to put up with this emotional roller coaster. I couldn't see him, make love with him, hear him tell me he loved me and wanted things to work out, and then find out the next day he'd gone to New York to see her.

Rod kept his rented house, and I continued to live in Carolwood. During one of our reconciliation discussions he'd begged me to put the divorce on hold, so I did, and that's where it remained, just like me—in limbo.

Chapter 22

I was so heartbroken at Rod's betrayal. I'd believed in him and I'd believed that our love and our marriage would last forever. Now my fantasy had burst. My whole world crashed in around me. My husband had left me for someone else, a model fifteen years younger than me. And he had done it all in such a blatantly public way—in front of his band, our friends, and the entire world.

All of this was bad enough, but it got much worse as I began unraveling the web of lies Rod had woven. Each new discovery was a fresh blow. I couldn't believe he had been deceiving me for so long.

It wasn't just me who was shocked and betrayed by Rod's behavior though. Even Arnold had told me once during one of our difficult times that "Well, honey, at least you don't have to worry about him fooling around. He never looks at another woman."

But apparently he did. First there was the model in Germany who had been with him in France just before the trip I met him on. And she had also been with him in South Africa. No wonder Elton had quipped it was a good thing I hadn't come.

And if all of this wasn't bad enough, I also heard that she had gotten pregnant and he paid for her abortion. The affair continued—until he met Kelly. She lived in New York, and that's why he'd always stop there on his way back and forth to Europe. And then of course there was the time he had visited her in Texas . . . for the car show . . .

I never confronted Rod to tell him I knew everything. What was the point? Nothing could change what had happened; too much damage had been done. I would have liked to have had some closure with Rod, though. I would have liked to have had a conversation during which we talked about our feelings—our deep feelings—over what had gone wrong between us.

In hindsight, however, I can see it wasn't just Rod's fault that the marriage had ended. I now clearly see my part in it too. He'd fallen in love with this fun-loving girl who, because of babies and health problems, had turned into a totally different woman, who was angry at him a lot of the time for not being who she wanted him to be.

But there was no way I could see that at the time, and there was probably no way he'd have been open to that conversation had I suggested having it. It was impossible to have a heart-to-heart talk with Rod about the breakup of our marriage. He was so closed off and avoided any kind of emotional confrontation with me. If he didn't like what I was saying, he'd walk away, or if we were on the telephone, he'd hang up.

He never said, "I'm sorry. I'm sorry I hurt you so badly. I'm sorry I broke up our marriage and our family." I think if we could have really talked it out, I probably would have been able to let it go sooner and move on. But that wasn't what was happening here.

Even the divorce dragged on longer than it needed to. It's not that it was overly complicated; it was more that neither one of us pushed for it, so it just stayed on hold. I think for Rod it was a great excuse not to get remarried.

In any case, I didn't handle the logistics of the divorce very well. I had deluded myself into believing that if I didn't try to take him to the cleaners, if I tried to keep things low profile, that he would respect me more and the nastiness wouldn't infect his relationship with the children. Boy, was I wrong.

Rod would have happily given me nothing, and I pretty much made that my guide in deciding what I should go after. I wanted the minimum—a house to live in until the kids were eighteen, a relatively small amount of alimony for two years after I moved out of Carolwood, and minimum child support.

I rationalized: I didn't need Rod's money. I was still young and I was sure I'd work—maybe even get a television series. I also figured I'd eventually get married again.

It was a terrible decision. I should have at least taken what was fair. I should have thought long and hard about the future—mine and the children's. I should have had college funds and trust funds established for them, but I just couldn't think clearly. Even when others—my friends, my attorney—told me I was making a mistake, I didn't listen. I foolishly believed I was doing the honorable thing.

I have to give Rod credit in one respect: he didn't try to rush me and the kids out of the house so he could move back in; instead, he continued to live in rented houses nearby.

Kelly and Rod were together a lot, either in New York, on tour, or sometimes in LA. I was adamant that I didn't want her around my children yet. It was just way too soon for that, and Rod complied, at least for a while.

The first time I found out she had been on tour while they were there, I hit the roof. Kim and Sean told me the minute I picked them up at the airport. But truthfully, they had to meet her sometime. I gathered that she was always very nice to my children, and when I was finally able to stop hating her, I was very grateful to her for that.

I was so fortunate that all of my friends gathered around me and none of them jumped ship to side with Rod, as is usually the case in Hollywood—friends generally flock to the one with more money and fame. That actually didn't happen in either of my marriages. George always said, "Alana got custody of all the friends." I think it was mostly because George and Rod both traveled so much, and Rod, especially, had come into my circle of friends rather than the other way around.

So yes, it was kind of a dark point in my life, but it wasn't all doom and gloom. We actually had some really fun evenings at my house playing Trivial Pursuit, which was a relatively new board game and all the rage at that time. Along with Farrah and Ryan, some of the other "regulars" were Ed Begley Jr., Jeff Goldblum, Melanie Griffith, Michelle Phillips, and a host of other pals.

It got very competitive, and there was a lot of good-natured arguing going on, but everyone really had a great time. Those Trivial Pursuit parties really took my mind off things.

One night Farrah, Ryan, and Ryan's son Patrick, who was seventeen at the time, stayed late after one of the games. I'm not sure how we got there, but somehow we ended up in Rod's closets. Rod had sort of moved out, but he left behind quite an array of his clothing. We decided to pick through his expansive wardrobe and have a little fashion show!

It was hilarious—everyone parading around in Rod's clothes. There was everything from leopard-skin stretch pants and matching jackets to Armani suits.

Then on impulse I said, with an expansive wave of my arm, "Take whatever you want." Rod's clothes were a little tight for Ryan, but they fit Patrick perfectly, and even Farrah found some great Thierry Mugler jackets from Paris that she loved.

We were all giggling like schoolkids. The three of them went out into the night, arms laden with piles of Rod's clothing. It was the best night I'd had in a long time.

Unfortunately, though, the dark days outnumbered the good. When would I meet someone and fall in love? Was I ever going to go back to work? When would my health be strong again?

Then out of the blue I got a couple of good TV guest-starring roles. I felt great about working and was hoping my career would take off again. I was going on auditions regularly and had joined the Groundlings, a well-respected improvisational comedy group in LA.

In June of 1986 I dropped Kim and Sean off in London with Rod and went to Cap Ferrat to take Ashley, who was now eleven, to George. He was doing a miniseries called *Monte Carlo* with Joan Collins that she was producing. She thought I'd be great for the role of the other woman and asked me to read for the director. It went very well, and I thought for sure I had the part. Joan wanted me, but CBS wanted another actress, so I didn't get it after all.

But George was wonderful. He told me to stay in Monte Carlo and paid for my room and all my expenses.

I consider myself very lucky that George has always been there for me. He'd always been a good man with a strong set of values. When I was younger, fairly innocent and naive, and fresh from Texas, I could have met an asshole. But George was and continues to be a really decent human being. And while I was in pieces over my divorce from Rod, he seemed to know exactly how to help me, at least for the time being. I really have depended a lot on him over the years. Despite divorce, there has always been a definite bond and a deep love between us that time still hasn't changed.

Back in Los Angeles Sean started having problems in school. After all sorts of testing, we learned he had attention deficit disorder and fairly severe learning disabilities. I racked my brain trying to figure out why. Was it a neurological disorder caused by the heavy pesticide they'd used when they sprayed our house for termites when Sean was a baby? Or the high fever and ear infection he'd had in London when he was only six weeks old?

I also read recently that so many kids are diagnosed with ADD because of the high rate of male children without fathers in the house. The lack of stability and security with their male role model causes great emotional damage that can manifest in these learning disabilities.

It made my heart ache to see my little Sean going through this. He so badly wanted his father to be around. He was such a sensitive little boy that I think Rod's absence affected him deeply.

In September 1986 I took the kids to London. Kelly wasn't around, and Rod invited me to join them for the concert at Wembley Stadium. It was so strange to be there watching him onstage again, with the children but not as his wife.

After the show Rod and I went out to dinner alone. We had some fun posing with knives at each other's throats when the paparazzi appeared, but over dinner we didn't talk about anything but superficial things. We had been married, and our marriage ended very badly, but not a word was spoken about it. It was all so strange.

When he dropped me off at the hotel with a kiss on the cheek, it was bittersweet. I felt lonely back in my room, and slightly depressed. It's difficult to explain. Perhaps I wasn't over him completely. But I also knew he had caused me so much pain that there was no way I could have been with him again. I just wished we could have connected better emotionally that night—and even afterward.

I know something about myself now that took me years to discover: when I'm deeply distressed, I get physically sick. I'm pretty sure this has had to do with my old tendency to stuff toxic emotions deep into myself and let them fester and infect me instead of letting them out.

Well, it doesn't take a genius to figure out what came next: I got sick. In fact, I got very sick over the next few days with something called the "Taiwan Flu," and I didn't get better for several months. Strangely enough, the Taiwan Flu brought a new friend into my life, with whom I became very close and who is still today one of my dearest friends.

Arnold Stiefel had been trying to get me and Carole Bayer Sager together for years. She too had the Taiwan Flu and called me to check in about symptoms. We bonded immediately and became the best of friends.

I knew I needed to close the book on my marriage to Rod. I knew it was time to get out of Carolwood. The house was so tied into my life with Rod as well as the anger and resentment I felt toward him and Kelly, and I needed to let all that go.

Earlier in the summer I had found a house in Brentwood Park, a lovely, homey, traditional English Tudor–style house set back from the quiet street, with gates, a beautiful large garden, and a swimming pool in the back. It was time to move myself and my kids into our new life.

Before I left, however, I couldn't help doing one thing that may have been a little vindictive, although my friends and I thought it was pretty funny. I started to notice that there were rats in the attic. I could hear them sometimes at night, scurrying around over my head, like they were having a party or something. Once a houseguest even saw one, the size of a small cat, and almost had a heart attack.

The rats seemed to be multiplying, and instead of calling the exterminators, I decided, why not let Kelly and Rod have a nice little group of guests greet them when they arrived! My friends and I joked about "Ben" and "Willard" and all their friends, in little berets, sitting on the bar stools, sipping martinis and smoking cigarettes while waiting to greet the new tenants.

I gave one final farewell bash at Carolwood, with my friends Stan Dragoti and Allan Carr, a New Year's Eve party to end all parties. It was quite amazing. We had a fabulous dinner followed by a live band, which played until all hours while we danced and drank Taittinger rosé champagne. At midnight, thirty bagpipers came marching through the ballroom playing "Auld Lang Syne." At 3 a.m. we had scrambled eggs and caviar and more pink champagne. It was the last hurrah at Carolwood, and I must say, we went out in style.

Chapter 23

Before we left Carolwood I went through every room in the house with a white candle, like Rosalyn Bruyere, a spiritual healer, had told me to do, leaving the old negative energy and taking my new energy with me.

The kids were sad and a little confused to be leaving the only home they'd known, and on top of that we had all just learned that Kelly was pregnant. It was a difficult time for all of us—for me because I felt like Rod had just taken what we had that was so special, discarded it, and was recreating the same story line with someone else. But for the kids, the thought of a new baby made them feel terribly hurt and upset. I wished he could have waited until the kids healed a little more.

I would later learn in therapy that I needed to pull back and stop protecting the children so much from emotional pain. I'd had such a painful childhood that I didn't want anything to hurt my children. But that's what I was doing.

So I made it seem like this new home was going to be so exciting. Kim and Sean were seven and six, and Ash had just turned twelve, so it was an adventure to them—especially when they saw the huge trampoline outside in the back garden that I'd gotten them as a surprise.

For myself, I threw a giant housewarming party to show my friends my new home. Elton John, who was one of the first to arrive, gave me the most beautiful diamond-studded deco watch. He'd always given me much better jewelry than my ex-husband had!

Elton truly is one of the kindest, most generous people I've ever known. In fact, another night when he was over, he wanted to play the piano after dinner. I told him I didn't have one.

"Bob," he said, to Bob Halley, his longtime personal assistant. "Make a note, dear. Have a piano delivered tomorrow morning." I thought he was joking, of course, but early the next morning the doorbell rang and a brand new baby grand piano was brought to my house. I've treasured it throughout the years, just as I've treasured my friendship with Elton.

In any case, the party was a roaring success, and everyone stayed very late. Rod even showed up with a woman who was not Kelly.

For the first time I started to feel sorry for her, stuck home and pregnant while Rod was out with another woman. I think it was at that point I stopped hating her so much.

Rod stayed until about 4 a.m. So did Elton and a few other friends. It still felt kind of funny seeing Rod. I knew by then I could never be with him again, but I still had some feelings for him. And there was still a big hole in my heart that was about to become a problem.

When my marriage with George broke up, I went out a lot. I had ways to escape the pain. I was healthy and younger, and with only one child at the time, I was, in a way, freer. Then I could drink and have fun with my friends and hide from the pain.

But I was just too sick at this point in my life to drink and party away the pain. I needed a new drug, a new escape. I'm not the first woman to ever try to heal a broken heart by trying to fall in love again, but this method for me this time was nearly my undoing.

Putting it all in perspective, after Rod left I completely fell apart emotionally. I was a shell of my former self. And although I had my kids and friends to keep my spirits up and started to do a lot of therapy, it was like there was a void in me that could only be filled in one way: by finding a man to love me. And at this point I was starting to know better!

In therapy I was learning why I went for the kinds of men I did, why I wanted men I couldn't have but didn't want the ones I could. I saw the patterns I'd been following in my life since I was a teenager, and I tried to work on myself to fix these terrible self-destructive tendencies. But I still wanted the "white knight" who would sweep in and make me feel safe and loved.

I obviously had another tough lesson to learn.

I continued working with Robert Lorenze, trying to sort it all out. We did a lot of energy work, and I cried and cried over that devastated little girl in me whose fantasy world was shattered with Rod. Robert said that it wasn't so much the relationship with Rod I was grieving over but rather my dreams being shattered just like when I was a child.

That should have made more sense to me. That should have made me not go out seeking a relationship but instead to turn inward and start seeking some answers within myself. But I wasn't ready yet.

Then, out of the blue, someone came into my life I would never have guessed, yet another high-profile man I'll just call "Sam." I don't want to spend a lot of time talking about Sam, but it's important I bring him up here because the pattern of our relationship and its overall effect on me nearly did me in. I was craving a new romance to help heal from the old, and voila! He had everything I was looking for—and shouldn't have been. He was powerful (a white knight!) and narcissistic ("sexy") and . . . married (unavailable!). What should have been three strikes against him was for me the magic formula. I didn't get completely involved with him right away (which I considered was me putting all that good therapy to use). I didn't hear from him again until almost a year later when he was finally divorced. But once we really started seeing each other, I was hooked.

There I was again, with that feeling of not having the ground beneath me, like when I was that baby crying on the train because there was no sense of being "held up" by anything. I told Robert that I was scared after my breakup with Rod, that I wondered what would happen to me.

From my work with Robert, I realized I mustn't try to find my safety and security in a man, that it had to come from me. That was the part I didn't know how to do, though, and it wasn't as if Robert could give me a magic pill that would suddenly enlighten me and give me healthy, grown-up feelings. The interesting part is that I knew I was strong, smart, practical, and could handle almost anything, and yet there was this other childlike part of me that was confused, frightened, and insecure.

So as much as I knew I should not be looking to Sam for grounding, the fact was that I just couldn't help myself. Sam had a reputation as a playboy and a womanizer; he would disappear, then call, then we'd have a great time together, then he'd disappear again. He was the most unstable force I could imagine, and here I was trying to find some sense of stability in him. Like the old saying goes, I was trying to build a house on sand.

I guess the signs were all there, but they were always so hard for me to see. I felt torn between wanting the romance and the excitement and seeing the reality of the situation. I read a book by a romance guru once that said something to the effect that if you ever feel this incredibly intense chemistry with a man across the room, you should run in the other direction as fast as you can. So a part of me was saying, "Run!" Unfortunately this was not the part of me I listened to.

So the patterns took shape as they always did. When Sam called, I was elated; when he didn't, I was depressed and anxious. Robert said this was pushing the buttons on all my old programming—fear of abandonment, neediness, looking for love and safety in an unsafe place—hoping this would finally be "it," that the "fantasy daddy" I'd always longed for would finally show up and love me and make me feel safe.

"Alana," he said, "on some very deep level, if you don't have validation from a man, you feel like you don't exist."

I went into a terrible depression after my birthday, one of those dark holes that I could barely pull myself out of. On top of the uncertainty with Sam, I had no work on deck and was having terrible stomach problems.

Robert told me, "Alana, you have to walk through the pain to prove to yourself you won't die from it. Stop distracting yourself with this toxic, idiotic romance."

But I didn't listen. I couldn't listen. The scarring from all that early abandonment was just too deep.

Now I had started having panic attacks. Robert reinforced his message: "If you want to stop the panic attacks, stop running from the pain of the past and face it." I knew that what Robert was saying made sense, but I didn't know how to go about doing that.

Robert continued to reiterate how dangerous Sam was for me and that I must end the relationship immediately. He said if I took action and pulled out of it, I'd feel stronger. I rationalized all of the red flags away.

Then Robert dropped a real bomb on me. He told me that if I saw Sam again, he wouldn't see me anymore. I had never heard of a therapist "firing" a patient because they wouldn't stop seeing a man! I was pretty angry about it. The one man I trusted to help and support me through this difficult time had, in a way, I felt, betrayed and abandoned me, just like all the rest. So I started seeing a new therapist, one who my friend Carole was also seeing.

The first thing Dr. Foster told me after I told her about my life growing up was that I should go to ACA (Adult Children of Alcoholics) and/or Al-Anon. She definitely agreed with Robert about Sam. She told me Sam represented power, safety, and "glitter" to me but that I already knew deep down he could never be enough for me.

I didn't listen to her about Sam either, but I did finally get up the courage to go to an ACA meeting. I sat down as far in the back as I could. I heard a young man telling his story, and it was so much like my own childhood that I started to cry. I knew that this was where I needed to be.

I soon started going religiously to the meetings. I still didn't have the nerve to share, but for the first time I was hearing so many stories like mine—about growing up in an alcoholic home, parents who were drug addicts and weren't present for their children, violence and shutting down emotionally because the pain was too terrifying to deal with.

Dr. Foster and I talked more about men—that my fantasy man would "save" me, that everything has always been centered around a man, that I only felt valuable and worthwhile if I was with a man, a man who was larger than life. She was hammering it home, and rightly so. I felt I was making progress and was starting to heal somewhat from the disastrous relationship with Sam, who was away in Europe working and whom I hadn't heard from in weeks.

Then one afternoon I arrived home to a huge basket of flowers, and back into my life Sam swept. I couldn't help it; whatever good sense I had went right out the window. I stayed in the quagmire with Sam even as it got deeper and more dysfunctional. I had to get out.

I had to make myself believe that I would be okay and not allow myself to live in this kind of fear anymore. I finally found the strength to end it; I did not feel better.

In fact, now I began to spiral into a terrible depression, so close to the despair I had felt when Rod and I broke up. I was frustrated and scared. I was supposed to be feeling better—wasn't that what healing meant? But no. I was starting to come undone.

The day after I broke up with Sam, I stayed in bed all day with horrible anxiety. I just couldn't face the world. What scared me the most is that this was what my mother had done—she had escaped into despair and apathy and took pills to do so. Things continued to get worse, and all I could do was stay in my room and cry.

My despair was deep and my thoughts grew dark. I started thinking that maybe I should kill myself and then the kids could go live with Rod and Kelly and have some semblance of a family life, that they wouldn't have to grow up the same way I had, with a mother who was there but never there.

The next few months were some of the most difficult of my life. I felt like I was completely alone, raising three children on my own, with fathers who were rarely in town. I was frightened and anxious, panicked about what was going to happen to me. I wasn't working, and my health was a mess.

The kids had suffered a lot from the divorce, and now they had to deal with Rod having a new baby on top of it. Kimberly, who was eight, was becoming very anxious and fearful and had been ever since we'd moved into the new house. She was afraid to go to sleep at night, and I'd spend hours rubbing her back, trying to convince her that we were all safe and fine.

Sean, who was seven, missed his father terribly and was having a difficult time at school. He seemed to be doing better after switching schools, but there were still problems. The school told me what I already knew—that a lot of his behavior and attention problems had to do with the fact that his father had a new baby and wasn't around very much. This, of course, only made me angrier and more resentful that I had to deal with all the problems alone.

And I felt horribly guilty because I knew that my health and my emotional condition weren't helping matters, either. I knew I must somehow pull myself together for my children. I had to get stronger—for me and for them.

I continued my ACA meetings and started Al-Anon, going religiously at least three times a week, and I was seeing Dr. Foster regularly. I had resolved to concentrate on my children and work—no liaisons with famous men, no party-girl image, no leopard skin. It took a lot, but I finally grew to know that I no longer wanted to be attracted to men like Sam or Rod. I knew my values needed to change. I didn't want to settle for a man who would probably always need other women to feed his ego.

One afternoon I walked into the house and saw a big bunch of flowers. My heart skipped a beat. I knew I had to stay away from him, but even though I was strong, I remained conflicted; I couldn't get him completely out of my mind. Dr. Foster was adamant that I stay as far away from Sam as possible. I knew she was right. I'd been working too hard on feeling good about myself, and there was no way I could ever feel worthy if I allowed a man to abuse me emotionally again.

Except I let him back in anyway. I was like an addict who couldn't say no to the drug. But soon enough the old patterns started again. I heard at an ACA meeting that we hold onto bad relationships in order not to have to face the loneliness and isolation we felt as children growing up in an alcoholic home. Was that what I was doing?

It was on my birthday, interestingly enough, that I knew it was finally over for me and Sam. We went to dinner and he gave me a beautiful antique ruby cross. During the course of the evening a friend of his joined us, and I excused myself to go to the ladies' room. When I got back, I heard Sam say, "Sure, give her my number."

At that moment something shifted in me. When we got back to my house, I told Sam I couldn't see him anymore. I felt sad, but strong; I knew I couldn't be with someone I could never trust.

Since then, I've dated casually through the years and even had a couple of boyfriends, but no one has ever quite knocked my socks off. A couple of years after Sam, a friend introduced me to a very eligible, attractive bachelor in New York who pursued me for months. I enjoyed his company immensely and particularly loved his sense of humor and his brilliance, but I couldn't bring myself to take it further than an occasional good-night kiss. He kept flying out to California to see me, obviously wanting more of a relationship, but I kept avoiding any intimacy. We made plans for me to come visit him in New York on several occasions, but both times I got cold feet and canceled at the last minute. Eventually, I had to end the relationship because I knew I wasn't going to get romantically involved with him, and I didn't want to lead him on. If he'd only known the way to win my heart was to be inconsistent, distant, or unavailable in some way!

Recently, I found a diary from high school. In one part I wrote about a boy I had a crush on: "I really like him so much. I wish he liked me more. Why can't I like Bill or Richard or somebody like them who really likes me? After I date a boy for a while, I just don't like them anymore." Interesting that I was questioning my patterns even then.

Back then I wondered if I'd ever be attracted to a different kind of man, and did that mean he had to be a nerd? One of those guys who wears yoga pants and Jesus sandals? I wanted a man who was exciting but also kind, compassionate, and loving. Did such a thing exist?

PART V

Starting to Heal

Chapter 24

After my breakup and emotional crash with Rod and then the subsequent breakup and emotional crash with Sam, I continued going to therapy and 12-step meetings regularly as I tried to hold it all together. Nothing made sense for me in those early days and months, but the more I worked through my issues, from the pain of my childhood and into my adult life, I started gaining more grounding and perspective.

I know now that everything happens for a reason. If I'd stayed married to Rod, if I'd stayed with Sam, I probably wouldn't have had to do the deep work on myself that eventually changed my life and made me the woman I am today. The pain from my childhood and over my mother and her death, even the rape, was so suppressed that it took a volcanic emotional event—two even—to force me to look within instead of continuing to just keep moving.

As I was to learn, there were many raw and scarred layers beneath that I needed to discover and heal. Because of the abandonment by my parents—both my dad's never being a part of my life and my mother's disappearance into drugs—I knew that I needed to learn how to reparent myself, to change my old beliefs, to grow up and become whole.

I started going to yet another therapist, Dr. Vera Dunn. She practiced Gestalt, a kind of psychotherapy that originated in Germany. Its purpose is to separate the child's feelings from those of the adult, the theory being that our "inner child" tends to run our actions and behaviors as an adult unless we deal with our past.

Vera said the reason I had so little sense of self was that I had never had the opportunity to bond with my mother. "When people don't have that initial parental bonding, they develop ways of coping, mechanisms that protect them from feeling their pain and anxiety," she explained. "They turn to alcohol, drugs, work, relationships, shopping, and so forth to distract them from dealing with their inner feelings."

That certainly made sense to me. I'd had no parental validation, so I looked to get it from people, places, and things, and I used men and relationships to keep from feeling the emptiness and pain.

I had never really grieved over the pain of my formative years. I could talk about the worst event in my life, and it was as if I was telling someone about a movie I'd seen, without showing any emotion. Then one day in an ACA meeting, I was sharing about something from my childhood and I started to cry. It was as if the floodgates had opened. It felt like I continued to cry for the next three years! It was very healing and cathartic, on one hand, but it sometimes seemed I was just getting in deeper and deeper and there was no end in sight.

I also discovered through therapy with Vera that I was emotionally unavailable. I may have picked men who were emotionally closed off, but I had my own suit of protective armor. I kept everything buried deep inside.

Vera would sometimes have me do "inner child" dialoguing and I resisted it. When I finally surrendered to the process, it was incredibly healing. What came up for me in one of the sessions was that all I had wanted as a little child was to have my mother put her arms around me and take care of me, and as an adult, I still desperately wanted that.

I ended up sobbing in Vera's arms. At first it felt weird and uncomfortable and my instinct was to pull back, but once I let her hold me and comfort me, it felt tremendously nurturing. We did a lot of inner-child work around my mother, and sometimes it felt as if the pain would never go away.

Eventually, I was able to open up more to people in the meetings as well. As I began to share more of my story, I started to let down my barriers and let people see who I really was. I slowly started to see that a lot of my life had been based on very superficial values.

Another thing that the program taught me was gratitude— something you don't learn in therapy. One morning when I was particularly low and depressed, I called my Al-Anon sponsor and began telling her all the things that sucked in my life. When I finally finished my laundry list of complaints, she was silent for a moment and then she said, "You need to make a gratitude list."

"A gratitude list? But, there's nothing in my life going right!" I argued.

"You can always find something to be grateful for," she told me. "You're alive, aren't you? You have three healthy children. Sit down and take a piece of paper and think of every single thing you have to be grateful for, no matter how small—what a beautiful day it is, the fact that you have plenty of food to eat. And then you can read it to me when you're finished if you want."

I hung up sort of hating her, but I grudgingly picked up a piece of paper and started writing. Something shifted in me as I wrote that list. I stopped feeling sorry for myself and started to feel some modicum of gratitude for the blessings I did have. I learned a valuable lesson that I will never forget: Gratitude is an attitude, it's an energy that attracts more of itself. The more you're grateful for, the more good you bring into your life.

The healing process seemed endless. Sometimes I felt resentful. Why didn't other people have to go through this? Why could some people just continue to live their superficial lives in a fool's paradise? In any case, I was on the path, and I had no choice but to continue on.

Things began to come up for me that I'd never acknowledged before. Fear, for instance. I had always had a lot of my grandmother's Texas gutsiness and feistiness, so I'd never thought of myself as a fearful person, but I realized what a terrified person I was underneath my controlled exterior.

After I hit my emotional wall and crumbled, it seemed that all my hidden fears bubbled up to the surface to be dealt with. The fear that would overwhelm me at times turned into occasional panic attacks and constant free-floating anxiety. I'd probably always had the anxiety; I just covered it with eating, shopping, men, and various other distractions.

I was terrified of ending up like my mother—broke, sick, and alone. Would I ever be involved in a relationship again? Would I ever fall in love again?

Maybe the area where I had the most fear was my health. After I was diagnosed with Epstein-Barr, I never really felt the same again. I would get so frustrated and so angry when I would get sick. My mind wanted to do so many things, but my body wouldn't always let me.

One night I had a frightening dream that my mother came out of a closet and I stabbed her in the head with a pair of scissors. I woke up barely able to get my breath, it was so real. Vera told me that a lot of the anger I felt over being sick was probably directed toward my mother. I couldn't consciously allow myself to be angry at her for not being there for me; instead, I just felt sadness for her. Her life was so tragic, and I felt it was my fault she had died.

I was tortured by guilt. I had to make an amends list and put on it everyone I felt I had hurt in some way. I wrote letters to my mother and grandmother. It felt so liberating, like a huge load had been lifted off me.

I even made amends to Rod.

A huge realization I made thanks to Al-Anon was that I couldn't continue to make Rod out as the villain and me the victim. If I was a victim of anything, it was of my upbringing and the deep emotional issues that I had never dealt with. Accepting responsibility for my part in the breakup was a huge step in my own healing.

So one day when he was visiting the kids and we were alone in the kitchen, I explained to him that I was in a 12-step program for families of alcoholics and that I had to make amends to people I felt I had hurt.

"I'm sorry for my part in the breakup of our marriage," I told him. "I'm sorry for the times I wasn't there emotionally for you."

He was quiet for a moment and then he said, "You know, I think I probably am an alcoholic."

I almost fell off my chair! Then he quickly added, "But I only drink wine with dinner now. It's very European." I didn't say anything. I'd learned in the program that it wasn't my place to tell anyone that I thought that their drinking might be a problem.

Rod never apologized to me for his part in our breakup, and as much as I would have loved total closure, I knew that my job was to sweep up my side of the street, without any expectations from him. Again, it was very liberating.

It had been a tough few years. Sean's school problems were progressively getting worse. He and Kimberly had both been going to therapy to help them deal with the divorce and Rod's new baby. The teacher at his school said that he was obsessing a lot over the new baby, feeling like he was being replaced in his dad's life.

The worst part was getting Rod on the phone. Often when I'd call about something important to do with the kids, his assistant would put me on hold, then come back on the phone and tell me he was in the bath. Once I said to him, "You must be the cleanest man in the world. Every time I call you, you're in the bath." I knew he avoided talking to me because he didn't want to hear about problems. It had always been easier to put his head in the sand.

And there was the never-ending battle about money. He still hated to pay bills, so when doctor or therapist bills for the kids would go to his office, they wouldn't get paid for months. The doctors would finally end up calling me and saying they couldn't see the kids anymore unless their bills were paid. There was nothing that made me feel angrier or more frustrated.

Kimberly was ten now, and she was also acting out, but her bad behavior was directed toward me and the others in the house. She was being terribly rude and talked back to everyone, most of all me. When I put her to bed one night, it suddenly hit me that maybe she was angry at her father and taking it out on everybody else.

"Honey, what if you could pretend you were talking to your dad right now—you know, 'tell' him, out loud now, everything you're feeling."

She did it, and it seemed to be a big release for her. I shared with her something else I had learned in Al-Anon. "You could also write him a letter," I suggested. "Then you can decide if you want to send it or not."

"It wouldn't change anything anyway," she said dejectedly.

I guess that's where kids get their feelings of powerlessness that stay with us as adults, the feeling that we just can't change things.

I think it was good for her, however, to express her feelings and for me to be able to hear them and try to comfort her.

Ashley had gone to boarding school, but now he was back home. Also around this time George busted him for having marijuana in his room. I was shocked. I couldn't imagine Ash doing drugs. I was determined to keep a close eye on him now.

He had suddenly grown up so much. He was fifteen and six feet tall. I felt like I had this tall stranger in my house. Connecting with him was so difficult; he was withdrawn and uncommunicative. Once I was able to draw him out a little and get him to talk to me. One of the things that came up was how hurt he was about Rod's leaving. He'd felt we were a family, and he adored Rod during the years we were together, but when Rod left, he didn't make an effort to see Ashley anymore. It had affected Ashley much more than I'd realized.

Then the big drama happened that almost caused the end of my relationship with George. One day he called me from South America to tell me that Ashley wanted to come to Aspen and live with him and go to school there.

I told George he couldn't possibly provide a stable home environment for Ash because he was constantly traveling all over the world. I tried to be as gentle as possible. "I know your intentions are good, but I don't think the best thing for Ash at this crucial age is to end up being looked after by a housekeeper."

When we hung up, I thought the matter was settled, but it wasn't.

"I'm going to Aspen," Ashley said when he came home that afternoon.

"Your father and I already talked about it," I told him. "I think it's best you stay here."

Ash started to argue with me.

"I told you, Ashley, you're not going. End of discussion," I said firmly and then left the house to do some errands. When I returned, the housekeeper told me that Ashley had called a taxi and taken a suitcase to his dad's house.

I called George's house several times that night, but there was always some reason Ash couldn't come to the phone.

Early the next morning, when I called Peggy, George's secretary, to try to locate George, I got a message that she had left for Aspen! Obviously she had taken Ashley with her.

I contacted my attorney, who advised me that since legally I had full custody, I should talk to the police. "We can telex the Aspen police to arrest your former husband," the police told me.

Arrest George? I never intended it to go that far. I finally got Peggy on the phone. "I called the police and they said they would have George arrested if Ashley wasn't brought home immediately."

I was so angry by now. I felt totally betrayed that George and Ashley would conspire against me and completely disregard my feelings. I decided I wasn't going to play the victim and, therefore, I wasn't going to back down from this fight. However, I knew I would never have George arrested.

George finally called and wanted to work things out, as I'd hoped he would. I agreed to let Ashley live with George temporarily as long as George was home with him. I realized there was no use forcing Ashley to come home where we would just end up arguing about everything, and that maybe he was at an age when being with his father would be more beneficial than being with me.

I felt like my relationship with Ashley needed to be healed, but I wasn't sure how to do it.

And George still jokes about the time I almost had him thrown in jail.

As I began to heal, it became increasingly important for me to be there more for my children. No matter how exhausted or ill I was feeling, I made myself rise to the occasion, attending every school function and every sports event I could.

My mother never went to a parents' night, a school play, or sports game, and I was usually the only kid who never had anyone show up for me. As I mentioned earlier, neither my mother nor my stepfather attended my high school graduation. I had no idea how much this neglect had affected me until I got deep into therapy, and I was determined that I was not going to let my kids down. Although I may not have always succeeded, I always tried my best.

My friends were also an important focus in my life at this time. Without a man in my life distracting me, I was able to spend time with my girlfriends and develop really deep and significant friendships.

Since my breakup with Rod, Farrah and I had really bonded. She was so down to earth and fun and so loyal. In fact, when I was about to lose my Screen Actors Guild insurance, she got me a small role in her upcoming miniseries, *Small Sacrifices*.

Carole Bayer Sager and I had become very close ever since we'd bonded over having the Taiwan Flu, and she and I started tossing around an idea for a screenplay. It was about a young woman, a raving hypochondriac, who meets and marries a famous rock star . . . sound familiar? Though Carol was an accomplished songwriter, neither of us had experience writing a screenplay, so I bought a famous book on how to write a screenplay and read the instructions to her while she typed out our story. After several months we completed *In Sickness and in Health*.

Carole's cousin, Rosalie Swedlin, a prestigious agent at CAA, agreed to read our screenplay and give us her opinion. "But I'm warning you—I'm a tough critic," she said.

"We want you to be honest with us," Carole told her. So we anxiously awaited Rosalie's critique, expecting the worse.

Carole called me a couple days later. "She loved it!" Carole said excitedly. "In fact, she wants to represent us!"

We were so surprised and so thrilled. This was more than we could have hoped for. Suddenly we both had new careers.

Carole also gave the script to her good friend Bette Midler, who really liked it but felt, as we did, that the part wasn't really right for her. However, Bette wanted us to write something she could do.

We came up with an idea about a down-and-out nightclub singer who meets a much older man in failing health, and decides to marry him for his money (and then try to kill him). Definitely a dark comedy. Bette had a production deal at Disney, so we pitched the idea there, but the head of Disney turned it down.

Shortly afterwards, I went to a Rolling Stones concert with my friend Joel Silver. On the way home I happened to mention our script idea and that Disney turned it down. Joel loved the idea and wanted to option it. Of course he wasn't known for his comedies, but that didn't bother us. We made a very lucrative deal with Joel and Warner Brothers to write the screenplay. We couldn't believe our good fortune!

Carole and I wrote daily, but soon other things got in the way. Burt Bacharach wanted her to spend more time with him writing songs, and he began to resent us working together. Then, out of the blue, he asked for a separation.

Carole was taken totally by surprise and wanted to do anything to save her marriage, which meant spending more time writing with him and putting a lot less time into our screenplay.

I can see now that Carole and I had probably developed a co-dependent friendship, and the situation brought up a lot of anxiety from our childhoods for both of us—I definitely felt abandoned. I felt very strongly the potential loss of not only our screenwriting career but, even more so, our friendship.

It turned out that Burt's "wanting some space" had to do with another woman (like I said, when a man asks for space . . .). Carole was devastated. A short time later, though, she met and eventually married Bob Daly and is still happily married to him today.

Bob was the cochairman of Warner Bros. Studio at the time, which could have worked out great for Carole and me work-wise, but he was a stickler for propriety. He told the head of development, Lorenzo D'Aventura, "I don't want anyone to think we're moving forward on this script because of my relationship with Carole. You know how strongly I feel about that." Lorenzo took this to mean he should pass on it—which he promptly did.

I was so disappointed, but I tried to keep a sense of humor about it. "Great," I said to Carole. "You had to fall for Dudley Do-Right. Why couldn't you have gone for someone like Jon Peters, who set his wife up in her own offices at Sony?" We've never let Bob forget that he was the reason our movie didn't get made!

In the meantime my health and spirit were in terrible shape. My doctor ordered some blood tests, and I was shocked to learn I had off-the-chart levels of active Epstein-Barr virus—far worse than the first time around. Why was this happening to me again?

I also started going to a new therapist. I know—what was I, nuts? Changing therapists like other people change their underwear? His name was Dr. Ron Furst, and he was recommended to me by my Al-Anon sponsor. But the fact of the matter was that this was a process, and it happened in phases, and each therapist I saw handled an important part of the process.

Anyway, on top of the depression and illness and disappointment, I was also turning forty-five. As much as I hated to admit it, I was really frightened of aging and losing my looks. I felt like no one would ever want me again. Would I ever feel normal? Would I even know what normal was if it ran me over in the street? It almost seemed like it would be easier just to give up.

I was fortunate that I'd learned now to have faith in a higher power, and I always thought about the saying, "It's darkest before the dawn." Sometimes the night seemed to go on forever, but I had to believe things would get better.

I spoke to a woman who had been in Al-Anon many years about how hopeless I was feeling about the Epstein-Barr coming back. She suggested that I ask God to show me what it was I needed to learn from this experience.

What could I possibly need to learn by getting sick, I wondered. What I eventually came to realize was that getting sick was my body's way of slowing me down; stopping me from focusing on all the distractions that kept me from doing the spiritual work I still needed to do.

Despite our recent hiccup over Ashley's living situation, George and I remained very close. He was like my family and my best friend and was always there to listen and to help me, as I was with him. When I told him about the Epstein-Barr relapse and the deep exhaustion and depression I was feeling, he sent me to see Dr. Deepak Chopra, whom he knew personally.

When I met Dr. Chopra, the first question he asked me after we said hello took me by surprise.

"Are you happy?" he asked.

"Well, no, not really," I answered, thinking that I probably wouldn't be here if I were happy.

"This hasn't been the happiest period of my life, that's for sure," I told him, then went on to list all the things that were wrong in my life, starting with my health.

After I finished he looked at me and smiled his lovely, kind smile. I waited for him to give me the secret to a happy, healthy life.

"Alana, do you know how to meditate?" he asked.

"Well, I tried transcendental meditation in the '70s but I didn't stick to it."

"I'd like you to try it again," he said. "Do you remember the mantra you were given?"

"Sort of," I said. "But that was so long ago. I'd prefer if you gave me a new one."

He smiled his gentle smile. "Fine," he said. "Then, I'd like you to go into silence for two days, when you don't speak to anyone, and start meditating twenty minutes twice a day. I'll give you your mantra now and we can meditate together if you like. Then I'll see you after your two days of silence."

"But what about my Epstein-Barr?" Surely, he must have some magical treatment plan for a miracle healing?

"Just begin meditating, Alana." He smiled, then added, "Happy thoughts make happy molecules."

I'll never forget that. In the beginning I remembered it because I couldn't believe I came all the way to Lancaster, Massachusetts, for the famous Dr. Chopra to tell me "Happy thoughts make happy molecules." It took some time for me to understand it fully, but as I said, I never forgot it. So simple, yet so magically true.

For the rest of the trip I devoured his books and watched his tapes and tried to understand it all. It started to make more sense to me. In the simplest terms, our thoughts and feelings create our physiology, and we have a choice as to how we think and feel.

That's where I got tripped up. I wasn't sure how to change the way I thought and felt. I wasn't sure how to choose happiness, but I was willing to learn. I'd start by trying this meditation thing.

He also said on one of his tapes that "Love is the strongest of all the happiness factors." But wasn't that my problem? Wasn't I desperately trying to find love so I would be happy?

I realized that I was only counting love if it came from a relationship with a man. I wasn't placing enough importance on the love I already had in my life—from my children and friends. I had a lot of love in my life, and perhaps I needed to appreciate that love more instead of constantly searching for it somewhere else.

I went into the two days of silence and attempted my meditation. I'd never gone without speaking in my life, and it was the most amazing experience. I felt this incredible feeling of peace come over me, a feeling I'd never experienced before.

Another doctor at the center had told me the first day I was there that the way to heal this deep fatigue that I was feeling was to calm the nervous system and thereby ground and balance the immune system. He said the key to healing was to restore harmony to the body, mind, and emotions by reducing stress, and the way they recommend to do that is through meditation.

Dr. Chopra told me in another session that I was "wound very tightly and needed to learn to let go." I'd never thought of it that way, but I realized it was so true.

I thought about the work I had been doing with Dr. Furst. During one of our meetings, when I told him about my childhood, he told me, "The way you grew up was like being a hostage," he said. "You always had to be vigilant. You could never relax."

I knew he was right. I'd been so vigilant all my life, never "letting go" for an instant. It was no wonder I had this deep fatigue.

I was supposed to stay at the clinic for a week, but then I got a terrible cold and bronchitis. How on earth could I get sick when I'm at a clinic that's supposed to help me get well? The doctors explained it was from all the toxins releasing. I was so sick that it sure didn't seem to me like it could just be toxins, but I had no choice but to stay another week.

It ended up being a blessing in disguise. I did a lot of writing and introspection, which I never would have done if I hadn't been forced to stay and be with myself. I realized that I never stopped "doing" and being on some kind of self-imposed schedule. Even when I was too tired to actively do much, my mind would still be whirling or I'd be on the telephone taking care of business. Maybe that was why my body broke down—to force me to slow down and be with myself.

Deepak said in one of his books, "A peaceful mind is all you need." I started to learn the value of being peaceful.

I continued my meditation with Deepak's mantra when I got home. There were times in my meditation that I actually felt a feeling of joy come over me. I was beginning to learn to go inside to look for my answers instead of desperately running around looking to others to give them to me, and I was feeling better. I had grown up seeing the universe as an unsafe, unpredictable place. Now I had to learn how to trust that, no matter what happened, I could handle it.

Another new development with Rod made it even clearer that I was the only one who was going to be there full-time for my kids. He had met a model named Rachel Hunter around the same time that he and Kelly Emberg broke up, and he asked her to marry him after two months. It really affected the children. I found Kimberly crying in her bed one night.

"Daddy doesn't love me anymore," she sobbed. "He loves Rachel more and only wants to be with her." Sean had said almost the same thing the night before. It was so incredibly painful to see my kids hurting and insecure. I reassured them that their father would always love them and they would always come first, but I knew the reality was that Rod did get very caught up with the woman who was in his life at the moment and that, between his new relationship and his career, the kids would not be his priority. I knew the next step would be yet more children, and Kim and Sean would have to face that as well. And I would have to bear the brunt of their pain (and anger).

Again, I really don't want to make Rod out as the villain or a bad father. He loved his kids. He just always had a lot going on in his life, and they suffered because of it. And like me, when he was growing up he wasn't given the tools he needed to raise kids and be there for them.

Chapter 25

When Ashley finished high school, I was concerned about what direction his life would take. I didn't feel like he was actively pursuing anything. Then I got a call from Patricia Green, the mother of one of Kimberly's best friends. Her husband, Gerald Green, was producing a movie in Africa.

"We've seen about three hundred young actors for the lead and haven't found the right one yet. Would you consider letting Ashley come in to read for the part?"

"I'll see if he'd be interested," I told her. As it turned out, he was, and they arranged a meeting with him. The minute they saw him, they knew he was their guy. Now he would have to go to Africa for two months!

I was terrified at the thought of letting him go off so far alone. He hadn't quite turned eighteen yet. He still seemed so young to me, but when Patricia and Gerald assured me they would watch over him like he was their own son, I reluctantly let him go.

As it turned out, Ash loved making the movie and acting. My friend Ed Limato at ICM Talent Agency thought Ash had great potential and took him on as a client. It was a huge step; Ed represented Mel Gibson, Michelle Pfeiffer, Richard Gere, Denzel Washington, and countless other big stars.

A few months after he returned from Africa I got the phone call that is every mother's worst nightmare. "Your son, Ashley Hamilton, is here in the emergency room," said the woman on the other end of the phone. "He's had a motorcycle accident."

"Is he okay?" I asked, feeling the blood drain out of my head.

"He's alive," she answered. "He's talking to us, but he has internal bleeding and will probably need surgery."

"I'm coming now," I said, though I could barely get the words out.

I was so shaken that a friend had to drive me to the hospital. As we raced there, I suddenly thought, "What motorcycle?" Ashley didn't own a motorcycle. We found out later he had bought one with some of the money he'd made from the movie. He kept it at a friend's house because he knew I would have a fit.

When I got to Ashley, he was lying on a bed in one of the curtained-off cubicles, just back from getting an MRI of his head. He seemed kind of dazed but coherent. His ear was bloody, and there was a bleeding gash in his head.

I ran to him. "Honey, are you okay?"

"My head hurts pretty bad," he said. I held his hand and reassured him he would be alright.

The neurosurgeon came in and said Ashley would need to have brain surgery right away; his skull was fractured and he had a blood clot on his brain. Time was of the essence. I was terrified but tried to hide my fear from Ash, and I just kept reassuring him that everything would be okay.

I called George, who made it to the hospital just before Ashley went into surgery. We each kissed Ash before they took him into the operating room and waited for two anxious hours before the doctor finally came out.

"The surgery went well," the doctor told us. "But the next twenty-four to forty-eight hours are crucial. He'll be in ICU until we're sure he's doing okay."

I was so grateful that I grabbed the doctor and hugged him tightly. "When can we see him?" I asked.

"In an hour or two," he said. "He's very lucky. He could have been paralyzed or killed."

When we went into ICU to see Ash, he was lying there, still sedated, with tubes coming out everywhere and a drain in his head. It was excruciating to see him like that and to know he still wasn't completely out of danger.

For the next two days I prayed like never before, and my prayers were answered. When the doctor told us that he had made it through the crucial time and could be moved into a regular room, I started to cry with relief.

"Will there be any aftereffects?" asked George.

"The brain takes time to heal," the surgeon explained. "There's a slight possibility he could have seizures during the first year. It's important that he doesn't smoke pot or drink very much alcohol either, as it can affect the brain."

I had an extra bed put into Ash's room, and I slept there every night with him. As I said, he and I had not been close the past few years, and there had seemed no way to break down the barrier between us. But now, because I had come close to losing him, I was able just to be there for him completely and love him with an open heart. He, in return, allowed me in.

While he recovered we started to really talk to each other and developed a closeness that we hadn't had since he was little. Our relationship was healed because of this terrible accident; it was a blessing in disguise.

Unfortunately, a whole new set of events with Sean were about to test my strength and my ability to get through scary and unfathomable circumstances.

Sean was now twelve, and his difficulties in school had been escalating. The school suggested I take him to a new therapist, who had grave concerns about Sean's emotional state. Ashley's accident had affected him much more than we'd realized; he had been terrified of losing his brother and still was. On top of that, Rod had already married Rachel, she was expecting a baby, and they were leaving for England for a month for Christmas.

Sean was angry, sad, and felt, again, like he had been replaced in his dad's life. Rod thought that I took Sean to too many therapists and that there was nothing wrong with him. He seemed to be in total denial about how fragile Sean was emotionally.

After Sean had set his T-shirt on fire while playing with matches and I had to rush him to the hospital for second-degree burns on his shoulder and chest, I was out of my mind with fear that he could do something to really hurt himself. I called Rod and told him that the situation was indeed serious, and he agreed to come with me to the specialist whom Sean's therapist wanted us to see.

After observing Sean and consulting other experts, Dr. Staring felt that Sean needed to be admitted to the Adolescent Neuropsychiatric Hospital at UCLA for four weeks, where he could have supervised treatment and be tested to find out exactly what was going on with him.

I couldn't stop crying. The doctor suggested he and Rod walk Sean over to the facility; they felt I would be too emotional to handle telling Sean, and I'm sure they were right.

When I said good-bye to Sean, he looked so young, so vulnerable, and so fragile that I thought my heart would break. Even Rod cried. I held Sean for a long time.

"I'll visit you every day," I told him, choking back my tears. "You'll be out of here in no time."

But as painful as it was, I felt a sense of relief that he was in a safe place where he would hopefully get the help he needed.

It had been one of the most traumatic months of my life, with Ash's accident and Sean's hospitalization all happening at the same time. I really didn't know how much more I could take. I'd heard a saying in Al-Anon that "God doesn't give you more than you can handle." Maybe that was true, but I felt like I had more than my fair share. When was life going to get easier?

I had hoped and prayed that Rod would cancel his trip to London or delay it until Sean got out of the hospital—but no. I was stunned when he told me over the phone that he was still going.

"How could you possibly leave with your son in the hospital?" I asked him. He hung up on me.

Meanwhile, all of this was affecting Kimberly as well. She seemed so angry all the time. Her therapist told me that she felt orphaned between Sean and Ashley and all their recent problems. She also felt abandoned by Rod and Rachel and felt that her dad didn't have any time for her and didn't want to be involved in her life. I felt horribly guilty that I hadn't been able to give her more attention.

When I put her to bed one night, she said, "Mom, you never laugh anymore." It was true. I guess I hadn't laughed in some time. I was too worried and sad. Once again, I felt overburdened, overwhelmed, and hopeless that things would ever change. And so very alone.

I talked about my anger at Rod and Rachel a lot in therapy and with my Al-Anon sponsor, and the bottom line was that my resentment only hurt one person—me. Again, I had to do some serious praying to try to forgive him, something that would take years to achieve.

The results of Sean's evaluation came in, and it seemed that many of Sean's problems stemmed from the emotional effect of his ADD and learning disabilities. Sean was often teased in school, and he had terribly low self-esteem, which was exacerbated by his pain and sadness about his father being absent so much. He also suffered from anxiety and depression, which I had inherited from my mother and passed on to Sean.

It was heartbreaking to watch my son go through such a difficult time. It made my heart feel heavy, yet I needed to be strong. It was a very stressful time, and I wasn't the perfect mother by any means. I was often irritable and sometimes lost my temper when the kids acted up. I always felt horrible afterward.

And it wasn't just the kids I lost my temper with.

Once I completely lost it at Rod's, and neither he nor the kids ever let me forget it. Rod had picked Sean up from school and had promised me he would take him to his therapist appointment. I went by his house later to pick Sean up for dinner, and when he got into the car, he informed me that he had missed the therapy session. Rod had just decided he didn't need to go. I told Sean to wait in the car while I went into the house to confront Rod.

"Rod, why didn't you take Sean to his therapy session? It's not something you can just decide not to go to!"

He turned on his heel. "Fuck off," he told me.

All of the past months of stress had mounted up, and I was running on empty emotionally. When Rod turned his back on me and walked away, I couldn't control it anymore. I would have liked to have hit him with a baseball bat, but as I didn't have one handy, I instead shoved one of his large art-nouveau statues off its pedestal. It crashed to the floor and broke into a million pieces. I have to admit it was a giant release of my pent-up frustration and anger with Rod—momentarily, that is.

Sean was in the car, thank God, but of course all the kids heard about it. As much as I had felt justified at the time, I had to apologize to Rod and to the kids for my behavior. No matter what, it wasn't okay for me to lose my temper and act out like that, and I felt terrible about it, mostly because I was setting a horrible example for the kids. I never heard the end of it from Rod until I finally paid him back for the stupid statue!

Chapter 26

Ashley's acting career started taking off. His agents sent him out on some auditions, and he immediately booked a role in a Jim Brooks movie. Then he was cast in the film *Beethoven's 2nd* with Charles Grodin and Bonnie Hunt. But when he returned home afterward he seemed to be going out a lot at night partying and sleeping most of the day. A couple times when he had friends over I thought I had smelled pot wafting out of his room.

"Ash, you remember what the brain surgeon said about not smoking grass?"

"It's not me, Mom. One of my friends had it," he explained. And I believed him.

Out of the blue, I got a call from a friend of Ashley's. "Alana," she said. "I need to talk to you."

"Is everything alright?"

There was a long silence on the other end, and then suddenly she burst into tears. She went on to tell me that Ash had been doing serious drugs for the past five months. "He'll kill me for telling you, but I couldn't live with myself if something happened to him," she sobbed.

I couldn't speak for the longest time. I don't even remember the rest of the conversation.

I called George immediately. From what Ash's friend had told me, I knew we had to get Ash to rehab and quick. I didn't know where to begin or whom to call to get help.

I don't remember how it all happened, but we found an interventionist and met with him. He arranged the intervention at my house. It was a very emotional gathering, of me and George and a couple of

Ashley's friends. We all spoke from our hearts, and afterward he agreed to go to rehab.

I hugged him tightly to me at the door. I felt so relieved and grateful that he had agreed to go. It was devastatingly painful to watch my son walk out the door on his way to rehab.

It brought up all the memories of my mother and her addiction. I had to really use the tools I'd learned in the program and the meetings to get me through this period. I knew that all I could do was turn it over to a higher power and trust that Ashley would be taken care of. But all the fear and anxiety were still there.

The next few weeks were like a roller coaster ride. Emotionally, I was all over the place. I alternated between pain, sadness, grief, and then numbness. I kept remembering my mother and my feelings of hopelessness around her addiction and her eventual death, and my inability to change it. And now my son had a drug problem, and I wasn't able to change it.

But I still had two other children to take care of, and they were traumatized by this new turn of events. It just wasn't fair that they should have to deal with so much. My heart just broke for them. And I didn't have the power to change anything—their father's new life, their brother's addiction, Sean's problems, my continuing health problems. All I could do was try to be there for all of them.

George and I attended our first family group meeting at the rehab, along with all the other families who had loved ones there. Ashley talked openly to George about some of his feelings growing up and they both ended up crying. Then it was my turn with Ashley, and he shared a lot of his feelings with me—the resentment and anger and pain he'd felt growing up. He said he had often felt like an outsider in the family.

I felt such unbelievable deep sadness for my beautiful son as I thought about all the pain and resentment he'd harbored all these years. The feelings were so painful that I just wanted to check out and leave my body. But I knew I had to walk through them and accept them and do whatever I could to make it right in the present. All I could do was ask his forgiveness for not having done it better.

The therapist said something to me that I never forgot. "Alana, some of Ashley's problems have your name on them and some of them have George's name on them, but the present has his name on it, and it's now up to him to change it."

As painful as this whole process was, it was very healing, not only for my relationship with Ashley but also for him and George.

Sixteen days after Ashley checked into rehab, he took off with a friend. He called the next morning to say that he had spent the night in a sober-living facility after going to two AA meetings and that he'd gotten a sponsor. I was so relieved I could have cried. Unfortunately, my relief didn't last long.

Ashley moved back into the house and continued going to meetings. Or at least he said he was. I thought things would now be quieting down. I didn't know it at the time, but the drama was only just beginning.

Chapter 27

⟨⟩

By the beginning of 1994 Deepak Chopra and I had become good friends. Because I was still feeling exhausted and sick, he suggested that I come down to his new clinic in Del Mar and stay for a week. Farrah had also been going through a terribly stressful period, so I invited her to join me.

The first night I was awakened at 4:30 a.m. by a small tremor. About a minute later Kimberly called and told me there had been a huge earthquake in LA. All the books had flown off the shelves and some of the glasses were broken in the bar, but there was no major damage in the house. Sean called on the other line and I turned on the television while I talked to them.

It was a massive earthquake. Almost nine thousand people were injured, and the damage amounted to $20 billion dollars, making it one of the costliest natural disasters in US history.

Farrah wasn't so lucky. The earthquake had literally split her house in two. Ryan and Redmond came to Del Mar, and she left with them after a few days to go home and deal with the damage. So much for her peaceful time.

As the kids were being looked after and no damage had occurred in our home, I decided to stay. Finally, after a few days of meditating and the relaxing Ayurvedic treatments, I started to feel peaceful again.

Once again, now that I had the time to quiet my mind, I could stop worrying about all the things that weighed on me—my children, my future. It was always during times like these, when I could get peaceful, that solutions I could not have imagined otherwise would come into my life. And this time, in the midst of all the drama, an incredible gift was coming my way.

Months before, I'd read an article about Oprah Winfrey, how she had started out with this little local talk show and gone on to become one of the most powerful and influential women in Hollywood. At the time I had mentioned to George that he and I should try to do a talk show together, but he only half-listened.

Well, while I was in Del Mar clearing my mind, George had made a splash as a guest host on *Regis and Kathie Lee.* His agents were excited about the possibility of him doing a talk show, and that's when he told them about my idea. They thought it was great—a talk show with his ex-wife! George called me in Del Mar to tell me; when I returned, there would be a meeting with George's agents, and an exciting new chapter of my life would begin.

Deepak was right: when I let go of the worry, I created a space for the universe to bring something into my life.

Then the other shoe dropped: when I got back home, I found out that Ash was still using. I tried to get him back to rehab, but it soon became obvious that there was nothing I could do.

I knew from Al-Anon that I couldn't control Ashley and his choices and that all I could do was turn him over to his higher power and pray for him. At the same time, I felt this horrible guilt that I hadn't done enough to "save" my mother, so I had to do everything in my power to save my son. It was a terrible struggle.

As it turned out, the next several months would prove to be a crazy dance between fulfilling my dream of doing our own talk show, and my worst nightmare: watching my son go down the same path my own mother had. The highs and lows crashed against each other for almost a year.

I really don't know how we got through it. Professionally, George and I did the best acting of our lives, staying focused on work while our son's life—and ours—was falling apart . . .

As challenging as it was, though, we managed. We had to. There were several big production companies interested in the show. Our agents, as agents tend to do, wanted to jump on the most lucrative offer. Rysher Entertainment, a relatively new production company, had the least experience but the biggest budget, so the decision was made to go with them.

It was amazing how quickly everything happened. Contracts were signed and we moved into our offices at CBS. We would be in pre-production for two months, then do two weeks of taping, which would be edited together and used to sell the show in syndication.

The first day I drove to the studio, it was really exciting to find my parking space with my name on it right in front of the building. But from that first day I noticed a peculiar smell, kind of a chemical odor. I had a lot of allergies and chemical sensitivities, and I was sure this was something definitely not good for any of us to breathe. No one seemed to be able to smell it but me, so I dropped it for the moment but insisted on getting an air purifier for my office.

But as the days went on I kept noticing the smell. I started to feel a little headachy and light-headed. When we went down to the stage the first day, the odor seemed even stronger. One day George mentioned he had a terrible headache. That was enough for me! I marched into our producer's office and said, "Paul, there's really something not right in the air. I don't feel well and neither does George."

Paul got on the phone to the studio. "Listen, you have to check out this smell that's in our offices. I can't have my stars getting sick!"

The next day a good friend of ours, the legendary producer of *Laugh-In*, George Schlatter, came over to visit with us. He, George, and I were chatting in our office, which opened onto the garden in the center of the building. Suddenly around the corner came a group of men all wearing hazmat suits, looking like they had come from outer space. They were scoping out the area, carrying a lot of strange equipment, examining every square inch of the grounds. George Schlatter doubled up with laughter and so did George and I, though George H. was torn between finding it hysterically funny and being furious at me for creating a problem.

Apparently there was oil pooling underneath the studio or something to that effect; the fumes were circulated throughout the air vents. We heard that it ended up costing the studio a fortune to fix. I probably wasn't very popular with the executives, but a number of people working at CBS approached me afterward to tell me they had been sick and were so grateful to me for bringing the problem out in the open. I felt like Erin Brockovich!

Now that we could work without getting sick, George and I threw all our energy into the show. We had terrific chemistry, and the producers were thrilled. I was so very grateful that God brought this wonderful opportunity into my life.

Meanwhile, Ashley checked himself back into rehab, and I was so relieved. But he soon checked out again and moved back into my house in Brentwood. After a short time I realized that he wasn't sober. As hard as it was, I couldn't let him stay in the house. I had to think about my younger children.

"Ash, I love you with all my heart," I told him, "and I'll do anything to help you get sober. But you can't stay here if you're not. You need to go back to rehab."

"Mom, I'm sorry," he said, "but I just don't want to be sober."

That was like a knife in my heart, but I knew what I had to do. Telling my son he couldn't stay in my home any longer was the hardest thing I've ever had to do.

They say in Al-Anon that you have to detach from the alcoholic or addict lovingly. I didn't understand how a mother could detach from her child when her heart is so involved. I cried every day. I'm not Catholic, but on the advice of my good friend Marianne Williamson, every day I went to church and lit a candle for him. And every day I lived in terror of getting a phone call telling me the unthinkable had happened.

Then I spoke to a friend of mine in Al-Anon. She told me that, instead of imagining the worst possible outcome, I should see him surrounded by white light—see God's love enveloping him and keeping him safe. See him smiling and healthy. I began doing that every day. I honestly believe prayer really works, and scientific studies have even proven it. I believe that putting prayer out into the world not only helps the person being prayed for but also the person doing the praying.

I didn't hear from Ashley for two long, painful months. Then a week before Christmas he called. He sounded terrible.

"Mom, I need your help." He began to cry.

"Where are you?" I said through my own tears.

I drove to the address he gave me—a dingy small house in Hollywood. It brought back such vivid and painful memories of my mother's apartments. It was dirty and dark and it even smelled the same, stale and dank. Ashley looked terrible—pale and gaunt. I hugged him for a long time.

After speaking with doctors at Cedar's, we decided Hazelden in Minnesota would be the best place for him. George and I would take him there.

I picked Ashley up at Cedar's, where he had been detoxing for a few days. He was wearing rumpled leather jeans, a Chrome Hearts wallet chain, a leather jacket with more chains, and his hair was long and disheveled. To top it off, he had a beard. I said to George later, "He looks like Jim Morrison on one of his bad days."

George met us at the airport looking like he'd just stepped off the cover of GQ—his suit was perfectly pressed, he was wearing a tie, and every hair was in perfect place, of course. Even in these serious circumstances, you had to see the humor in it.

While we were walking through the airport, with Ashley shuffling along behind us, one of the heads of Rysher spotted us and came rushing over.

"Hey, what are you guys doing here? Where are you headed?"

"Minneapolis," we answered. We introduced him to our son, who mumbled hello as the man enthusiastically shook his hand.

"I'm going to Minneapolis too! What are you going for?" he asked.

"Family," I answered quickly.

"Great," he said. "Maybe we'll get together."

Rysher sold the *George and Alana Show* in 98 percent of the markets, and it would make its national debut in September. It should have been one of the most exciting times of my life, and yet I was so wrung out physically and emotionally that I wasn't able to fully enjoy it. I was still suffering from all the effects of the stressful past months with Ashley. I could hardly eat, and I was getting thinner and thinner. And I was beyond exhausted. But so much was happening that I just had to keep going.

Ashley left treatment at Hazelden, much to our dismay. He finally agreed to go to a rehab in London where a close friend of his had gotten sober. He completed his stint there and moved into an apartment under the doctor's supervision. We were in the middle of preproduction when I got a call that Ashley had just been found in a coma from an overdose, and I had to leave work to fly to London. After we brought him back, the drama continued. I was living in a constant state of anxiety and fear that my son could die.

George and I were terrified that Ashley's "rock-bottom" might be the end of his life, and we were determined to do anything in our power to prevent that. We finally got him into another rehab and tried to remain hopeful.

And then came the moment that changed everything. As Ashley later told us, he had a moment of clarity and realized he didn't want to live like this anymore. You don't get sober until you are ready, and now it seemed as though Ashley was finally ready. A wonderful man from AA came by to talk to him at the rehab. He drove a Harley, and I think might even have been a Hell's Angel, but he had been sober for many years. He brought the big book of AA with him and sat with Ash for some time. He came back every day after that and became Ashley's sponsor. I am eternally grateful to him.

So in the end, it was Ashley himself who finally made the decision to get sober. This time he really committed to getting sober, and this time he stayed sober. In thirty days Ashley moved back home. What a relief it was to all of us. George and I had our son back, and Sean and Kimberly had their brother. I realized that we had so much to be grateful for. I felt like God had truly blessed us with a miracle.

At last it was time for the show to begin. Because of what we had been going through with Ashley, George and I hadn't been there to oversee things as much as we should have. We were back from England just days before the show debuted. I was beyond exhausted. In fact, one day during a press tour in New York I lay down on the floor of the hotel suite and sobbed. I literally couldn't get up. I was terrified the Epstein-Barr had resurfaced. I was sure it was either that or I was dying.

George was incredibly supportive; he took me to the doctor, who said I was suffering from complete nervous exhaustion. My stomach was in total spasm as well as my neck and back, and my blood sugar was dangerously low from not eating. He gave me some Librax to relax my stomach and pumped me full of B vitamins. I felt somewhat better afterward, but I was still facing the absolute terror of doing the first show.

D-Day came, and I was in total panic. We were taping the show live in front of three hundred people in the studio audience, but it would be seen by millions (hopefully) all over the country. What if I froze and no words came out?

I prayed for strength and inspiration as I walked onto the set. The audience was applauding, and I swear to God, I barely remember the rest except that we had a great time and we got a standing ovation. It was an incredible feeling. The producers and the syndicators were ecstatic. George was terrific, and he and I made a great team.

The ratings for the first show were great and everyone was very excited. The rest of the week flew by. I absolutely loved doing the show more than anything I'd ever done professionally.

It's hard to imagine how demanding it is to work on a talk show if you've never done it. I know it looks like it's easy—just sit and chat with guests, sipping coffee. But that's only what you see on the screen. We spent hours preparing when we weren't on the set—reading books and watching film clips so we would be able to interview our guests intelligently. Sometimes we'd start at six in the morning to do promos and morning radio. We'd have producers' meetings, run-throughs, and, of course, wardrobe, hair, and makeup.

Then, the live show, followed by more meetings afterward to discuss how the show went as well as the material for the following day. I'd get home barely in time to see the kids before they went to bed; then I'd stay up until midnight or later preparing for the next day.

It would have been a crazy schedule for anyone; with the health problems I'd had it was exhausting. But I loved it and made myself keep the pace. "You sure have determination when you want to do something," George said. "I've never seen anyone come so alive!"

We had a lot of fun on the show. I constantly teased George about his idiosyncrasies and, of course, he did endless routines about mine. I had given him the bigger office and dressing room, and he'd spent days having them decorated in perfect Ralph Lauren style. He even had a cigar humidor built in his office. When he wanted to put sun furniture on the roof so he could sunbathe during breaks, it had to be forklifted up the side of the building because they couldn't get it up the stairs. "You better hope this show's a huge success or Rysher is going to throw this ridiculous furniture off the roof and us after it!" I told him.

Then there was the time I pulled up to work and there he was, holding a meeting in the parking lot, sun reflector perched under his chin, as the staff sat sweating in the sun around him.

Back on the home front, Kim and Sean had just turned sixteen and fifteen, and they weren't interested in spending much time with me. I was having major concerns about them. I found out that Kim was going out to clubs and drinking on weekends and that occasionally Sean had too. Apparently, the people who ran some of the clubs knew who they were and would let them and a lot of their underage friends in. I was absolutely furious.

I called the managers of every single club and told them if I heard of any of these kids coming into their clubs anymore I would call the police and report them. That stopped that, at least for the moment, but I was the most unpopular mother in town with all the kids.

The show started out strong. There were huge billboards all around LA of George and me and full-page ads in all the magazines and in the industry trade papers. I felt so incredibly grateful to be working at something that I loved doing so much. I felt like I had really found my niche. And I was making a terrific salary.

But slowly our ratings began to drop in some of the markets. Some of our shows were in bad time slots (like in Chicago, opposite Oprah!). Unfortunately, the executive producer they had hired had never produced a talk show, and that certainly didn't help.

Then George told me in confidence that the executives at Rysher had told him they thought perhaps it would be a good idea to let me go and put a new spin on the show, to either hire someone new or have George do it alone. They thought that maybe the reason the ratings weren't better was that I was "too thin and too pretty," that the average woman across America didn't identify with me. George stuck up for me. He told Rysher that he wouldn't do the show without me. I will always remember his loyalty and be grateful for it.

Another producer, who had produced several successful talk shows, was brought in for the next season and gave the show a whole new life. He wouldn't let us prepare in any way for the opening or even talk to each other right before we went on. He would come up with ways to cause us to push each other's buttons, and what came out of it was totally spontaneous and funny.

One morning in the producer's meeting George and I had strongly disagreed about something and tempers flared.

"You're a pain in the ass and I'm never going to work with you ever again!" he said.

I was so mad that I threw a bottle of Evian water at him. I wasn't trying to hit him but instead just threw it in his general direction; it splattered against the wall. He was furious and refused to talk to me.

When we went out to do the show, he still wouldn't talk to me and sat there in stony silence to punish me while I had to carry on alone. Finally, I told the audience what happened. We ended up airing all our "dirty laundry" on camera, and it was one of our funniest openings.

The show started to really cook and the ratings were going up. But when we lost our time slot on CBS in New York, it was too late for Rysher to make a deal with another station there, so they panicked. I got a call from George one morning just before leaving for the studio. "They're not going to pick up the show," he told me.

We were so disappointed, especially as the show was finally getting its "legs." But there was nothing we could do about it. In hindsight I realize that Rysher didn't have the kind of experience and savvy that could have kept us on the air. I learned a valuable lesson from the experience: the offer with the best money may not be the best offer at all.

I took the cancellation much harder than George did. I was simply devastated. I had put my heart and soul into the show and worked so hard to make it happen. And then there was the realization that George and I wouldn't be working together anymore. For the past two years we'd been joined at the hip working on the show as well as dealing with all the crises with Ashley, and now it was over. It felt like getting divorced all over again.

On the plus side, though, doing the show had given me a confidence as a performer that I couldn't have expected. I had gone into an arena I had absolutely no experience in, faced my terror, and done a job I could be proud of. That made so much of a difference in my life.

One positive and interesting thing happened the day before the show ended, however. I had never been able to find any relatives that were alive on my father's side, and I always felt a kind of emptiness and a lack of closure around my father. I felt like a person with a piece missing.

Because of my visibility on the show, my father's stepson, Chuck, wrote me a letter. He and my father's brother, Richard Collins, and his family came down to the show to see me. It was surreal in a way finally to meet these people whom I was related to. Suddenly I had an uncle and two cousins.

They all came to the house the following week to meet my kids. They brought my father's army trunk for me to keep. It was filled with lots of photos of my father, of my mother and him together, and some of me. I was able to find out a lot of information about my dad and fill in a lot of the blanks.

After my father and mother split up, he moved back to Santa Ana and went to work as a bartender. He drank, gambled, partied a lot, and, after a while, married a woman he'd dated in high school. He never had any other children, although she had two sons from a previous marriage.

He continued to drink heavily, and during the next twenty years his life went steadily downhill. In his early forties he suffered a stroke and was warned to stop drinking. He chose to ignore the doctors' warnings and continued to drink from morning to night.

My uncle said my father died from an overdose of prescription drugs. No one knows for sure if he committed suicide or, in a drunken haze, accidentally mixed together too many different drugs. What seems to be certain is that he had simply given up on living and drank himself to death.

How sadly ironic that both he and my mother would die under such similar circumstances, he at forty-six and she at fifty-two.

Addiction is known to run in families, and with two parents dying so young from drugs and alcohol, it was no wonder I had my work cut out for me with my own kids.

Chapter 28

I'd grown up a lot since my split with Rod, and I definitely learned to become a better parent to my kids over the years. However, I wished that I could have been one of those calm, centered people who never felt overwhelmed or raised her voice, but unfortunately, my nervous system wasn't made that way. Dr. Furst explained to me that children raised in homes like mine have nervous systems that are wired to be hypervigilant, have a low threshold for stress, and tend to live in a state of constant anxiety. That surely applied to me, but I kept working at it.

Now a whole new phase of my life was about to begin. Kimberly was turning seventeen and increasingly headstrong; we clashed a lot. We had a therapy session together with my new therapist, Liz LoPresti (yes, another one!), who was actually the therapist who helped Ashley get sober. I was so happy that Kim was at least open to working on our relationship. I'd had a deep sense of sadness and loss because we weren't as close anymore; I don't think she had any idea how important she was to me and how much I loved her.

In our session with Liz, Kim told me that she was dating Scott Caan. His father, James Caan, had been a friend of mine for many years. At first I was really concerned because Scott was twenty-one, but I realized it was far better for Kimberly to be dating someone who was sober and responsible than another seventeen-year-old who was drinking and driving too fast.

Scott spent a lot of time at our house, and I grew to really adore him. They were together for three years and remain close friends; I always tell them I wish they would have gotten married.

Sean was still struggling with his ADD and learning disabilities, and there was also the perennial issue of craving more time with Rod, but Rod was absorbed in everything else going on in his life.

Ash was a year sober now, and seeing him take his cake at a meeting was such an amazing experience. I was so incredibly proud of him. We had a closer relationship now than ever. One night we were talking on the phone and he said, "Mom, hearing your voice on the phone really makes me glad I'm sober." I couldn't have received a better gift than hearing my son say those words.

I felt so lucky and grateful that I had my kids in my life and had their love. In one of our sessions Liz told me how proud I should be for doing so much work on myself and really trying to be a better mother. I started crying. It was so hard for me to give myself any credit. I always felt like I hadn't been a good enough mother and had failed my children terribly. But she was right—I had worked really hard to be a better parent.

I was also learning that I had a lot of inner strength and could get through whatever life might bring my way, although that's not to say I still didn't have a lot of fear from time to time. I read spiritual books constantly and went to a Science of Mind church in the Valley. I was learning how much our thinking and beliefs affect what happens in our lives, and I kept remembering Deepak's words: "Happy thoughts make happy molecules."

I read in one of the books that fear was a belief in the negative and faith was a belief in the positive. I could now see how my fearful, negative, critical thinking had affected my life in so many ways. If I thought positive thoughts, I would attract positive experiences, and if I thought negative, fear-filled thoughts, then I would attract those kinds of experiences. I had to just keep replacing the fear with faith and accept that I had an inner power and strength to draw upon.

I hadn't really tried to calm my mind since the show ended, and I realized I needed to stop obsessing over finding another job and just let myself heal. When I could find peace, the universe would provide, as it always did.

Legally, I still had the Brentwood house to live in until Sean was eighteen, but we got an offer from singer Melissa Etheridge to buy it. I didn't really want to leave the home the kids and I had known for so long, but I asked Rod, if I let him sell it a year early, would he give me a share in the profits? He balked at first but finally agreed.

This move was way more traumatic than the one from Carolwood. A whole chapter of my life was ending; I was leaving the house where my children had grown up, and they wouldn't be going with me. It all felt unreal. This part of my life had passed way too quickly.

At the same time I was having terrible problems with Sean. He was seventeen now, but because of his ADD, the doctor said he was much more immature emotionally.

Sean was still my baby boy, and I couldn't bear the thought of sending him away to a boarding school, but it was getting to the point at which I had no choice. It seemed like every other day I'd get a call from the school that Sean was in trouble again—skipping class, smoking behind the school, and so forth.

"If this keeps up, you're going to have to go away to school," I warned him. But it didn't seem to sink in. When he got busted for pot, it was the last straw.

The school and the therapist were both recommending a very structured environment for teens with behavioral and learning problems. The therapist helped me find a school in northern Idaho, the Boulder Creek Academy. Sean needed to grow up and learn responsibility and respect, and we hoped this school would help him.

When I told Rod that Sean had to go to the school in Idaho, he agreed to come with us to take him there. Ashley came along as well to support his brother. It was an incredibly emotional and sad day for all of us. We all cried when we said good-bye.

I found a small house to rent off of Mulholland, down a quiet little country-like road. Moving in was such a huge life change for me. It was the first time since before I'd moved in with George almost thirty years ago that I had lived on my own.

For so many years my life had revolved around my kids, and suddenly they weren't there; it left a huge void in my life. However, there was also a part of me that was deeply exhausted; my little house was very peaceful and healing in many respects, and I enjoyed living a much quieter life. I rarely went out with friends, and it was a period of my life when I was very quiet and introspective.

Fortunately, some career things did start to happen. My friend Diane von Furstenberg called me. "How would you like to have a jewelry line on the Home Shopping Network?" she asked.

I happily accepted, working with the designers to come up with pieces based on jewelry I had personally owned or vintage pieces that I had collected.

The Alana Stewart Jewelry Line launched quite successfully, and I flew back and forth to the Home Shopping Network studios in Saint Petersburg, Florida, for a year. It was fun being back on television.

Then my agent got me the female lead in a movie called *Mom, Can I Keep Her?* I played the stepmother to a young boy who finds an escaped gorilla and tries to keep her as a pet.

I had long scenes with pages and pages of dialogue every day, and the director liked to shoot everything in one or two takes. There was no room for flubbed lines or not hitting your marks. We worked twelve- to fourteen-hour days in the San Fernando Valley with temperatures that shot up to well over 100 degrees. By the time I got home at night there was very little time to learn my dialogue for the next day. It was like being thrown in the deep end with very little time to prepare.

At one point in my life these conditions would have really bothered me; instead, I made a commitment to myself not to complain about anything, to be a team player and keep a good attitude, and to be grateful for the opportunity to be working. It was a valuable lesson for me, and it made all the difference in the world.

I left to visit Sean as soon as we finished filming. He hadn't been allowed visitors his first two months, so I couldn't wait to see him.

He looked and acted like a different boy; he looked alive and not angry and shut down. He was talking about his feelings to his therapist and learning how to express them to his dad and, hopefully, accept that he was still valuable even if he didn't always come first in his father's life.

I wished so badly that talking to Rod about our son could be easier. I could never really know whom I was going to get—Dr. Jekyll or Mr. Hyde. Sometimes he could be really caring and start to get involved, but then he would turn around and be so totally cold and distant. I really wanted to have a relationship where our kids were concerned, but I never felt like I could get through that invisible armor he put up.

Sean desperately wanted his dad to come up for the next parents' weekend. Rod and Rachel had broken up a couple of months before, and Rod was in terrible shape. All the kids rallied around him in support. One night we all went out to dinner together. It was the first time I'd ever seen him looking so frail and vulnerable, and I really felt sorry for him. No matter what had gone on in the past between us, I wanted to be there for him as a friend.

Rod chartered a plane, and Rod, Kimberly, and I flew up to see Sean. Sean was so happy to see his dad, and we all had a really nice time together. We spent the night in a charming little inn in the mountains near Sean's school. Rod and I talked about Sean, and he said how much closer he felt to all his children. He was so different when he was on his own, without a woman in his life.

It felt kind of strange being on the trip with Rod, but it made me remember some of the things that had endeared him to me. When he was the "good Rod," he was so funny and eccentric. We went into a grocery store to buy some cough medicine for him, and it was like he'd never been in a grocery store before. Come to think of it, he probably hadn't! And, of course, his lifestyle was very seductive—the private plane, everything and everyone at his disposal, the houses, the cars, the wealth. I felt like the poor relation!

Sean left school after a year at Boulder Creek and moved back in with me. He started dating a really nice girl, Michelle, who, fortunately for me (but not for her) was a first-class Al-Anon candidate. She kind of took over where I left off.

It wasn't long before trouble began again. I found out that Sean was drinking and doing drugs. The next couple years became a blur of rehabs and crises. I always slept with my phone on because I never knew when I'd get a hysterical call from Michelle that Sean had an accident or got into a fight or was in the emergency room. It was the nightmare with Ashley all over again.

Chapter 29

Finally, Sean was in a safe place, at Impact Recovery Center in Pasadena, and he couldn't have visitors for a month. Farrah and I had desperately wanted to get away to someplace warm, and we chose the Bahamas. She'd been having her own problems with her son, Redmond, and she needed to escape as much as I did. I was still afraid, though, that Sean wouldn't stay at Impact. It was a tough, kick-ass place—just what he needed, for sure, but when someone is over eighteen, they can leave of their own accord.

Sure enough, I'd been in the Bahamas two days when I got the phone call that Sean had left. I was heartsick, but there was nothing I could do. I could only pray for a miracle. I just kept praying and seeing him in God's hands. Then I got a call from Gary, Sean's counselor, that he was in sober living. At least he was safe and I could hopefully now relax—at least for the moment.

Farrah and I did absolutely nothing that trip. We slept late, ate, and lay by the pool, and if we had enough energy, we read. It was just what we needed.

Shortly after I returned home the phone rang at 3:00 a.m.—never a good sign. It was Michelle. She was hysterical. "Alana, Sean's been arrested!"

I called the jail and spoke to the arresting officer. "Your son has been charged with a felony, ma'am. Assault with a deadly weapon," he told me.

"What kind of weapon?" My heart was pounding out of my chest.

"A foot shoe," he replied. "A what?" I thought I'd misunderstood.

"A foot shoe," he repeated. I felt like I was having a conversation with a robot.

"What's a foot shoe?" I asked, perplexed.

"A shoe that's worn on the foot, ma'am."

This sounded crazy. Where else would you wear a shoe?

"I don't understand. My son attacked someone with a shoe?"

"Yes, ma'am. He kicked the other party," he replied.

"What kind of shoe was he wearing?" I asked.

"An Adidas sneaker, ma'am."

I started to feel like I was Alice in Wonderland. "An Adidas sneaker is a deadly weapon?"

"Yes, ma'am. It is a foot shoe, and that is considered a deadly weapon," the officer replied. He explained to me that Sean would be held unless we posted bail.

I called Rod's house, but the French houseman told me he was sleeping.

"It's an emergency," I told him. "Please wake him up and tell him that his son's in jail."

The houseman put the phone on hold and never came back. As usual, I was on my own.

Somehow, I found a bail bondsman, something I'd never thought I'd be doing, and made the arrangements to get Sean out pending the hearing. The following week he was arrested again for drinking and having Vicodin in his pocket.

Even though I got Sean straight into rehab after the second incident, the judge sentenced him to three months in jail and four years probation. We were all shocked. The attorneys said that was an unusually stiff sentence for the offense.

Sean should have been sentenced to a long stint in rehab, where he would get help, not to jail, where he would get none. In the end we were able to get the judge to agree to let Sean serve his three months at a city jail in Monterrey Park instead of county, where the most dangerous and seasoned criminals are housed.

The day I saw Sean off to jail, I went to Johnny Rockets afterwards and numbly ate a double cheeseburger with a vanilla coke. I sat at the counter with tears running down my face, crying into my cheeseburger, hoping no one would notice.

"Stand by Me," the old Ben E. King song, came on the jukebox, and I cried even harder. It had been Sean's favorite song when he was young. I just wanted to get home, put on my flannel pajamas, and stay in bed indefinitely.

Sean called four times the next day. I was surprised he had such free use of the phone.

"Honey, how are you?" I asked him, praying he was alright.

"Okay," he said. "I guess a little scared. And lonely. I'm in a cell by myself."

"Oh," I said. "Well it's better than being in county in a cell with twenty gangbangers beating the crap out of you every day—or worse."

"Yeah, it probably is," he said.

The following Sunday Michelle and I went to visit Sean. The officer who took us to see him was really nice and said because it was Sunday, he would let us have a "contact visit," which meant we got to sit in a small room with him instead of having a fifteen-minute visit through glass with a phone.

I was so nervous to see him—to see what shape he was in. I expected him to burst into tears when he saw us like the first time I visited him at boarding school, but he was in surprisingly good spirits.

He was sitting at a table in his green prisoner's jumpsuit. When he saw us, he jumped up and hugged us both. When we sat down, the first words out of his mouth were "I kind of like it here. Everybody's really cool."

You could have knocked me over with a feather! He said he'd been really lonely in his cell alone, but now he was in a cell with three other guys—one who didn't speak English, an Asian fellow who had also gotten into a fight, and a Mexican drug dealer.

They kept him separated from the high-risk, longer-term prisoners, but Sean said he would rather be with them because they had a lounge where they could watch television. He said he'd talked to a couple of them, and they were "really nice guys." Sean was always unique, bless his heart.

When it came time for him to be released, everyone advised us to get him out of town to make sure he didn't get in trouble again. I called his therapist in Idaho to ask her advice. "Why doesn't he just come and live with me for a while?" she suggested. It was the best idea I could imagine; at least I knew he'd be safe and sober.

On top of everything else, I was having terrible anxiety about my living situation. When I had moved to my little house off Mulholland, I had planned on being there a year and then buying something. But property prices kept going up, and I couldn't find anything I could afford. Before I knew it, four years had gone by and I'd wasted a lot of money in rent. My lease was up, and I had to be out of the house in a couple months. I woke up every morning feeling like there was an elephant on my chest.

Unbeknownst to me, Kimberly had gone to her father and asked him to help me with a house. She suggested he take it out of whatever inheritance she would get someday, but that didn't happen.

Finally I called Rod and asked him if he would help me with a down payment and he could be part owner in the house and share in any profits we made. He agreed. I was so grateful and so relieved.

I found a small, two-bedroom house in the hills off Laurel Canyon that was reasonably priced. I made the offer on it and had five days to put down a deposit. I called Rod to come see it so we could make the arrangements, but he didn't call me back. I called several times, but still no return call. When I finally got him on the phone, he told me he had changed his mind and really didn't want to be in the house business.

So I lost the house. I was not only terribly disappointed that Rod let me down, but I also had no idea what I was going to do. Luckily, though, two of my closest friends told me they would loan me the money for a down payment when I found a new house so I wouldn't have to be in that position again; in return I would give them part ownership. I felt (and still feel) incredibly fortunate to have friends like that in my life, and I will be eternally grateful to them.

Chapter 30

My agent called me just after I'd made an offer on a new house I'd found. "How would you feel about doing a show for ABC called *I'm a Celebrity, Get Me out of Here!*?" he asked. "It's going to be shown for two weeks, live, during February sweeps, and it's kind of a celebrity survivor show."

He went on to explain that it was a big hit show in England and that ABC had picked it up. I'd have to leave in a few weeks for the Australian rain forest.

"I'd have to sleep outside in the jungle?" I asked in horror. "Are you out of your mind?"

Then he told me how much they were paying and I almost dropped the phone. I couldn't turn down that kind of money!

"You can do it," he said. "They want you to come in and meet with the producers and the execs from ABC day after tomorrow. They have to cast right away."

I went to the meeting, hoping they'd change their minds and not want me after they heard some of my phobias. My first words when I walked into the meeting were "I just have two questions. Will there be someone to carry my luggage and where will I plug in my hair dryer?"

Everyone laughed. They proceeded to sell me on the idea. They told me that the location was beautiful and everyone from the English cast had loved it so much they hadn't wanted to leave. I left thinking it actually did sort of sound like fun. And I simply couldn't turn down the money.

The ABC promotional campaign started immediately. There were photo sessions, fittings, interviews. A camera crew came to my house to shoot footage of me. It was all happening so fast that my head was swimming.

Then the morning I had to leave for Australia I woke up with a raging flu and bronchitis. I couldn't believe it. It was probably caused by all the stress and anxiety I felt over going to the jungle. I knew I had to just get on the plane and tough it out, no matter what, so I started antibiotics and every kind of medicine for flu available. The plane ride was a nightmare; I coughed all night long.

When we arrived in Sydney after a fifteen-hour flight, we changed planes to go to a smaller city, and then they drove us to the Gold Coast. The minute we arrived at the hotel, we were whisked straight off for wardrobe fittings. I was so sick that I could barely get through them.

The next day they filmed us while we were being instructed on what we were about to encounter. Much to my dismay, I learned during the training that the most dangerous snake in the world, the black snake, lived right where we were going! It was enough to make me want to run away and just keep running.

After filming all day we changed clothes for a press conference and photo session and fell into bed, only to get up at 4:00 a.m. to leave for the jungle.

When I found out that we were being helicoptered to the edge of the rain forest and then would have a three-mile hike to our camp, I freaked. I seriously didn't know if I could make it. I was still so sick; the plane flight had only made the bronchitis worse.

The producers had someone ready to fill in for me if I couldn't make it, but I'd made up my mind that nothing was going to stop me. I was either going to make it and get better or I was going to die in the damn jungle!

They gave us the clothes we were to wear with one change. We couldn't take any face creams, sunblock, hair products, or makeup. They said they would have moisturizer and sunblock there for us to use. We were allowed only two personal items. I took an eye mask and lip gloss. They body-searched all of us before we got onto the helicopters to make sure we didn't have anything else with us. I cleverly smuggled blusher and a bottle of Valium in my boot! I was more afraid of not being able to sleep than I was of the spiders and snakes.

At 6 a.m. we were herded onto helicopters for the trip to the edge of the rain forest. Everyone started out friendly and supportive—it wasn't long before that would change.

The hike, which the producers had sworn was "no big deal," was a treacherous three-plus-hour trek through the mountainous, overgrown rain forest. We stumbled our way up and down the steep terrain, through the tangled foliage, with our water bottles and backpacks. I was still very weak and sick, but at least I wasn't worse. I just kept repeating two Bible verses over and over in my head: "I am strong in the Lord and the power of His might" and "I can do all things through God who strengthens me."

There was no food, and we were starving halfway through. Along with the blusher and Valium, I had also smuggled two croissants in my boot, and I shared them with everyone else.

When we finally arrived at the campsite, I wanted to fall down and kiss the ground. I couldn't believe I'd actually made it. I guess I was stronger than I gave myself credit for.

From everything the producers had told me in our first meeting, I had envisioned a kind of Fantasy Island with a beautiful river in an idyllic forest. Not even close! The camp area was a relatively small, damp circle next to the river, which was freezing cold.

We started setting up our campsite by building a fire, carrying logs, and putting a plastic curtain around the outdoor hole in the ground that was our toilet. If you had to go to the bathroom in the night, you had to take a lantern and brave the trek up the hill in the darkness. And the spiders were as big as my hand.

We were each allotted a small portion of beans and rice each day, and we had to cook them in a big pot over the campfire. The only way to take a bath was in the river. And the mosquitoes were fierce. There was a case with supplies in it, along with toothpaste, moisturizer, sunblock, and mosquito repellant. For our drinking water, we had to take water from the river and sterilize it by boiling it over the fire.

This took roughing it to a whole new level.

Several of the others had prepared for the trip, some working out and getting into great shape. I realized I probably should have prepared a little more. I knew nothing about camping. I didn't have a clue how to set up my cot or even my sleeping bag. Thank God Bruce Jenner helped me.

What they also hadn't told me was that it was the beginning of the rainy season in Australia, and from the minute we arrived at the campsite, it began to rain, first sprinkling and then coming down in torrents. We had no tents—only sleeping bags on small cots out in the open. When the rain started, two men appeared from nowhere and put up a tarp in the trees to stop the rain from pouring down on our cots, but it didn't help much.

When it was time to go to bed, I crawled into my sleeping bag and took one of the Valium I'd smuggled in. I put on my eye mask and finally went to sleep, hoping a snake or a spider wouldn't crawl on me and that I wouldn't wake up with pneumonia.

It soon became clear who the really competitive ones were and who wanted to be leaders. Little cliques started to form. Meanwhile, I was still recuperating from the flu and bronchitis, and I wasn't feeling my best.

One night, around 3 a.m., I had to get up to pee. I didn't feel like navigating up the hill through the pounding rain and the dark. I figured everyone was sleeping, so I snuck into the woods where there were no cameras. Or so I thought.

The next morning Julie Brown, who was camp leader for the day, brought everyone together and announced, "Last night the infrared cameras caught on tape someone peeing in the woods." She went on to say that it just wasn't acceptable, that it was breaking the rules (what rules?), and that it could pollute the water.

A horrible feeling of shame washed over me, like a kid in grade school caught by the teacher. I was so taken aback that I didn't stand up and say what I should have said, "Excuse me, but that was me who peed in the woods last night. And by the way, a number of the guys have done it, so what's the big deal? It wasn't anywhere near the river, and even if it was, don't you think animals have done a lot worse in the river?"

Later, when I had to do my on-camera interview, I brought it up, adding, "Animals pee in the woods, the guys pee in the woods, and I think it's ridiculous for Julie Brown to single me out to try to embarrass me."

For some reason Julie had it out for me. At one point she literally threatened me. She had heard I had said something about her that she didn't like. She got right in my face and whispered so the mic wouldn't pick it up: "If you ever say anything like that about me again, I swear, I'll hurt you!" she said. Of course the mic picked up every word.

I'd had enough. This Texas girl wasn't about to shrink away from Julie's threats. "Julie, you get the fuck out of my face, or I swear I'm going to deck you!" I said, keeping my voice even, but meaning every word.

On the fifth day I was voted by the viewers to do the "Bushtucker Trial." This was an event in which one contestant had to try to win meals for the rest of the team, which always involved something disgusting like spiders or snakes—or worse. When I found out I'd been chosen, I started to cry. I knew my fellow camp members didn't have very much faith in my ability to even win one meal, much less ten. I hadn't had a very good start in this adventure; starting out sick had definitely put me at a disadvantage and made me look like a weakling.

After making my way a short distance through the jungle and crossing a rope bridge hanging perilously over the water, I arrived at the trial area where the host, John Lehr, and a number of large silver dome–covered dishes awaited.

"Alana, do you know what you're supposed to do?"

I did, and I was terrified. I hated spiders and snakes and the like, and that was just what I was about to be dealing with.

John explained, "I'll lift the lid of each container. Underneath there will be critters of every sort. Buried among them you'll find a wooden star with a small handle on top."

I knew what was coming next, and I cringed.

"Alana, your task is to pull the star out with your teeth. Are you up for it?"

I took a deep breath. "Yes."

"You'll only have a matter of seconds to collect each star. I'm going to tell you before I lift the cover what you can expect, and you can refuse. But, if you refuse . . . you go home."

"Okay," I said. "I'm ready."

I was absolutely out of my body with sheer terror! It didn't console me any when I saw the group of doctors and emergency medical technicians standing close by the stage. Oh, and did I mention my hands would be tied behind my back?

I prayed under my breath, "God, just let me get through this. You do it for me." Suddenly, this feeling of calm strength and determination came over me.

"Come on, girl," I said to myself. "You're from Texas. Where's that feisty spirit of yours? You're not going to be a wuss on national television!"

It was time for the first cover to come off. John asked, "Do you want to know what's inside?"

"No," I answered quickly. "Let's just do it." Better I didn't have time to think about it.

He lifted the first cover and there was the gold star, buried beneath a mountain of wriggling worms. Without giving myself time to think, I ducked my head down into the mass of creepy crawlers and grabbed the star with my teeth. One down!

If I could do one, I thought, I could do two.

"Okay, let's do the next one," I said, without hesitating.

John pulled the cover off to reveal a vat of leeches. I grabbed the star with my teeth. One more down!

"Okay, next one," I said. If I could do two, I could do three.

The next one contained what I feared the most—huge spiders! Without pausing, I dove in and grabbed the star—with my teeth, of course. I could feel several of the spiders in my hair. I shook my head as hard as I could, sending the spiders flying. Yuck! But now I'd done three. Surely I could do four.

The next was filled with electric eels in water. I didn't allow myself time to think whether or not I would get shocked—I just did it. I was on a roll.

The next ones went quickly. I didn't allow myself to hesitate. The worst one was the one filled with rats. Yes, it was disgusting, but I just did it. I couldn't stop now. My adrenaline was flowing.

It was time for the tenth and final trial. This one was different—a covered cage instead of a silver-domed dish. "You may want to know about this one," John warned.

"Nope," I said. "I don't. Just uncover it."

When he did, what I saw was enough to send chills up my spine. Crouched over in the cage was a black "thing" that looked kind of like a skunk. Its teeth were bared, and it was hissing at me. And it was sitting on the star!

The handlers and doctors moved closer, and out of the corner of my eye, I could see concerned looks on their faces.

Suddenly, one of the trainers stepped up and said he had to call a halt to the trial. The creature, which I found out was a wild Australian possum, was particularly agitated and he couldn't put me in that kind of danger.

"Do I still get the star?" I asked.

"Well, no," said the producer.

"Why not?" I asked. "You guys stopped the trial, not me."

"But we can't give you the star if you didn't get it yourself," he replied.

"Then I want to continue the trial," I said.

"But it's dangerous," the producer said. The doctors and trainers agreed.

"Look, you either give me the star or let me get it," I insisted, stubbornly.

They all looked at each other, conferred for a brief moment, and then agreed to let me go ahead.

The doctors and EMTs all moved in closer. As I lowered my head toward the cage, the creature hissed louder and louder and bared his teeth threateningly.

God, what am I thinking?, I thought to myself.

I put the back of my head in first because I quickly deduced that if he went for me with his sharp claws and teeth, he'd get the back of my head, not my face. Vanity first! With the back of my head, I gently pushed him off the star. In a flash I grabbed the star with my teeth and jerked my head out of the cage. My legs buckled and I collapsed on the ground, limp with relief that I still had a head.

Everyone on the set went wild with applause and cheering. The producers were all ecstatic. They said it was the best trial they had ever had. They would never have expected it of me. Ha! Neither did I!

I was so proud of myself. I couldn't believe I had actually done it. I would never be frightened of spiders, snakes, or any other critter again. As I walked back into the camp, the other cast members all looked at me questioningly. They had no clue what had happened, but I could see by their faces that they didn't expect to eat that evening.

I put on a long face. "Well, guess what happened?" I said dejectedly.

They waited in silence.

"I won all ten!" I shouted gleefully. They were all totally shocked. Most of them hugged and high-fived me, but there were a few players who actually looked disappointed that I had done so well. I had to accept that a few people—Robin Leach, Julie Brown, and Melissa Rivers—were never going to like me. The only two people I really felt comfortable hanging out with were Bruce Jenner and María Conchita Alonzo.

After a week it was time to vote the first person off. The audience voted for the people they wanted to stay on and continue the trials; by that time I desperately wanted to get out of there. I had told myself that if I could last a week, I would consider it a success, and so far I'd made it eight days. But I didn't want to be the first one off. After that, I'd be happy to leave.

The first to go was Robin Leach. I was so relieved it wasn't me. However, I went the second day, which was sort of okay with me. I couldn't wait to use a real toilet! That night, when I got back to my beautiful suite at the Versace Palace, I have never enjoyed a bath so much. And a wonderful dinner. My manager had flown over to join me, and we had a wonderful rest of the week, waiting for the others to come back one by one.

It turned out to be an incredibly positive experience for me. I had to see it as a success, not as a failure. I'd lasted nine days in the jungle, for God's sake! And I had walked through all my fears. I had done things I had never dreamed I could do. And I had been honest about how frightened I was in the beginning.

Interestingly enough, from the time I got on the airplane to go home, people, especially women, came up to me and said they couldn't believe how brave I was to do all that, that they could never have done it. I felt like it was a great lesson in trusting in God and facing my fears.

Chapter 31

Back in Los Angeles, I was now the proud owner of my first house. George, who was now living in Florida, came to stay with me for a few weeks to help decorate. We certainly disagreed a lot. George had very strong opinions, and so did I. And he was messy and I was obsessively neat. And forget about his clothes. Every time he came to stay, he brought enough clothes for ten people. His clothes were everywhere—his closet, my closet—it just drove me crazy.

However, it was great having him around. We went out to dinner and the movies and had so much fun together. Our friends always said we should get back together, but despite the affection we shared, it wasn't meant to be.

And while I was trying to get the house finished, my other ex-husband did something that really surprised me. I opened an envelope with a check for $25,000 and a nice note from Rod enclosed, saying that it was to help me furnish the new house. I think it might have been his way of saying he was sorry for backing out of the house deal, but whatever the reason, it was a wonderful gesture. I was incredibly touched and appreciative.

Even though I had moved into my own house at this point, there was, as usual, a lot going on with my kids. They were adults now, but I was still focused on them. It was like they were my whole life, and I got so upset whenever they were going through challenges—totally contrary to everything I'd learned in Al-Anon, by the way.

My close friend Marianne Williamson, who also happens to be a leading figure in the spiritual world, shared with me what she had heard—"You're only as happy as your least happy child." Boy, was she ever right. Now, it seemed, instead of a man or a job, my happiness depended on my kids.

I was really worried about Sean. He had come back from Idaho, and I suspected he was drinking again. Ashley had returned from England, where he'd become quite a successful songwriter and musician, and he was staying with me in Los Angeles. Unfortunately, he was struggling with sobriety again. How I hated this disease that plagued my family. Kimberly was living in London for the moment. Her modeling career was taking off, and she had a television show there as well, but our relationship was still having its ups and downs.

I was struggling with more than my kids and their problems at this point. Nothing seemed to be going right in my life in any area. After the show in Australia I'd done a couple less-than-memorable movies and several plays, but I hadn't worked in a while, and there didn't seem to be anything on the horizon. And I was running out of money! Acting roles were scarce for women over fifty, and to make matters worse, my agents had decided they were going to focus on young talent and had let me go. And let me tell you, being fired by agents who weren't that great in the first place is a pretty low blow.

To be honest, a part of me didn't want to live in this superficial Hollywood world anymore. Everything seemed to be based on wealth, power, and fame. And youth. And I didn't fit into any of those categories. I felt tired of trying to be accepted in Hollywood—as an actress, as a talk show host, as a person in my own right and not somebody's ex-wife. Sometimes I really felt like moving out of this town, but my kids and my life were here.

It was an incredibly frustrating time for me. I visualized, I prayed, I meditated, but nothing seemed to work. I was once again plagued with that familiar, debilitating depression. It was so painful with everything hitting me at once—no financial security, no work on the horizon, no relationship, and watching my adult kids struggle.

Finding myself now in the throes of yet another emotional crash, I decided to call Marianne. She offered to do a session with me. It really opened my eyes.

"Alana, you need to acknowledge the shame, regret, anger, and sadness you're feeling over not taking care of yourself financially in your divorce," she said. "It's time to forgive yourself and move on."

Marianne also told me that I was exhausting myself by constantly striving for approval and that I had to stop trying to "make it happen" all the time. "Remember the Bible verse, 'See ye first the kingdom of God and all these things will be added unto you,'" she told me, and then she suggested I start "The Course in Miracles," a program of spiritual study. The goal is inner peace, based on the practice of forgiveness.

But most importantly, she gave me a prayer to pray every day: "God, show me how to be the woman that you would have me be in order to do what you would have me do."

It was the beginning of a big change in my life. I realized that every spiritual teaching I'd ever studied always said how important it was to stop thinking about oneself and give back—to do some kind of service. I knew I wanted to do something to help others; I just didn't know what.

I had no idea at the time that the work I did with Marianne was going to change my life in a way I never could have imagined.

Even though I was doing the Course in Miracles, things didn't change overnight. I was still feeling exhausted and depressed most of the time. George had told me about this clinic in Germany where he'd taken a friend of his who had cancer. I didn't want to go off to Germany, but he insisted I go. He even arranged everything for me as my birthday present.

I ended up spending two weeks there, and the doctors I met were quite amazing. What they were doing seemed so much more advanced than anything that was happening in the States in the treatment of chronic fatigue, cancer, and other diseases. They were incredibly helpful to me. I had taken antidepressants on and off for years, but at the clinic I got natural substances that helped me immensely. I still take them to this day.

A few months later I took Sean to the clinic with me because the doctors felt they could really help him with his ADD. They found he had a huge amount of mercury and other toxic metals in his system, and this could have been one of the reasons he had difficulty staying focused.

While we were at the clinic in October 2006, Kimberly, visiting from London, came into my room and told me she had just read on the Internet that Farrah had cancer. I was sure it couldn't be true, but I called Farrah, and she tearfully confirmed it. She had decided to start undergoing treatment at UCLA immediately. I told her I'd come home early so I could be there with her.

Farrah had already been going through some tough times. Her son, Redmond, had gone down the same addictive path as my sons, and we grew even closer bonding over our pain and helping each other get through some of our more difficult times. Although she and Ryan had broken up several years before, they were still close, and when he'd been diagnosed with leukemia a few years earlier, she was there for him. They had reconciled but continued to live separately.

Her parents also depended heavily on her, and she had lost her sister to lung cancer a few years back. Her beloved mother had recently died, and the loss had devastated her. Suffice it to say, it had already been a very stressful period for her.

Farrah had always been fearless. She had never backed down from a fight—and she didn't back down from this one, either.

I won't get into too much of my experience with Farrah at this point; I wrote about it extensively in *My Journey with Farrah*, a tribute to the most courageous woman I've ever known. But for two years we went back and forth to the clinic in Germany to try to win her battle.

I became single-minded about helping Farrah find a cure for her cancer. I was determined to be there whenever she needed me. I loved her so much that I would have done anything for her. But I think it went deeper than that. I think it also had to do with me not being able to help my mother all those years ago, to give her what she needed. I think part of the reason I threw myself into helping Farrah fight this incredible battle was that I hadn't been able to help my mother fight hers.

On her first trip to Germany Farrah handed me her small hand-held video camera. She wanted me to start filming all the doctor's visits and procedures so she would have a record of everything. At the time the video was just meant to be for her.

I'd never filmed anything before, but after she showed me how the camera worked, not only did I get the hang of it but I also began to really get into it. There were times I'd shut the camera off when I thought it was too invasive, like when she was violently vomiting for hours, but she'd tell me, "Turn it back on. This is what cancer is like." Farrah wasn't afraid to show herself in the most vulnerable and painful situations.

About a year into our filming, networks began to make offers to Farrah to air our footage as a documentary. She hesitated at first, but as thousands of people had written her over the past year, telling her what an inspiration and hope she was to them in their own battles with cancer, she began to realize that she could hopefully make a difference by sharing her illness. She was in remission at this point; our film was supposed to be about our finding a cure for her cancer, to give hope to others. But life took a different turn.

Farrah's Story was screened at the Paley Theater in Beverly Hills for the network people as well as friends and family on May 13. At the end of the film nearly everyone in the theater was sobbing. Farrah had touched everyone so deeply with her honesty and her undaunted courage.

People were raving about it. Ryan said one of the reasons the documentary turned out so well was that it had such a feeling of intimacy about it. There was no film crew, no lights, no director; it was just Farrah and me.

I was proud to have been a part of it, but I almost felt embarrassed by the praise I was getting. I felt like all I had done was hold the camera. The saddest part of the evening, though, was that Farrah wasn't there to take the credit that only she deserved. Almost a month after her passing *Farrah's Story* was nominated for an Emmy.

It's hard to believe that during that harrowing and scary experience we also had a lot of good times. Farrah had the most amazing attitude as she went through painful and debilitating treatments and procedures. She would always find something to laugh or joke about. A lot of the time we were like two girlfriends on a trip—being silly, laughing, and having a good time. It was an escape from the reality of what she was dealing with.

Occasionally, when she was in intense pain, she would cry or falter in her determination. But it never lasted long. One time she said to me, "I'm sorry. I don't mean to be such a baby."

"Are you crazy?" I said. "I've never met anyone as strong and determined and inspiring as you. You're the bravest person I've ever met!"

"Really?" she said. That was Farrah. She never really saw herself as everyone else saw her.

One of the things I always loved about our friendship was that we always had so much fun together no matter what we did. Farrah and I shared a close-knit group of friends, and we always celebrated our birthdays together. And the past number of years we'd spent Christmases together with Ryan and our kids. She and I would bake on Christmas Eve—our famous pies from her mother's and my grandmother's recipes. The last time we baked was Christmas Eve 2008, and she was so weak that she had to lie down on my sofa and rest often. She and Ryan and Redmond even made it for Christmas dinner the next day. We didn't know or maybe we didn't want to believe that it was her last Christmas.

On June 3, 2009, Farrah went into the hospital for some routine tests and procedures, but complications arose and she ended up in intensive care. There was no way to get her home. She died on June 25, 2009, at 9:36 a.m.

Ryan called me at 6:00 that morning. "You should come now," he said. We were there with her when she passed away, holding her hands. It was surreal. My old familiar numbness came over me—it was too painful to accept that I was losing my friend as she peacefully slipped away.

After her passing Ryan and I were criticized by a few people who thought we had kept them from seeing Farrah in the weeks before she passed away. What they didn't understand is that Farrah hadn't wanted to see anyone, and we were just respecting her wishes. Each time someone would ask, she would get quiet for a moment and then say, "You know, I'm sorry, but I'm just not feeling up to seeing anyone right now. Maybe later." I think she didn't want to see anyone because she was so frail and didn't want her friends to remember her that way.

Right to the end, Farrah made her own decisions about everything, whether it was business or what she wanted to eat and when. The doctors and nurses said they had never seen anyone so determined and who had such a strong will. She was going to do it her way—that was Farrah through and through.

After Farrah's funeral I was horribly depressed for months. I had a couple sessions with my friend David Kessler, a wonderful author and speaker who is also a grief counselor. It was extremely helpful. One of the things I learned is that I just had to allow myself the time to grieve. I couldn't expect just to carry on with my life. I think it really took a good year before the pain started to lessen.

I didn't have a lot of time to either grieve or recuperate, though. Out of the blue I'd been offered a really good role in a movie called *Delivered*, playing the mother of a young American soldier who comes back home after being severely injured in Iraq.

In the middle of shooting the movie I had to go to New York to do all the press for *My Journey with Farrah*, as the publishers had, against my wishes, pushed up its release. Thinking about doing interviews so soon after my friend's death was extremely difficult. I was emotionally and physically depleted. I flew to New York and somehow got through it, then came back to LA and finished the movie.

I was in the middle of the West Coast part of the book tour when I got a call from Kimberly's best friend, begging me to come to London and surprise Kim for her thirtieth birthday. She said Rod wasn't coming, and Kim wouldn't have any of her family there if I didn't come. I didn't see how I could humanly do it, but I just knew it was something I had to do; there was just no way I could miss such an important birthday.

I canceled a couple television interviews and made my plans to leave the following day. While I was at the LA airport, I got a call from my publisher. *My Journey with Farrah* had debuted at number nine on the *New York Times* Best-Sellers list. I was surprised and thrilled, but a part of me felt guilty that good things were happening in my life but Farrah was gone.

I was so glad I went to Kimberly's birthday party. I didn't feel great while I was there, but seeing Kimberly's face that night made it all worth it.

When I came back to Los Angeles, my beloved dog, Lolita, started to have trouble walking. When Farrah was so ill, I would come home at night, terribly dejected, and Lolita would lie down beside me and just look at me, as if to say, "It's okay." She was such a comfort to me. Poor Lolita had surgery for a large cancerous tumor on her spinal cord, and she died two days after the surgery. I was inconsolable. I went to bed and cried for days. Having this happen so soon after losing Farrah was more than I could bear.

A couple days after Lolita died a woman called who said my publisher had given her my number. She was a psychic and a medium. "I've been getting very strong messages from Farrah," she said. "They kept getting stronger and stronger. She wants me to tell you that she has your dog."

I went weak in the knees. No one could have known about Lolita—certainly not my publisher or this woman in New York. She went on to tell me that Farrah said she knew after Lolita's surgery she wasn't going to make it.

"Farrah says to tell you that she waited for her and that she's okay." I had chills all over. I started sobbing again. "She says to tell you that it was Lolita's time but that she waited because she knew you needed her." I know it sounds crazy, but I knew it was true. Since then I've gotten other messages from Farrah, messages so strong that they were undeniable.

Farrah had set up the Farrah Fawcett Foundation two years before she died because she wanted to fund cutting-edge cancer research as well as help people battling cancer, especially children. She had appointed Bernie Francis, her business manager of thirty years, as executor of her estate and chairman of the foundation. After she passed away Bernie asked me if I would consider acting as president and running the foundation. I was thrilled and honored to have the opportunity to carry on Farrah's legacy. It is one of the most meaningful roles I have ever played.

Some months after Farrah's death I went back to my friend's house in Mexico, where I had been last with Farrah. One day, while I was lying by the pool, I looked over at the empty chaise next to me where Farrah had laid in the sun every day when we had been there together. I could still see us sipping our fresh watermelon juices, feasting on guacamole and quesadillas, just two girlfriends hanging out in the gorgeous Mexican sunshine. Suddenly, I felt a giant wave of sadness wash over me. I had never missed her more than I did in that moment.

After a while I got up and went inside. I got a piece of watermelon and sat down on the sofa. The entire back of the house was completely open to the pool area and the beach and ocean beyond.

All of a sudden something small and white came fluttering up to the house from across the pool. At first I thought it was a bird, but as it flew into the house I realized it was a very large white butterfly—the largest butterfly I had ever seen. I was mesmerized as it fluttered closer and closer to me and finally landed on the edge of the plate of watermelon sitting on my lap. It perched there for about ten seconds and looked at me intently with its large black eyes. Then it flew away, into the garden and out of sight.

I had chills all over my body, and tears were streaming down my face. I knew it was Farrah. She had come to me in the form of that beautiful white butterfly to let me know she was still there in spirit and not to be sad.

I know that Farrah still watches over the people she loves. She will always be our special angel.

PART VI

Finding Peace

The past several years have brought a lot of good things into my life. Running the Farrah Fawcett Foundation has been an incredibly fulfilling experience. I feel like I'm doing something that hopefully will make a difference in the battle against cancer and help to carry on my dear friend's legacy. One of the most important lessons I've learned is that turning my focus away from myself and my problems to help others is what makes life rewarding. I believe doing so ultimately brings the happiness that, in the past, I've searched for and never found in the material world.

Last year I was honored by the John Wayne Cancer Institute with the True Grit Humanitarian Award. I also received a GENII Award for Excellence in Documentary Filmmaking for filming and producing *Farrah's Story*. I could never have imagined that my life would take the turn that it has, and I owe it all to Farrah. I feel like she's the one who should be getting the awards, not me, and in my heart I feel I'm accepting them on her behalf.

Delivered, the film I did shortly after Farrah died, has been shown at several film festivals and gotten some positive attention. It was entered in WorldFest, an international film festival that takes place in Houston every year. Being nominated for Best Supporting Actress was an honor in itself; I never expected to win, but much to my surprise, I did. It may not have been an Academy Award or an Emmy, but for me, it was so exciting that I was being recognized for my work as an actress. I've only had one acting role since then, and I still don't even have an agent at the moment, but I've been so busy with the foundation and the book that I haven't really had time to focus on it. My career is a way to support myself; I no longer need it to boost my self-esteem.

Another huge blessing for me is that I no longer live in fear about the future—well, at least, not all the time. I know that my security is not going to come from work or a relationship but rather from my connection with a power higher than myself. I've found a level of peace in being able to surrender the need to know how a problem will be resolved, in just trusting that things will be taken care of, that the answer will come. So although I can still get absolutely terrified if I allow myself to, I work through it. I get still and I go within. I now have tools and a higher source to turn to.

I still worry about my kids when they're going through difficult times. I know they each have their own paths and their own lessons to learn—just as I have—but it's still painful, especially when I can't do anything to help. I just spent the weekend helping Kimberly with my baby granddaughter, Delilah. She's ten months old and the most beautiful, enchanting little creature. It's so wonderful to watch my daughter with her daughter and to see what a wonderful mother she has become and how devoted she is to Delilah. I'm so incredibly proud of her. It really makes me think about the miracle of life as I look at this baby girl with her whole life before her. I think how quickly mine has gone by thus far. It makes me feel that life is so fleeting, so we had better treasure every moment we're here on this earth and cherish those we love. It's a lesson I learned from my experience with my beautiful friend Farrah. Life can change in a heartbeat.

Kimberly and I have a much better relationship now. Delilah has brought us much closer, although we still have our differences. She's a Leo and I'm a Taurus, and we will probably always butt heads because we're both strong willed and opinionated. But she knows how much I love her and that I will always be there for her and Delilah as much as I possibly can, as I will for my sons.

Ashley and Sean are sober today, and I'm so very grateful for that. I can't bear the thought of ever going through any of the past experiences again, but I know, of course, it's one day at a time. And I have to stay focused on today, not the past or the future.

Ashley has a role in *Ironman III*—a huge break for him and a wonderful opportunity. I'm so proud of where he is today. He's turned into the most wonderful man, and we have an amazing relationship.

Sean's focusing on several projects now, and I know that the right one will work out for him. He also started a soccer clinic at the Union Rescue Mission for the homeless kids whose families are staying there. The Union recently honored him at a fund-raising luncheon for the work he's done. I'm so proud of him for doing it and keeping his commitment. He has the most wonderful heart and is so wacky that he keeps everyone laughing. And no matter how old he gets, he's still my baby boy.

I've tried to teach all my children how important it is to help others, and each of them do it in their own way. Ashley gives back through 12-step programs and community service, and Kimberly went to Haiti for three weeks to help the people there. She also completed an EMT (emergency medical training) course so she can aid people in those kinds of situations. She's very committed to being a serious actress, but most of all to raising Delilah. I'm very proud of all of them for realizing the value of helping others and having such kind and generous hearts.

As for Rod, our relationship is friendly, but superficially friendly. We don't talk about deep, meaningful things, but then again, we never did. Even though Kim and Sean are grown, there will always be issues that, as their parents, we need to talk about. It's very important to the kids that he and I have a good relationship.

Rod may not have the same views as I do in terms of how much involvement parents should have in the lives of their adult children, of how much support, both emotional and financial, his kids may need, but I do believe he loves his children. When he's in town, all his kids hang out at his house and love spending time with him. In all fairness he's much more understanding than he used to be. He's become much more loving and supportive with Sean, and there's nothing in the world that means more to Sean than having a relationship with his dad and having his approval.

As for George, we will always play important roles in each other's lives and be there for one another, no matter what. George has been dating a German doctor for several years who is much younger than he is. I admit I had to get used to the idea at first, but I really do like her. She cares about George, and strangely enough, I think that his having a serious girlfriend has freed me up to get on with my life as well.

I'm sure that, on some level, I've kind of avoided a serious relationship because of my concern for George. I was always worried that he would be alone in his later years and there would be no one to take care of him. There is no way I would ever let that happen, and I assumed that unless he found someone, we would probably grow old together. But everything happens the way it's supposed to happen.

As I think about the person I am today as opposed to the woman I was when I started on a path of spiritual seeking, I can't believe how much I've changed. I realize that God has truly answered my prayer that Marianne suggested I use: "God, show me how to be the woman you would have me be." I believe that, for the most part, I have become the kind, compassionate, loving person I asked to be. Sure, I have my moments when I still get angry or impatient, but they're rare and it takes a lot to get me there today. I actually like who I've become, and I'm proud of the work I've done on myself and the changes I've made.

I've dated over the years, but I haven't met that special person for whom I would want to give up my independence. I'd rather be on my own than settle for someone whom I'm not deeply in love with. I don't need to be married or be in a relationship to feel okay about myself. I'd love to be in a wonderful, loving relationship, and if it happens, that would be great. And if it doesn't, I know now that I'll still be okay.

At least today I know what love isn't. It's not that desperate, obsessive feeling of wanting to possess another person. Love isn't about jealousy or longing or anxiety. Love isn't critical or judgmental. It isn't about changing another person to fit your picture of how they should be. It's accepting someone as they are and supporting them in expressing their uniqueness. Love is about being kind, respectful, and appreciative of the other person and wanting them to be happy and fulfilled, and about being the best person you can be for the person you love.

My values have changed so much over the years. I used to believe that material things would make me happy, but they never did. I know that the most important thing in life is love, the people we care about, and finding the joy in life on a daily basis. Money and power don't buy happiness, nor do they enable you to avoid the tragedies of life.

I still carry Deepak's words in my heart: "Alana, if you want more love in your life, be more loving. If you want more appreciation, give more appreciation." I practice it on a daily basis by trying to be loving, kind, thoughtful, and considerate—not just to those I love but to everyone. Not an easy task. Especially when you encounter a first-class a*#hole. But part of being a more loving person is being forgiving of those who have wronged you. It's hard to have love in your life without forgiveness.

I practice it even when I'm driving. If someone tries to cut me off or get in front of me, I simply let them get on with it. If I see someone trying to get into a busy lane of traffic, I'll stop and let them go in front of me. It makes me feel good, and it probably makes them feel good too. It's just a small way to practice the "be more loving" concept. As I said, it's not always easy, and I don't always do it perfectly, that's for sure. I just wish that I'd practiced it more and been a better example when my children were growing up, but you learn when you learn.

It's been really interesting going back and reading all my old journals that I've kept all these years. I was often in such emotional pain, fear, and anxiety about life. I so often seemed to be a victim of my circumstances. I guess there comes a point in life when you have to say "Enough!" and make a decision to be happy. Abe Lincoln said, "A man is just about as happy as he makes up his mind to be," and that's so true. We have to choose happiness and work on disciplining our thoughts.

One of the most valuable things we can ever learn in life is how to discipline our minds. I just read a book called *The Happiness Makeover* by M. J. Ryan, and something the author said stood out to me: "You have to retrain your mind, and by creating new habits of thought, you generate positive feelings." Our thoughts control our feelings, and believe it or not, we can control our thoughts. I can't allow myself to wallow in emotional pain and self-pity when things aren't going well. I spent so much of my life seeing everything that was wrong instead of being grateful for what was right.

Obviously, no one can be happy all the time, especially if we're going through a crisis or if some tragedy occurs, but we can choose happiness as a goal and focus on the good in our lives, even when we're going through the toughest times.

These are some of the spiritual principles that one has to learn and practice. They don't come naturally—or at least they certainly didn't for me. The minister of my church, Dr. Mark Vierra, once said, "If you study any spiritual teaching for two years and practice it, your life will change for the better." I've done it all—Al-Anon, Science of Mind, Kabbalah, Christian Science, A Course in Miracles—and they have all helped get me through some very difficult times and to where I am today. It doesn't matter what one chooses to study; it just takes the first step and a commitment to do the work in order to have a better life.

So I guess it never ends, this journey of self-discovery that we're all on—at least not until we die—so I figure we better enjoy every day that we have here on this earth and be grateful for it.

We're not in this life alone, and we can turn to that power within us, that higher power, spirit, divine mind, or God, as I choose to call it, to guide us and care for us and get us through whatever we might be facing. And I believe that if we have trust and faith, we always come through our challenges better and stronger than we were before. And I know, most importantly, that we have to live in the present moment, choose to enjoy our lives, be more loving, and keep our hearts open.